Praise for *Justice Is Served*

"The highest of recommendations for this unique and gorgeously written recipe for happiness. Surprising, captivating, and as delicious as a perfect meal, I love this book beyond all reason."

—HANK PHILLIPPI RYAN, *USA Today* best-selling author of *Her Perfect Life*

"[A] delectable page-turner . . . part memoir, part culinary odyssey, and part historical account of an extraordinary evening. I was salivating from beginning to end."

—REYNA GRANDE, author of *A Dream Called Home*

"Leslie Karst's celebration of women's progress wrapped up in the tale of one stupendous and life-changing dinner is . . . chef's kiss. Quietly patriotic, passionate, and oh-so readable, this book is a feast."

—CATRIONA McPHERSON, Anthony and Agatha Award-winning author of *In Place of Fear*

"[A] captivating chronicle of one woman's commitment to the law, to the culinary arts, to family, and to finding her life's purpose. . . . Karst has masterfully woven her own story with that of the beloved Supreme Court justice, creating a narrative of two inspiring women whose paths cross for one special night."

—ELIZABETH McKENZIE, author of *The Dog of the North* and *The Portable Veblen*

"*Justice Is Served* is a delightful romp through a daunting culinary challenge. But even more so, it's an homage to family bonds, committed partnership, and the hard-won battles that move society forward inch by inch. Even if you've never spent the better part of a year—or a day—planning a meal, you will relate to Leslie Karst's quest to prepare a perfect dinner for a thrillingly formidable guest. You'll also feel like you're right there at the table. How lucky we are to be invited."

—MEGHAN DAUM, author of *The Unspeakable: And Other Subjects Of Discussion*

"[D]elicious and delightful. . . . Whether you love food or the law—or both!—you will savor every page."

—ADAM WINKLER, author of *We the Corporations*, National Book Award finalist

"Verdict: A delicious and soul-satisfying read, the perfect recipe for anyone hungry to discover her passions and follow them, one bite at a time. Laced with tempting tidbits of cooking advice and insights into Ruth Bader Ginsburg's life and career, Leslie Karst's *Justice Is Served* will show you another side of the justice and her husband, make you hungry, and leave you plotting your way to get invited to the author's home for dinner!"

—LESLIE BUDEWITZ, attorney and three-time Agatha Award-winning author of the Spice Shop Mysteries

"A literary meal that's heartwarming, suspenseful, humorous, and entertaining. . . . An absolute delight."

—ELLEN BYRON, *USA Today* best-selling author of the Cajun Country and Vintage Cookbook Mysteries

"Leslie Karst delights and tempts your appetite in this lovely memoir. . . . *Justice Is Served* is a dish you'll savor and enjoy."

—**EDITH MAXWELL (aka MADDIE DAY),**
Agatha Award-winning author of
the Country Store and Cozy Capers
Book Group Mysteries.

"For readers who love food and admire the fascinating life of Ruth Bader Ginsburg, Karst's book is an irresistible and loving look into not only cooking the big dinner itself, but also her exploration of what this dinner meant and how it changed her life."

—**LUCY BURDETTE**, author of
A Dish to Die For

Also by Leslie Karst

The Sally Solari Mysteries

Dying for a Taste
A Measure of Murder
Death al Fresco
Murder from Scratch
The Fragrance of Death

JUSTICE IS SERVED

A Tale of Scallops, the Law, & Cooking for RBG

LESLIE KARST

SHE WRITES PRESS

Published 2023
Printed in the United States of America
Print ISBN: 978-1-64742-458-9
E-ISBN: 978-1-64742-459-6
Library of Congress Control Number: 2022919513

For information, address:
She Writes Press
1569 Solano Ave #546
Berkeley, CA 94707

An excerpt from an early version of *Justice Is Served* was published in January 2011 by *California Lawyer* magazine.

Interior design by Tabitha Lahr

She Writes Press is a division of SparkPoint Studio, LLC.

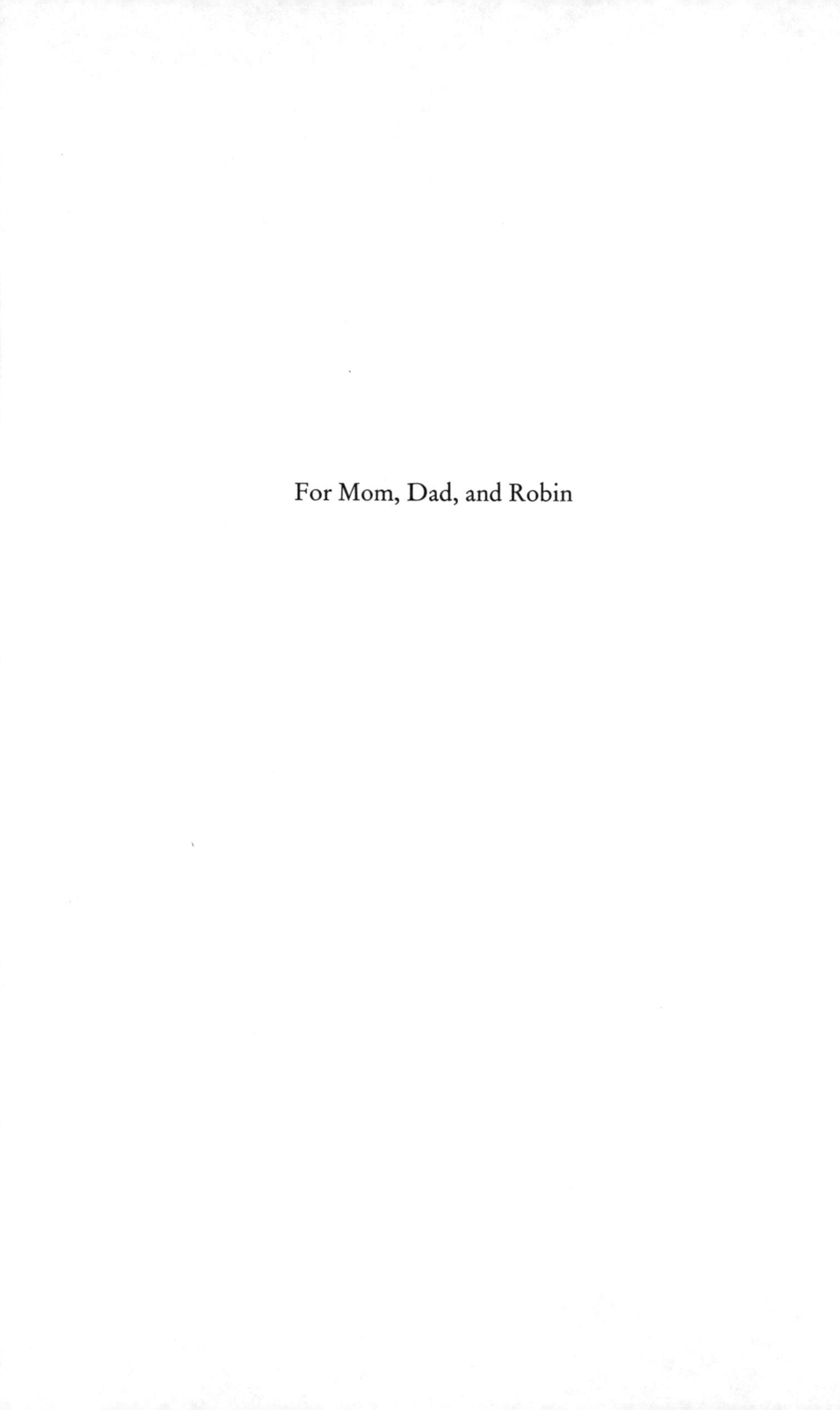

For Mom, Dad, and Robin

Contents

Prelude

Dinner cooked by Leslie January 28 would be fine. R.B.G.

So read the message on the screen, an email forwarded from my father. Blinking rapidly to keep my contact lenses from wigging out, I had to stare at the words—succinct though they were—and concentrate, to make sure I was reading them correctly.

Yes. It *did* say that.

I leaned back in my chair to let the significance of the text wash over me, then laughed out loud—one of those giddy, explosive laughs, akin to the bark of the fat sea lions that like to hang out at our fisherman's wharf.

My partner, Robin, wasn't home, so no one heard me but our dog Rosie, who'd been asleep on the couch. She lifted her head at the sound and looked my way expectantly, her enormous bat-like ears at full attention. Then, when I kept on chuckling and shaking my head and slapping my knee, she decided something was up and jumped off the couch to investigate.

I took Rosie's soft face in my hands and looked into her soulful eyes. Even though she was half Border Collie, I knew she could not be expected to understand the full import of the communication I had just received. But I had to tell *someone* the exciting news.

"Rosie," I announced proudly, "*I* am going to cook dinner for United States Supreme Court Justice Ruth Bader Ginsburg."

Turning to stare once again at the email message on my computer screen, I took a deep breath. It was May 3, 2005, and I had nine months to plan the most important and elegant dinner party of my life. With a slow exhale, I did my best to ignore the wave of heat that had swept over me like a Santa Ana wind.

And then I smiled.

CHAPTER 1

From Pescara to Paris and the Pacific

The email didn't come as a complete surprise. Some months earlier, my father and I had been discussing his upcoming retirement after forty years as a constitutional law professor at the UCLA School of Law. We were seated at Robin's and my dining room table, cups of coffee and the morning newspaper spread out before us.

"You know that I've kept in touch with Ruth Ginsburg, right?" Dad asked.

"Sure," I said. "At least I remember her being one of the 'law people' you and Mom used to refer to back when I was a kid. And I always assumed you stayed friends over the years."

"Well, it wasn't as if we were ever close *friends*. 'Warm colleagues' is probably a better description." Dad tapped an index finger on the side of his ceramic mug. "Back when she was still teaching, we used to exchange friendly notes and reprints of the legal articles we'd published, and then after she was on the bench, I'd occasionally recommend students to clerk for her."

"Uh, huh . . ." The wheels spinning in my brain were trying to ascertain where exactly this conversation was going.

Dad took several sips of his black coffee, in no hurry to get to the point, then finally set down the mug and cleared his throat. "So anyway, ever since Ruth was appointed to the Supreme Court, I've been trying to convince her to come give a talk at the law school, but she's never accepted my invitation." A pause. "Until now . . ."

"What? You mean this time she said *yes*?"

His mouth twisted into a sly grin. "She didn't exactly commit to coming, but when I told her that next year would be my final one teaching—and hence her last chance to come speak at my invitation—she did indicate that she *might* accept."

"Ohmygod," I blurted out. "If she does say yes, you and Mom should invite her for dinner, and I can come down to your house and cook." I'd mostly been joking and expected him to merely laugh in a "ha-ha, that's a ridiculous notion" kind of way. But instead, Dad cocked his head, a serious look in his eyes.

"That sounds like a great idea," he said.

Whoa. Had I really just agreed to host a dinner party for *Ruth Bader Ginsburg*? What on earth had I gotten myself into?

• • •

My father and Ruth Ginsburg had met in the 1960s, when he'd been teaching at Ohio State and she at Rutgers. At the time, the two were both involved with comparative law, Dad focusing on Latin American land reform issues and Ruth on Swedish civil procedure.

I still have a vivid picture of my mom recounting the first time she met Ruth at some "law thing" in Italy. It was the summer of 1970, and I was almost fourteen and not the least bit interested in the Congress of the International Academy of Comparative Law, except that it meant my parents would be away for several weeks, leaving us kids in the care of a hired sitter.

We adored Mitzi, who let us pretty much run wild and who quickly exhausted all the money my folks had left for expenses, spoiling us with all kinds of decadent junk food my mother would never buy. Little did I suspect—as my adolescent taste buds were reveling in frozen pepperoni pizzas, Doritos, beef jerky, and ice cream sandwiches—that some thirty-five years hence I'd be preparing a lavish, gourmet feast in honor of one of the attendees of that "law thing" in Italy.

Meanwhile, during one of the free days at the comparative law congress on the other side of the globe, some of the law professors and their spouses went to the beach at Pescara, on the Adriatic Sea.

"I walked down to the water," my mother later told me. "It was calm. More like a lake than the ocean. And the water got deep, up to your waist, and then shallow again as you walked out." Mom smiled at the memory. "And there was little Ruth in her bathing suit, testing the water with her toes. We waded out together, giggling."

She demonstrated for me, prancing about with her arms half raised, looking just like a schoolgirl. (I suspect, however, that this reenactment more accurately represented my ever-schoolgirlish mother than it did the demure law professor.) "And that's how I first met her," said Mom. "Who would have guessed that little Ruth, the shy Swedish civil procedure professor, would someday become Justice Ginsburg, seated upon the United States Supreme Court?"

INTERLUDE

Lund, Sweden is not where the young Ruth Bader would likely have imagined herself living at the age of twenty-nine. The granddaughter of émigrés from Central Europe and Russia, Kiki (as she was known from childhood through college) grew up in the Flatbush area of Brooklyn, home to Irish, Poles, Jews, and Italians—but not a whole lot of Swedes.

Staying close to home, she attended Cornell University, spent two years at Harvard Law School, and then—following her husband back to New York—transferred to Columbia University, where she finished at the top of her graduating class. Nevertheless, not a single law firm in the entire city of New York would consider hiring her. It was simply too much, she would later say: a woman, a mother of a young child, and a Jew.

Small wonder then, that after completing a judicial clerkship with Judge Palmieri of the Southern District of New York, the young lawyer Ruth Bader Ginsburg decided not to seek employment at a high-powered law firm. Instead, she accepted an offer to coauthor a book on Swedish civil procedure.

Did she need to know Swedish for the project? No problem: she would spend the next year studying the language with a former lead male dancer at the Stockholm Ballet now enrolled at Columbia, who gave Swedish lessons on the side. And then, once the new language was under her belt, she would head off to Lund, leaving her six-year-old daughter temporarily in the care of her tax attorney, but eager-to-do-whatever-I-can-to-help-my-wife's-career husband, Marty.

So began a lifetime love affair with procedure and comparative law. Upon completing her Swedish adventure (which also included helping translate the Swedish Code of Judicial Procedure into

English), Ginsburg was offered a position teaching civil procedure with the law faculty of Rutgers University. And shortly after this, she began attending and speaking at comparative law conferences—such as the one in Pescara, Italy, where she and my mother waded out together that day into the calm sea.

• • •

Three months after my conversation with Dad, I still hadn't heard if Ruth had accepted his invitation to speak at the law school. As a result, I'd pretty much put the whole thing out of my mind—until I received his email.

At which point it all became very real indeed. You see, I'm not a chef, and I've never cooked on any professional basis. When I so boldly offered to prepare dinner for Justice Ginsburg, I was a small-town lawyer who, to add a bit of spice to the daily grind of pumping out those billable hours, had merely taken up cooking as a hobby. I enjoyed throwing small but stylish dinner parties and took pride in being able to serve my guests a series of tasty and artistically presented dishes over the course of an evening. One night it might be pan-fried pork chops in apricot-brandy sauce with roasted potatoes and sautéed leeks. On another, mussels steamed in butter and Pernod with a tossed green salad and a crunchy baguette. And for dessert, I'd add a decadent pastry that I'd purchase at our local bakery. That was about my speed.

But I'd never done any entertaining on *this* level before. Preparing dinner for someone as prestigious as a Supreme Court justice wouldn't be the same as having a few of my good friends over for a fancy meal. No. This momentous event called for a sophistication and grandeur on a scale I'd never even considered attempting. Yet I'd volunteered to do so as casually as if asking, "How about coming over for pizza and beer?"

I had little time to worry too much about the significance of the upcoming event, however, because—as fate would have it—the very day I received the email from my father, Robin and I were leaving for a month in Paris. My sister, Laura, a French instructor at a college not too far from Santa Cruz where Robin and I live, was in Paris teaching a class for the quarter, and Robin and I had decided, what better excuse to spend some time in the City of Lights?

Laura and I had first visited France with my parents in 1972, during a sabbatical year my father had taken in Oxford, England. And although I didn't end up making France and its language my primary vocation as did Laura, over the course of several subsequent return trips, I too fell in love with the country—its passionate and gregarious inhabitants, its vibrant cities and picturesque villages, and above all its glorious cuisine.

I therefore resolved that this trip with Robin would be a quest to seek out the very best recipe ideas for My Dinner with Ruth. Shooting off a quick response to Dad's email message, I wrote: "Yippee! I'll be looking for menu possibilities while in Paris!" I was now headed to France not simply as a tourist but as a woman with a purpose.

I was between projects at my law firm, so the timing was perfect. And I was ready for a break from work—which is a massive understatement. In fact, I was ready for a *permanent* break from my job. I just couldn't figure out how to make that happen.

I'd been surrounded for most of my life by people whose *raison d'être* was the law—first, my father and his law professor cronies who'd pass entire evenings at my parents' house in animated discussions of constitutional issues; later, law school pals who relished analyzing whichever arcane case law we'd been assigned for class; and then fellow attorneys from work who'd spend many a late night boning up for their trials.

But the truth is, although I was very good at my work, I never *loved* the law. Not like my dad did, and not like my passionate colleagues, including the senior partner, Fred, who—not willing to go even a day without working on one of his beloved files—would show up every single weekend at the office. Sure, it was always satisfying to find that perfect case, the one that would prove a key point of law in one of my briefs, and I'd certainly get a massive rush of delight whenever I won a motion or an appeal. But it was never *a calling* for me; it was simply a job.

Fresh out of law school, I'd decided to focus on research, a specialty that calls for a lot of writing. From undergraduate papers I'd penned about John Donne and Virginia Woolf to song lyrics for a New Wave rock band I formed after college to trying my hand at the beginnings of a romance novel, the craft of wordsmithing had long provided me with great satisfaction. So why not write as an attorney, too? It seemed the perfect compromise, combining my love of writing with my desire to earn a good living.

My job at the law firm entailed drafting appellate briefs and trial motions to be filed in court, which called for persuasive writing, and research memos for the various attorneys in the office, which required that I explore both sides of an argument. It's a rigorous occupation—not unlike working on a term paper every single day of your life—and demands intense concentration as well as strong organizational and writing skills. But one of the nice things about the work was that, since I didn't have my own clients or files and instead assisted with the other lawyers' cases, I had the flexibility to take time off between projects.

Hence, the month in France.

The best aspect of my job, however, and the primary reason I accepted the offer, was that I was able to negotiate a thirty-hour week—highly unusual for newbie lawyers—that allowed me to have a life outside the tedium of legal briefs and appeals. And working part time turned out to be a wise decision, as it didn't take long for me to discover that the law was not my passion; I clearly had to look for that elsewhere.

Shortly after I started work as an attorney, my sister Laura and I formed a country-rock band called Electric Range.[1] Splitting my days between music and the law, I quickly began to think of my work as an attorney as my "side gig" and the band as the primary focus in my life. Singing, playing guitar, and especially writing the songs for Electric Range proved far more fulfilling than drafting motions to compel discovery of medical records.

But as so often happens, the band eventually broke up, and I once again found myself hunting for some other nonlegal activity to satisfy my need for creative expression. One day, as I tried unsuccessfully to concentrate on the statutory history of a confusing section of the probate code, I had the thought: *What about cooking school?*

Notwithstanding my adolescent love affair with Doritos and beef jerky,[2] I'd long been drawn to the culinary arts, going back to my junior high school days when my best friend, Nancy, and I had frequently cooked together. The Time-Life *Foods of the World* cookbook series was just being released, and when a new volume would arrive in the mail, we'd lie next to each other on her living room floor listening to Mamas and Papas and Beatles LPs, flipping through the pages of glossy color photographs until we found a dish that looked fun, and then we'd consult the smaller spiral-bound book to see how difficult the recipe was.

---

1. Yes, I know that gas is far superior to electric for stove-top cooking, but the name "Gas Range" for a band doesn't have quite the same pizazz.
2. Okay, so I admit to still indulging in them occasionally even now.

Nancy was studying Russian at the time, so we spent long hours perusing that particular volume, fascinated by the intricately painted red and orange Easter eggs on its cover. In particular, I remember making a crispy meat and egg pastry called *pirozhki*—a deliciously exotic food spiked with dill and other flavors previously unknown to me. Nancy and I also made a sweet, yeasty Russian Easter bread called *kulich* which I found especially fascinating as it was baked in a coffee can and because it contained saffron—also new to me—dissolved in rum. Nancy and I would then gorge on the results of our experiments, blissfully ignorant of the youthful hormones that allowed us to consume an entire *kulich* in one sitting with nary an adverse result.

Since that period of teenage enthusiasm, I hadn't done a whole lot of cooking other than whipping up the usual college student fare of bean and cheese burritos and vegetarian chili. But right around the time Electric Range disbanded, my interest in food was rekindled. I'd been smitten by a luscious cream of mushroom soup I'd ordered at a local French bistro and, intent on recreating it at home, had surprised myself by how close I'd come to the restaurant's version. The secret, I deduced, was adding sherry—an ingredient I'd previously not thought to use. I now buy it by the half-gallon.

This resurgent interest in cooking appeared in an appellate brief I wrote at the time, into which I managed to slip a citation to a "learned culinary treatise" (as I referred to it)—*The Joy of Cooking.* Our client had testified that he'd consumed "a glass or two" of wine, and we needed to prove this was only a small quantity of alcohol. Because Mrs. Rombauer's declaration in her cookbook as to the size of "an average serving of wine" is, of course, a genteel, small amount (three to three-and-a-half ounces), I thought I was terribly clever in using her as a citation. And yes, we did prevail on appeal.

Soon after the break-up of Electric Range, I enrolled in a few culinary arts classes at Cabrillo, our local community college, and was hooked from day one. The mysteries of all those French sauces, of pâtés and *galantines*, of *liaisons*, and of stocks and consommés, were unveiled for me. I discovered how to carve eye-dazzling garnishes out of simple carrots and tomatoes, how to choose and best prepare the myriad cuts of beef, how to bone out and stuff a chicken and fillet a fish, and how to make my own sausage.

Like an addict, I quickly consumed all the courses necessary for a degree in culinary arts and then proudly hung my diploma in my office, right above the one from law school.

Fitting credentials to prepare dinner for a Supreme Court justice, *n'est-ce pas?*

• • •

Robin was as thrilled as I by the news that I'd be cooking for Justice Ginsburg—perhaps in some ways, even more so. She'd long had a love of all things legal and had even been accepted years earlier for admission to the UC Berkeley law school. But at the last moment she'd declined the offer, having just been hired by her (and my) alma mater, UCSC, as the facilities manager for Kresge College. As Robin put it at the time, "We already have one lawyer in the family. And besides, I would hate the clothes I'd have to wear." (This was back when female attorneys were still expected to dress in skirts and dresses, the thought of which made Robin shudder.)

Moreover, unlike Robin, my excitement about the dinner had almost immediately been tempered by abject fear: Why had I offered to cook for such a monumental event? The Ginsburgs were no doubt accustomed to being wined and dined by celebrity chefs and heads of state. How could I possibly hope to match those meals? *What had I been thinking?*

I was a nervous wreck, but, doing my best to quash my doubts, I focused on the positive. We were about to spend an entire month in Paris—the gastronomical center of the universe! Surely I could come up with some fabulous menu ideas while there. Once Robin and I arrived in Paris, we therefore became obsessed with food, incessantly seeking out possibilities for "the dinner," as we now referred to the coming event.

Robin isn't much of a cook, but she does love to eat and was more than happy to assist me in my pursuit of the perfect menu for the one and only RBG. Whenever we went to a restaurant, we'd order as many different items as possible, Robin and I—and Laura, when she could join us—sharing all the dishes to obtain the maximum tasting quotient. We gorged ourselves on *steak-frites*; duck breast pan-fried rare; mussels and oysters; foie gras; braised rabbit; white bean salad; goat, cow, and sheep's cheeses; baby green beans (which we Yanks call "French beans") lightly sautéed in garlic butter; *frisée* salad with *lardons* and poached egg; tender white asparagus; tiny lima beans; liters of cream sauce; and fresh-out-of-the-oven crusty baguettes.

Then for dessert we'd try crème brûlée, chocolate mousse, *tarte tatin*, and my favorite, a *coupe chantilly*, which is essentially a mammoth scoop of incredibly thick whipped cream flavored with just a hint of sugar and vanilla.

All of this, of course, had to be washed down with delicious French wines, usually red, but the occasional white would do the job in a pinch. And we could never get over the fact that you can buy highly drinkable wines from Bordeaux, Bourgogne, the Rhône, or the Languedoc for only a couple of euros. How can you not love a place where wine *in a restaurant* often costs less than a Coca-Cola?

One day, Robin and Laura and I set out in search of lunch in the Marais district, one of the few areas of Paris that wasn't razed during the massive renovations of the city made by

Baron Haussmann under Napoleon III. Remembering a small bistro near the Musée Picasso that Robin and I had been to several years earlier, I suggested it for our meal. We'd stumbled on the place by accident while wandering the neighborhood's delightfully narrow and winding streets and had decided to eat there simply because Robin was getting cranky with hunger. It was one of those, "Well, dammit, let's just eat here" moments, all too common for tourists.

The weather was pleasant, so we sat outside where we could watch the world go by. Their special that day happened to be frogs' legs, which Robin had never tried. When I told her they taste "a bit like chicken, but sweeter," she decided to order them. Now, one of the things I love about Paris is that, unlike many places in the world where it can be risky to simply eat at the first place you come to because your partner is getting whiny from lack of food, in Paris your chances are quite good that the meal will be excellent. And it was. The frogs' legs came drowning in garlic butter and were served with a generous portion of *pommes de terre Dauphinois*, creamy scalloped potatoes with a scattering of Gruyère cheese. *Voilà*! Crankiness vanquished.

Robin, who loves potatoes as much as I love cream, was in heaven. And when it came time for dessert, while I ordered the usual *crème brûlée et un café*, Robin asked for another side of the potatoes "for dessert." Our waiter was greatly amused by this strange behavior, and no doubt informed the kitchen staff of the odd American who loved their potatoes so very much that she needed an extra helping right there and then.

Back again in Paris for the first time since that earlier trip, I was eager to find the small bistro once more. "I bet if I taste those scalloped potatoes again, I can figure out the ingredients and recreate them at home," I said to Robin and Laura, beginning to salivate at the thought of the creamy, cheesy dish. "They might make a good dish for the Ruth dinner!"

"Sounds great to me," replied Robin. "But I don't remember the name of the place, or even where it was."

"That's all right. I'm sure we can find it." Now on a true mission, we hurried down the cobbled streets of the Marais in search of the elusive bistro.

Alas, as my mom always liked to say, "You can't go back to the Shire." When Robin and Laura and I finally found the restaurant amidst the neighborhood's irregular, seemingly random streets, we were disappointed to learn that they no longer had potatoes *Dauphinois* on the menu, and although Robin was able to order frogs' legs, they were dry and overcooked and certainly *not* drowning in garlic butter.

Okay, I told myself, *so even Paris can sometimes disappoint.*

But then I had a far more disquieting thought: If even restaurants in Paris could disappoint, what was to keep *me* from doing the same? *What if the dishes I prepare for the Ruth dinner end up dry and overcooked like these frogs' legs?*

Staring across the street at an ornate, 17th century building with a rainbow flag strung across its upper balcony, I resolved to make damn sure that didn't happen. I'd do my homework to find the perfect recipes, carefully test them out in advance, and then . . .

Well, at that point, I'd simply have to hope for the best.

• • •

For one of our weeks in Paris, Robin and I traded houses with a couple who owned a flat in Saint-Germain-en-Laye, a charming town just outside the city with its own 16th-century château and conveniently located on a train line into the center of Paris. To my delight, we had a small but well-appointed kitchen where I could experiment with potential recipes for the Ruth dinner.

Grocery shopping became an adventure. We tried every *boulangerie* in town until we found the baguettes with the crunchiest outside and the chewiest inside. Then there was the cheese—which *crèmerie* had the widest selection and best prices for Petit Basque and Banon?

And the twice-weekly outdoor *marché—oh là là!* I spent hours wandering down its rows of stalls in the dappled sunlight filtering through the ubiquitous plane trees. Drinking in the saturated colors of the fresh vegetables and bowls of North African spices, I'd gaze hungrily at the dozens of varieties of olives and roasted nuts. Next I'd move on to the *charcuterie* stall, where I'd greedily accept samples of dried sausages and cured meats as I chatted up the butchers in their blood-stained smocks—who for some reason the world-over always seem to be the biggest flirts.

I would then lug all my goodies home, Robin would pour us both a *pastis*, and I'd set to work cooking. One night we had paella made with bright yellow saffron strands and *merguez* (a spicy North African lamb sausage), chicken legs, and fresh mussels. *Maybe this would work for the dinner*, I mused.

But no, I realized as I monitored the rice to ensure it was forming a crunchy, brown crust on the bottom of the pan without burning. Although delicious, the dish would be far too complicated. For I would also be a *guest* of the dinner party, not simply the cook. So I certainly didn't want to spend the whole evening in the kitchen. The menu therefore needed to not only consist of interesting, tasty, and elegant dishes but also needed to leave me plenty of time to socialize.

Was such a thing even possible?

One evening while in Saint-Germain-en-Laye, Robin and I hosted a dinner party for several Parisian friends. We started with aperitifs and tiny *picholine* olives, and for the main course,[3] I prepared one of my favorite recipes: chicken

---

3. I've always thought it odd that Americans call the main course the "entrée," given that this French term refers to the *beginning* course in France, the word deriving from the French verb "to enter." In France they call the main course *le plat*, which literally means "the dish," and the *entrée* is the first course.

with mustard sauce. I was thinking it might work for the Ginsburg dinner, as the combination of Dijon mustard, brown sugar, balsamic vinegar, and butter makes for a heavenly glaze, and it's an easy, stick-it-in-the-oven-and-pretty-much-forget-about-it dish that works great for a dinner party.

But I wanted to try the chicken out on some folks with discerning palates before making any decision, and this group—devout foodies, all—was ideal for the task. Besides the two of us and Laura, there were three guests that night: our friend Philippe; my father's Harvard Law School classmate, Aram "Jack" Kevorkian (no, not *that* Jack Kevorkian); and his French wife, Eve.

Robin is an opera lover who met Philippe online through a site devoted to the mezzo-soprano, Tatiana Troyanos, and at the time of our dinner party, he was working as an agent for singers in Europe. I knew he'd be a terrific taste-tester, as he'd introduced us to some fabulous Parisian restaurants over the years and was never shy about telling us exactly what he thought of the food.

Robin and I had first met Jack, about whom my father had spoken fondly over the years, on a previous trip to Paris, at which time we learned he was the only American licensed to argue cases before the *Cour de cassation*, the French equivalent of our Supreme Court. Short, rotund, and as full of warmth, wit, and mirth as anyone I've ever encountered, Jack loved nothing more than an animated discussion of politics or music over a hearty meal of *steak-frites* and a bottle of fine Bordeaux.

In contrast to her gregarious American husband, Eve came across as withdrawn and genteel. But because her French was so rapid and full of colloquialisms and her English almost nonexistent, I must admit I never got to know her well. (Philippe, who spent much of that evening in discussion with Eve, has since assured me that she was quite the dynamo.)

Once we were all seated at the table, our plates of mustard-glazed chicken, roasted baby red potatoes, and butter lettuce salad before us, Robin raised her glass of Haut-Médoc and called for attention. "I just want you all to know that you were invited here tonight as guinea pigs."

At a blank look from Eve, Laura leaned over to translate this expression for her into French.

"Leslie's trying out this recipe on you tonight," Robin went on, "as she's thinking of cooking it for a dinner party this coming winter for a very special person—Supreme Court Justice Ruth Bader Ginsburg."

Eve's blank look returned, and even Philippe appeared unsure exactly who this famous person might be—though he did seem to appreciate her import by virtue of the title preceding her name.

But I could tell Jack was impressed, notwithstanding his feigned indifference. "Ruth . . . Ginsburg," he said, pretending to have to think about who she might be. "Ah, right. That young gal not too many years behind Ken and me at Harvard. I hear tell she's done very well for herself." And then he grinned. "So why are you cooking for the esteemed justice? Is she going out to the West Coast to see your father?"

While he dug gleefully into his meal, I explained the history behind the dinner, and how I now found myself nervous as hell, even though the event was still many months off.

Jack waved a dismissive hand. "No need to worry," he said, mouth full of chicken. "You make this delicious dish, and she'll be completely at your mercy."

"Right," I said as he let out a hearty laugh, then drank down his glass of wine. The idea of the justice being at anyone's mercy—least of all mine—struck me as highly improbable.

That night, once the guests had taken their leave and I'd stowed away in the fridge what little remained of the meal, Robin and I curled up in bed with her laptop to watch

Something's Gotta Give. In the film, the Diane Keaton character talks incessantly about going to Paris and how she has a favorite restaurant there—a *brasserie* called le Grand Colbert—where they make "the best roast chicken."[4]

"I wonder if it's as good as your mustard chicken," Robin remarked during the restaurant scene, then turned to face me. "Maybe you *should* cook that for the dinner, hon. Everyone seemed to really like it tonight."

"Maybe."

I've never been good at making decisions like this. When out to eat, I'm always the one who has to order last, not having yet made up my mind, since I find it excruciating to have to forego one item in place of another. And if I couldn't make up my mind what to eat at a restaurant, how was I going to decide on an entire menu as important as this one? It was a daunting task.

As a result, throughout the rest of our time in Paris, like a sauce left to reduce on the back burner, thoughts of the Ruth dinner continued to simmer away in my mind. And as I scanned a menu or tried a new dish, I'd be thinking: Is this something that would work for our meal? Would it work for a dinner for six? How much needs to be done at the last minute? Can this sauce be made in advance and then sit and be reheated?

In addition, I realized as I wandered up and down the aisles of the *marché* searching for that "perfect" food idea, I had no idea what the justice and her husband—who was also coming—even liked to eat or what they might not be able to eat because of food allergies or restrictions.

And then, standing in front of the *boucherie* stall, staring at the coils of fat sausages behind a glass case, I had a thought:

Ohmygod. What if they keep kosher?

---

4. Inspired by the movie, Robin and I tried to eat there one night during that trip, but it was a Sunday and—like most Parisian restaurants—the place was alas closed that day.

CHAPTER 2

Seasonable Doubt

D minus eight months.

The moment I returned to Santa Cruz from Paris, I was eager to write the Ginsburgs to find out if they had any food constraints, but I forced myself to hold off. It was only June, after all, and the dinner wasn't till the following January. I didn't want to seem *that* eager; that would surely be uncool. But there was no need to hold off on the bragging front. After all, hosting a celebrity such as Justice Ginsburg was truly something to crow about, particularly amongst my fellow attorneys.

Back in 2005, "RBG" was not the cultural phenomenon she is now, her face and dissent collar emblazoned across T-shirts and coffee mugs far and wide. And although I'd heard her name from a young age because of my father, it wasn't until law school that I became aware of how truly important she was. When we learned in our constitutional law class what a fiery advocate she'd been during her pre-jurist years, I began to fully appreciate how central a role she'd played in changing the law of the land regarding gender equality—and how awesome it was that my dad actually *knew* her.

Ruth Bader Ginsburg was, I now understood, a superstar in the world of women's rights. And I was going to have the opportunity not only to cook a dinner for the justice but to spend an entire evening in her company.

Wow.

And *Yikes!* I thought as realization hit. Stopping in the middle of the sidewalk, I startled Rosie, who'd been trotting ahead of me on our morning walk. What the hell was I going to *say* to her? Dad would have no doubt told the justice that I was an attorney. What if she wanted to talk *law* with me? A shiver of apprehension passed over my body, and I shook out my arms to release the nervous tension now gripping them.

Here I'd been spending all my energy worrying about the food for the dinner but hadn't even considered the conversation. Should I bone up on all the work she'd done as an attorney for the ACLU? Did I need to read about the cases that would be before her this term on the Supreme Court?

And then there was Ruth's husband, Martin, who my dad had told me was a celebrated tax attorney in DC. With four lawyers in attendance at the dinner, not to mention the almost-attorney, Robin, it was a sure bet the law was going to come up in conversation—a lot.

But I'm not like them, I whined internally. *I don't really even* like *the law.*

In fact, several years earlier, I'd become so unhappy in my work as an attorney that I'd come close to quitting. A blackness had started to greet me every morning when I awoke, and it had been getting worse. I'd lie in bed dreading the day ahead, wishing with all my might that I could call in sick or, better yet, simply give my notice and be done with it.

But then a strange thing happened. I was reading Henry Miller's *Tropic of Cancer*, the novel/memoir in which he's scrambling to eke out a half-starved existence in depression-era Paris[5], and when I got to the bit where he takes on a series of pseudonymous writing jobs, it made me pause. For even though Miller loathed the gigs, he was thankful for the work, which allowed him to eat well for a time and—more importantly—continue his life in Paris.

It struck me that what Henry Miller had wanted more than anything back in his Paris years was to write. And even if it was ghostwriting someone else's psychology thesis or hashing out pamphlets advertising a brothel, at least he was *writing*.

As was I, in my work.

I should be happy to be a legal writer, I reasoned—*thrilled, even. There must be thousands of writers out there who'd kill for a job like mine. So why on earth are you whining?*

It actually worked for a while. Because it was true. I may not have been working my dream job, but I began to appreciate how good I had it. Two of the things I loved most—besides food and cooking—were words and language, which were the exact tools of my trade.

Before long, however, the feeling of drudgery returned, and I was once again finding myself staring in misery at the legal casebooks spread out before me as I did research in our firm's law library, wondering why I'd ever chosen this line of work. And now I was going to be on show in front of one of the most famous attorneys who'd ever lived.

A vision of the time I'd been asked about my moot court project during law school swam before my eyes—when I'd blanked out and couldn't even remember the topic I'd been assigned for the damn brief. What if I had a similar episode the night of the big dinner and made a complete fool of myself? My stress level, which had already been sky-high at

---

5. I have a love/hate relationship with this book because, although it contains some gloriously poetic language and insightful looks at human nature, Miller also shows himself to be a narcissistic misogynist of the first degree.

the prospect of simply cooking for the Supreme Court justice, now increased tenfold.

But I tried to hide it and returned to work after my Paris sojourn full of my news, collaring all the other attorneys at the law firm as they pulled files in the hallway or looked up statutes in the law library, to tell them about my upcoming dinner with Justice Ginsburg. If I could delude them about my anxiety, perhaps I could delude Ruth. Not to mention myself.

INTERLUDE

Martin and Ruth Ginsburg have provided different versions of why she ended up deciding to go to law school. He liked to recount that after the two of them became romantically involved at Cornell, they came up with the idea of following the same career path so they'd have each other to bounce ideas off of and would always have something in common to discuss over dinner. Marty started out as a chemistry major but had switched to studying government when the chem labs conflicted with his golf-team schedule, so medical school was out—as was business, since the Harvard Business School didn't accept women. Therefore, by process of elimination, the Ginsburgs chose to pursue careers in law.

Ruth, however, told a different—and I suspect more likely true—story: Her undergraduate years at Cornell coincided with the Red Scare, when Senator Joe McCarthy was hauling people before the House Un-American Activities Committee to be interrogated for having belonged to socialist or communist organizations. After a Cornell teacher who refused to name fellow members of a Marxist study group was stripped of his teaching duties, the young Kiki Bader was horrified.

She had a professor of constitutional law at the time, Robert E. Cushman, who tried to make his students understand how the country was straying from its most basic values. He pointed out that it was lawyers who were standing up for these people, reminding Congress that we have a constitution that says we prize, above all else, the right to think, to speak, to write as we will without Big Brother looking over our shoulders. And so it occurred to Ruth that the legal profession would offer her the opportunity to get paid for her work and at the same time aim at something outside herself, to help repair the tears in society and make things better for other people.

Her family, however, was not pleased by this career choice because, as she put it, nobody wanted lady lawyers in those days. There was no Title VII[6], and discrimination was up front, open, and undisguised. How could she possibly make a living? they worried.

But then, when she married Marty upon graduation from Cornell, her family's attitude changed: Well, they now said, if Ruth wants to be a lawyer, let her try. And if she fails, she'll have a man to support her.

So marriage, rather than hindering her career—as was the case for so many women of her era—helped advance it.

• • •

Unlike Ruth Ginsburg, I did not end up in law school for altruistic reasons. Rather, I'd simply been casting about for a "real career" after spending several years post-college singing in my new wave rock band and waiting tables to pay the rent and had finally decided that graduate school would be an

6. Title VII of the Civil Rights Act of 1964 prohibits employment discrimination based on race, color, religion, sex, and national origin.

effective start to this new life. I was leaning towards the idea of the law, in part because it was likely to lead to a well-paying job, but also because I knew it would make my father proud. But I was also considering a master's degree in music, art, or romance languages.

I'm more or less an amalgam of both my parents, having inherited in equal parts their two very different natures. Although Dad was passionate about music and art, he always leaned far more towards the cerebral, finding solace in puzzles, language and word games, and thorny issues of legal construction. Mom, on the other hand—though possessing a keen, analytical mind herself[7]—was drawn to the arts, and spent her days creating whimsical ceramic sculptures and penning children's picture books and young adult novels.

I've often struggled to find a happy balance between these different natures within myself, at various periods of my life dipping into the worlds of music, foreign languages, painting, photography, and writing. In simplistic terms, then, the question ultimately came down to this: did I want to follow my mother's path or my father's?

Ultimately, the scales tipped in favor of law school after a discussion I had with Barbara Gunther, the teacher of a life drawing course I was taking at Cabrillo College in my late twenties. One day after class, Barbara happened to glance down at her roster and notice my last name.

"*Karst*?" she said, her eyes growing wide. "Are you *Ken and Smiley's*[8] daughter?"

And suddenly I realized why her name had seemed so familiar to me: Barbara's husband, Gerry Gunther, had been

---

7. After my sister Laura started kindergarten, Mom went back to school to finish her undergraduate degree, then went on to receive a master's in Latin American Studies from UCLA.

8. Smiley had been a family surname several generations earlier and was Mom's given middle name—though she went by Smiley (supremely appropriate to her warm and sunny personality) her entire life.

my father's classmate at Harvard Law School (along with Parisian ex-pat, Jack Kevorkian), and he and Barbara had been long-time friends of my parents.

After law school, Gerry went on to teach at Columbia, where—in a lovely twist of fate, at least with regard to the events of this story—he became one of Ruth Bader Ginsburg's professors. Knowing what a stellar law student she'd been, Gerry was outraged when he learned that Ruth had been unable to secure employment upon graduation. He promptly wrote a letter to New York District Court Judge Edmund L. Palmieri, telling him in no uncertain terms that he would never recommend another student to the judge if he failed to give Ruth Ginsburg an interview and promising that if she didn't prove worthy, he would send the judge a highly qualified male substitute.

It worked; Judge Palmieri hired her as a law clerk. And the rest, as they say, is history.

Gerry eventually moved on from Columbia to Stanford law school, where I ended up as his student as well.[9] I also worked as his research assistant, helping with the Learned Hand biography he later published, and Gerry and Barbara eventually became close friends of both Robin and me in addition to my parents.

So my signing up for a drawing class with Barbara turned out to be quite serendipitous: once it dawned on me who Barbara and her husband were, it occurred to me that—being familiar with both the art and legal professions—Barbara was in the perfect position to render an objective opinion about my choice of career path. Yes, I could have asked my parents, but I knew they'd be swayed by their own subjective desires and expectations. I needed a nonpartisan ear.

"Become a lawyer," Barbara responded without hesitation. "That way, you'll always be able to do your art or music or

---

9. I'm proud to be the only person ever to have been both Gerry and Barbara's student.

follow whatever passion you have on your *own* terms without having to sell out or scramble for money."

It seemed like sage advice. And at the time, attending law school struck me, too, as the logical choice—even if it wasn't necessarily my *heartfelt* choice. After all, ever since junior high school, plenty of Dad's UCLA colleagues—with whom I'd engage in verbal sparring matches whenever they'd come over for dinner—had been telling me I'd make a great lawyer. And, it turned out, I was in fact very good at my job.

One would think this history should have helped reduce my stress level about the upcoming dinner. But no. The fact that I could draft a mean legal brief or that I enjoyed a lively argument with someone I'd known since I was eight years old did little to increase my confidence regarding the evening I'd be spending with the Ginsburgs.

Nevertheless, since I couldn't come up with an immediate solution to reduce my anxiety about the dinner conversation, I did the next best thing: I simply pushed it back to the far reaches of my brain and focused instead on the menu for the meal.

During this time, I was the treasurer of my local chapter of Slow Food, an international non-profit organization that promotes "rediscovery of the pleasures of the table," while at the same time working to protect cultural identities tied to food, traditional cultivation and processing techniques, and heritage species of animals and vegetables. Largely because of my involvement in the Slow Food movement, I'd become interested in supporting local food growers and suppliers, patronizing farmers markets, and trying to purchase only humanely raised, pastured beef and pork and free-range poultry and eggs.

I also started paying more attention to seasonal foods, for instance, buying peas and baby lettuces in the spring and early summer; apples, corn, and red peppers in late summer and autumn; and broccoli and root vegetables in the winter. This, of course, is the way most of the world has eaten for millennia.

But now that we get imports year round from Florida, Central and South America, Hawai'i, and South-East Asia, it's easy to forget in the middle of December that the tomato in your salad has traveled thousands of miles to reach your mouth.

Because the dinner would be in January, I thought the menu should reflect—at least in part—that the event would be taking place in the dead of winter (though the chance of the temperature being in the 70s that time of year in Santa Monica where my folks lived was actually fairly good). So even though we were still in high summer, I started experimenting with wintry kinds of dishes.

I prepared *coq au vin*, following the five-page recipe in Julia Child's *Mastering the Art of French Cooking*. And, yes, the full-blown recipe truly *is* better than the shortcut versions. In particular, sautéing the mushrooms and onions separately and adding them at the end rather than just tossing them into the stew pot to cook along with the chicken allows the various components of the dish to maintain their own distinct flavors.

A few days later, I slow-cooked short ribs in equal parts Coca-Cola and dark beer till they were falling off the bone and swimming in a thick, savory-sweet gravy. Then I read up on how to braise vegetables in my *Larousse Gastronomique*, and Robin and I feasted on fennel and leeks that I'd baked in the oven with butter and chicken stock and finished with a dollop of cream and grated Romano cheese.

It did feel a bit odd to be doing so much cold-weather type cooking in July and August, but our perennial coastal fog in the summer months made it a little less strange. Santa Cruz isn't far from the Bay Area, and around here we're all too familiar with the famous Mark Twain quote about his summer in San Francisco.[10] In fact, more than a few times in

10. The quote, "The coldest winter I ever spent was a summer in San Francisco," though attributed to Twain, does not actually appear in any of his written work, and there is doubt amongst scholars that he ever even said it.

the heart of a Northern California summer, I've found myself looking forward to sitting down to a dinner of steaming pot roast with mashed potatoes.

While waiting for my beef or leeks to braise, Robin and I would spend cocktail hour on our bench in the front yard, enjoying the day's last lingering rays of sunlight. We'd raise our glasses of bourbon and branch to the passing cars, bicyclists, and pedestrians, and sometimes folks out for an evening stroll would stop and join us for a drink.

One such day that summer, our neighbor Joe walked slowly up to our bench, weighted down by a large cardboard box. He set it and himself down on the grass with a heavy *thunk*, and asked, "You gals like winter squash?"

"Sure," I responded, though at the time I didn't know a whole lot about how to cook the stuff. But the cogs in my head had started turning. *Winter* squash . . .

"My friend drives a truck for Safeway, and a crate of these here squash fell out onto the road. Ya can't sell 'em once the crate's broken, so he gave 'em all to me. I thought you might like some." He nodded toward the box.

There were acorn, butternut, and hubbard squash, and Robin and I ate them for weeks. I sliced them in half and baked them brushed with butter and then stuffed the cavities with leftover chicken stuffing. I made squash soup. I blanched diced pieces of squash and sautéed them with onions, pine nuts, and fresh mint.

Robin, who wasn't overly fond of winter squash to begin with, finally balked. "Can't we eat something *else* for a change?" she said, returning home from work one day to discover me slicing up yet another enormous, orange-fleshed monster. Then, "You know what? That's it. You can do whatever you want, but I'm done with squash. I'm heading down to the taquería for dinner."

"Fine. I'll eat it myself," I replied, trying to keep the hurt from my voice. But I knew she was right. No rational person would want to eat—or cook—winter squash every single day for weeks on end.

I really needed to take a break and decompress for a while. But how could I do so when my brain was so fixated on the search for that perfect dish to serve the Ginsburgs for dinner?

• • •

Summer gradually faded into fall. September and October are commonly the hottest months in coastal California, and this year was no exception, the weather warm and mercifully fog-free. I took idyllic bike rides, cruising up the coast along the Pacific Ocean. My vegetable garden was flourishing, and we were overrun with tomatoes, basil, yellow and red bell peppers, green beans, and zucchini. Our fruit trees were weighted down with enormous, crunchy Bosc pears and tiny, tart, Calville Blanc d'Hiver apples. We ate loads of caprese salads—vine-ripened tomatoes, mozzarella *di bufala*, basil, and balsamic vinaigrette—and baby spinach with pear slices and bleu cheese and walnuts.

Too bad the dinner is in January and not August or September, I thought ruefully as we gorged on nature's bounty from our own garden. What a shame it would be to have to *buy* fruit and vegetables.

Finally, when the weather abruptly changed and the mornings became chilly and the days noticeably shorter, I could wait no longer. It was November 3—exactly six months to the day since I'd received Dad's email informing me that the dinner was a go. Time to take the plunge. I wrote my father to get the email address for Justice Ginsburg's assistant at the Supreme Court.

CHAPTER 3

Of Fin Fish and Partnerships

D minus three months.

Dad wrote back almost immediately with the address for Linda O'Donnell, Justice Ginsburg's assistant. Nevertheless, now that I finally had no reason to postpone what I'd been so eager to do for the past five months, I was hesitant. It's not every day, after all, that one communicates with somebody in the justices' chambers at the United States Supreme Court.

What exactly would I write?

I'd actually met both Justice Ginsburg and Linda O'Donnell once before. When Robin and I had visited Washington, DC five years earlier, my father had contacted Linda and arranged for us to sit in Justice Ginsburg's "box" during oral arguments one day. Each justice has three reserved seats in the court room for their family or guests,[11] which are to the justices' left, across from the reporters' section.

I have to say that watching and listening to oral argument at the United States Supreme Court that day was one of the

11. The seats are technically in name of the justice's spouse (if there is one), but of course the justice's chambers decides who will fill them.

most awe-inspiring experiences of my life. (Two others that rank as highly were seeing hot flowing lava up close on the Big Island of Hawai'i and watching the aurora borealis chase across the sky in Fairbanks, Alaska.)

In order to better understand the lawyers' arguments and the justices' questions, Robin and I had studied up beforehand by reading the Circuit Court opinions in the two cases being heard that morning: there was a car search case and a case involving some complicated insurance law issue that I promptly forgot as soon as we left the courtroom.

We were both impressed beyond measure by the justices, who knew the law and the facts of each case inside and out and asked probing and deeply insightful questions of the attorneys, never letting up the pressure. The lone exception was Justice Thomas, who, as is his wont, never said a ding-dang word during either of the two cases on the docket that morning.

I'd often heard it said—and this experience proved it true—that the justices' questions can be more for the intended edification of their colleagues than for the purpose of actually hearing what the attorneys have to say about the case. And some of the questions were not what you would expect, either. Justice Scalia, for example—not noted for his liberal views on civil liberties issues—skewered that poor prosecutor in the search and seizure case with his exacting questions about what constitutes probable cause for a vehicle search.

Robin and I have since commented that the sheer amount of gray matter up there on that bench was truly astounding. I'm not by nature a flag-waving sort, but seeing the Court in action that day made me mighty proud of our judicial system.

At the conclusion of oral argument, we were escorted up to the chambers where Linda introduced us to Justice Ginsburg. The justice was polite and gracious, asking after my father and about our visit to Washington, but she was certainly no chatterbox. After a few awkward minutes standing around the lavish chambers, Robin noticed a photograph of Justices Ginsburg and Scalia on stage in powdered wigs. Knowing the justice to be an aficionado of opera like herself, Robin asked about the photo.

"That was taken on stage at the Washington National Opera," the justice replied, "when Justice Scalia and I were supernumeraries in *Ariadne auf Naxos*." And then, without any further elaboration, she picked up a brief sitting on her desk and said, "Now, this case on tomorrow's docket presents some fascinating issues of law."

Definitely not one for small talk, was she.

Five years later when I wrote to Justice Ginsburg's assistant, I reminded her of who I was and explained that I would be cooking dinner for the Ginsburgs and needed to know of any dietary constraints or food preferences they might have. Having been told by my father that Martin Ginsburg liked to cook, and not wanting to interrupt the justice at work (I envisioned her in the middle of drafting an important opinion about wiretapping or federal preemption, only to be interrupted by a frivolous query regarding onions), I suggested to Linda, *Perhaps you could forward my email to Mr. Ginsburg.*

I'll be happy to forward your email to Professor Ginsburg, she replied.

Merde. Faux pas number one. *He's a* Professor, *you numbskull, not a mere Mister.* I shoulda done my homework before simply shooting off correspondence to the Supreme Court. Chagrined, I wrote Linda again: *Oops. I didn't realize he was a professor; I was under the impression he was a partner in a DC tax firm.*

He is of counsel at a law firm and teaches at Georgetown, came the response. Ah, he's a floor wax *and* a dessert topping.[12] I didn't feel so bad anymore.

---

12. For you non-boomers, that's a reference to a Gilda Radner and Dan Aykroyd *Saturday Night Live* skit, *circa* 1976.

I also asked Linda about the federal marshals, as I was aware that these law enforcement officers travel with the Supreme Court justices when they're on the road. Robin and I had met two of the marshals at Stanford Law School a few years earlier when we attended the memorial service for my dear friend and former professor Gerry Gunther. Justice Souter had been a guest at the service, and when Robin and I noticed two men in suits on the periphery of the gathering who didn't look the least bit like law professors, law students, or lawyers, our curiosity prompted us to chat them up. They were forthcoming about being marshals and quite friendly and happy to tell us about their detail with Justice Souter.

We'd told my parents about meeting the marshals at Stanford, and it had thereafter become a running joke among us all—how there would be US marshals coming to my folks' house for the Ruth dinner. Before long, however, it progressed beyond a mere joke, as the four of us became more and more preoccupied with questions about them: *What* about *the marshals*? my father asked in an email. *Do you think they will come to the dinner? And if so, will they wait in the car or will they come inside*?

Then during a call with my mother, after wondering aloud how many marshals she and Dad should expect at their house, she raised a vitally important question: "Do you suppose they'll expect to be *fed*?"

So when I wrote back to Linda, I asked our burning question, putting it as a post script in a lame attempt to be casual: *P.S. I know that the US marshals tend to accompany the justices when they're out and about. Will they be with the Ginsburgs the night of our dinner; i.e., should I plan to prepare extra food for them?*

Linda answered that the marshals would be driving the Ginsburgs, but she didn't know exactly what they would do. *They haven't been assigned yet, so I will have to wait and ask when we are nearer to the event*, she wrote.

Oh boy, double uncool. *I'm so overeager with my trivial queries—months before the actual event—that the marshals haven't even been assigned yet. Oh well,* I figured; *she's probably used to neophytes.* Now wishing I could turn back the clock and wait an appropriate few more weeks before sending my query to Professor Ginsburg, I anxiously awaited his response.

I didn't have to wait long, for he replied but two hours later. At the sound of the high-pitched *ding* on my work computer, I glanced down at the bottom of the screen where it briefly reveals the sender's name and the title of the message. It was from *him.* Abruptly stopping work on the trial brief I'd been composing, I took a deep breath and opened the message:

> *How nice of you to ask. I eat anything (except poi); RBG likes fish and shellfish (as do I) and does not eat red meat. We have no known allergies. I'm sure the marshals will be with us. If offered superb food, doubtless they and we will be grateful—who would not be—but if offered none they will suffer stoically and say never a nasty word.*

And then I laughed out loud. Mostly from amusement at the message, but also from relief.

Remember, my only other interaction with either of the Ginsburgs had been that short meeting with the justice in her chambers when she had been friendly but distracted by her work. And then there was her short note to my father accepting his invitation to dinner. So from what I could gather, this was a woman who didn't waste words. I'd therefore been fretting not only over a menu and the idea that the justice might want to talk to me about law; I'd also been churning over the possibility that both she *and* her husband might be reserved and taciturn.

I consider any dinner party to be an utter failure unless everyone is talking at the same time at least once during the evening, but I now knew I need not worry. Professor Ginsburg was not only a warm and friendly guy, he was *funny*. And he clearly loved *food*! Although I'd never met the man, after reading that single email message I felt as if I knew him on some level. Not in any deep or fundamental way, but I had the feeling that I would like the guy and be comfortable around him. And that we perhaps shared a certain sensibility about the world.

Not wanting to appear over-anxious, I waited until the next day to reply to the professor. I thanked him for the information and noted that I, too, will eat pretty much anything—other than kidneys. I also assured him I would happily cook extra food for the marshals and asked, *Are there usually two of them?*

Prompt again, his answer came within the hour: *Usually 2, sometimes 3, in my experience. I like kidneys. Tripe too.*

I knew I was gonna like this man.

INTERLUDE

Kiki Bader and Martin Ginsburg met while both undergraduates at Cornell. The amiable and outgoing Marty, always ready with a witticism or one-liner, turned out to be the perfect match for the more serious and shy Ruth. He was one of the few people who could always make her laugh, and unlike most of his male counterparts at the college, wasn't put off by her intelligence, but rather, attracted to it. As Ruth later put it, he was the first boy she'd ever met who cared that she had a brain.

Not that Marty didn't have a brain of his own. He loved to downplay his own accomplishments, often quipping that at Cornell, where he played on the golf team, he stood low in his class—which he didn't—and that he'd done well at Harvard Law School because, unlike at Cornell, they didn't field a golf team.

The truth is, after graduating magna cum laude from Harvard, Martin Ginsburg went on to become one of the preeminent tax attorneys in the country, advising powerful clients such as Ross Perot on their corporate tax matters. (In his characteristic wry manner, Marty once stated: "A disproportionate part of my professional life has been devoted to protecting the deservedly rich from the predations of the poor and downtrodden.") And then, after tiring of the life of a full-time corporate lawyer—and having accrued considerable wealth doing so—he accepted a position as professor of tax law at Columbia University.

But perhaps his greatest accomplishment was the fierce and ceaseless support he provided his wife as she rose from student to professor, to advocate, to judge, and finally to justice of the United States Supreme Court.

Since her days in Sweden, Ruth Bader Ginsburg had spent her life striving for equality between the sexes, which, she consistently asserted, was as much about men entering the women's sphere as vice versa. And in Marty—who was always far more proud of his wife's accomplishments than his own—Ruth found a man pretty darn close to this ideal.

As a new father, he enthusiastically took part in caring for the baby Jane, happily managing the middle-of-the-night feedings since he knew his wife had a difficult time falling back to sleep. And when Ruth first went off to Sweden, Marty readily agreed to keep the six-year-old Jane with him in New York until they could join her.[13]

When Ruth was appointed to the DC Circuit Court of Appeals, Marty—without a moment's hesitation—gave up his position at Columbia so he could move with her to Washington, taking a less prestigious professorship at Georgetown University. And when

13. He wasn't perfect. There were quite a few years where he was more of the traditional absent father, because of the pull of the corporate law firm culture. But he later expressed regret about this.

it became clear that she had a realistic shot at a Supreme Court appointment, he campaigned tirelessly on her behalf, sending letters to and visiting everyone in DC with any sway over the matter and convincing his law partners and friends to do the same.

It worked. And Justice Ginsburg was the first to admit she would not have been on that high bench had it not been for the efforts and support of her husband. "I had a life partner who thought my work was as important as his," she stated soon after his death from cancer in 2010, "and I think that made all the difference for me."

• • •

I was now finally able to turn my attention to the menu for the dinner. Fish and shellfish, Marty had said. No red meat.

Oy, I thought with trepidation. Fish can be tricky—even for a trained chef with years of experience, which I most certainly was not. Not only is it easy to overcook, but sourcing good fresh fish and then scaling and filleting it can be difficult as well. I'd have to pull out my old culinary arts class notes to remind myself what I learned in the fish and shellfish lessons.

But for now, it was time to start making some decisions about the different courses for the dinner: what exactly would I cook?

We'd definitely need a soup course. Soup was classy, especially if served in the proper bowls with an artistic and tasty garnish. And it would satisfy my desire for the menu to have a wintry theme. I had been considering a recipe for roasted butternut squash soup that I'd recently clipped from the *New York Times Magazine*. It looked intriguing, but I had yet to try it out, as I'd run across the recipe only after finishing the last of the squash from the broken Safeway crate. I'd have to prepare a batch of the soup to see if it proved worthy of this momentous occasion.

But just how many courses should we have? It seemed appropriate to follow the traditional, "classic" approach to the menu, with an appetizer, soup, fish, salad, main, and dessert. But if fish was going to be the main course, would it be proper to serve a traditional "fish" course beforehand?

I know, I thought. *We can have one shell-fish dish and one fin-fish dish. Scallops! That's it; I love scallops!*

But was I brave enough to take on something as exacting as scallops for this event? I'd never prepared them myself but knew from my cooking school classes that if you weren't careful, they could turn into tough little balls of rubber. They required a deft hand, the little mollusks: a flash-searing till caramelized a toasty brown on the outside but only warmed—still virtually raw—in the center.

Pulling out all my cookbooks, I spread them on the floor and searched the indices for scallop recipes. I found lots of traditional options like *coquilles Saint-Jacques gratin*, scallops in white wine sauce, and scallops wrapped in bacon. Well, I certainly wasn't going to prepare a dish with bacon, and besides, I wanted something more out of the ordinary than all of those.

The next time I visited Bookshop Santa Cruz, I flipped through a few cookbooks, looking for likely scallop recipes. Nothing inspired me. Then I remembered a meal I'd eaten in Hawai'i years earlier when Robin's brother Russell and I had prepared dinner for our respective spouses and my parents. Russell, who loves to cook anything on the barbecue, grilled ahi tuna steaks, and I made a fresh tropical salsa to serve as a garnish for the ahi. It was a sort of Hawaiian *pico de gallo* made of equal parts coarsely chopped papaya, avocado, and red onion tossed in lime juice and a bit of chili powder.

That was the answer—I could do a similar *pico de gallo* salsa for the scallops! Okay, so it didn't really go with my wintry theme, but it sure as heck tasted good. And no one but me would even notice its non-wintery character. *Bingo*, I though with a smile of satisfaction. That's what I'd make.

When I told Robin of my idea, however, she shot it down. "It's too strong a taste to go with the scallops. You need something more subtle, or their delicacy will be overwhelmed."

The stubbornness in me pushed back against her. "What do you mean it's too strong? People serve all sorts of strong-flavored things with scallops." Once I finally settle upon something—which can take a long time, given my indecisive nature—I often have a hard time letting it go. Plus, I now realize I was so very eager to have at least *one* of the menu items for the dinner finally decided that my protest was more of a knee-jerk reaction than anything else.

"Whatever," Robin replied with a shrug. "It's your dinner; do as you like." But I knew in my heart she was right. I needed to come up with a different idea.

Lying in bed at night, I obsessed about scallops. Should they be served in a sauce, and if so, what kind—lemon-caper, East Asian, white wine, a *velouté*? And did I want to pan-fry them or perhaps bake or broil the delicacies? Whenever we went out to eat, I'd check to see if they were on the menu and how they were served. And if I was downtown, I'd cruise the bookstore magazine racks, flipping through the pages of *Food and Wine* and *Gourmet*, scanning for scallop recipes.

Now that I'd become fixated on scallops for the menu, I was unwilling to even consider another type of shellfish. Partly it was because of how much I personally loved to consume the dish; nothing truly compares to the savory yet slightly sweet taste of the scallop, with its hint of the briny depths and its near-perfect pillowy texture. But also, I wanted to prove to myself that I could do it—that I could prepare the perfect scallop dish, one that rivaled the offerings of the finest restaurants in Northern California. Yep, stubborn, that's me.

Then one day Robin suggested, "Why don't you just Google it?"

Although not a *total* dweeb when it came to computers, back in 2005 when I was on this recipe hunt, I hadn't yet gotten used to the idea that you could use them to search for information. If I had a question about something, I still tended to look it up in a book, perhaps in *Webster's Dictionary*, Bartlett's *Familiar Quotations*, or the old US history text I'd bought at a garage sale. But, of course, Google could do most of these things at the mere flick of a mouse. So I took her advice and sat down at the computer.

¡Ay chihuahua! There were five gajillion scallop recipes online. I was overwhelmed.

Okay, girl, you've got to limit your search; you can't simply type in "scallop recipes." But as I was helplessly scrolling down through the countless ways to cook the delectable shellfish, I noticed that many of them shared a common denominator: *cream*. As I mentioned earlier, it's no secret that I adore cream. *So*, I thought, *let's do a search with "cream" and "scallops."*

This decreased the search results to merely one gajillion recipes. Undaunted, I started scanning through them. Many, it turned out, were similar: lots of dishes with cream and white wine or cream and garlic. And then I saw that quite of few of the recipes also featured ginger. *Ginger and cream?* I liked that; it offered some of the tropical flavor I was going for in my vetoed salsa idea but was more subtle—not to mention creamy! Then I stumbled upon a recipe with a ginger-lime cream sauce. Now, *that* sounded delicious. I hit "print screen."

• • •

Squash soup and scallops. Two courses down—or at least tentatively on tap. Given my propensity for indecision, there was every likelihood I'd change my mind somewhere down the line. But for now, I'd move on to the rest of the menu.

So what about the salad course and main dish?

Not long before, I'd thrown a dinner party for which I prepared a salad of baby spinach, foie gras, pine nuts, and pear slices poached in red wine. I then made it again for another meal, this time substituting prosciutto for the foie gras and blood oranges from our own tree in the back yard for the poached pears. It was a good palate-cleansing dish, the saltiness of the prosciutto complementing the sweet/tart blood oranges. And it looked attractive as a composed salad, the red flesh of the oranges set off against the dark green spinach leaves. *And*, I noted with satisfaction as I considered the possibility of using this salad for the Ruth dinner, blood oranges are a *winter* fruit.

Perfect.

Then my shoulders slumped. *Wait. Ruth doesn't eat red meat; I can't use prosciutto in the salad.* And even though foie gras is technically poultry, that whole force-feeding thing could turn some folks off, so it would probably be best to nix it from the list as well. *Sigh* . . . Briefly, I toyed with the idea of making that second version of the salad and simply leaving the prosciutto off Justice Ginsburg's plate but quickly rejected it. She would be the guest of honor, after all, and therefore the dishes should be based on *her* palate. But what if I could find a worthy replacement for the prosciutto?

For two days I angsted about my salad, brainstorming salty and savory ingredients worthy of a Supreme Court justice. *Smoked oysters?* No. We already had shellfish on the menu, and I wasn't sure how well the flavor of oysters would pair with blood oranges, in any case. *What about anchovies?* No again; Robin would hate that—far too fishy for her taste.

And then, as I was flipping through a treatise on landlord-tenant law—my mind more on salad ingredients than forcible eviction—I hit upon the perfect solution. "Bleu cheese!" I said aloud, startling my fellow attorney, Bob, who was seated across from me at the firm's law library table.

"Huh?" He looked up at me, confusion in his eyes.

"Oh, sorry. Just thinking about the salad course for my Ruth Ginsburg dinner."

"Ah. Well, that sounds good to me," Bob replied with a grin. "You can never go wrong with bleu cheese."

As he returned to his Insurance Code annotations, I pretended to study the page open before me, all the while musing about cheeses. *A rich, crumbly one, like Gorgonzola.* And it would pair perfectly with what Robin calls my "house dressing," I noted with satisfaction.

In my family we're all salad freaks. When we kids were growing up, Mom would prepare enormous tossed green salads in a big wooden bowl, and the rule was: "No one leaves the table until the salad's gone." As a result, after Robin and I met and I started cooking for her, I was dismayed to see her only pick at the salads I prepared. "What, don't you like it?" I'd ask when she took only a small helping from the bowl.

"No, it's not that. I'm just not a big fan of salads, is all."

"Really?" This seemed unfathomable to me. So I set out to change her mind.

Knowing that Robin had a powerful sweet tooth, I started experimenting with sweet ingredients in my salads such as red seedless grapes and dried cranberries, to try to win her over. In addition, having learned in cooking school that the secret of a tasty salad dressing is often the addition of a little sugar, I started preparing my own slightly sweet dressings. A favorite is my Japanese-inflected specialty: mayonnaise, a touch of white sugar, soy sauce, and sesame oil—all thinned with a little milk. And what came to be called my "house dressing," a lovely Dijon vinaigrette made of mustard, balsamic vinegar—which is sweet itself—garlic, black pepper, olive oil, and a little brown sugar.

It worked. Robin now ate as much salad as I did and even held her own at Karst family dinners when the gigantic salad bowl was passed around the table.

My salad musings were interrupted by Bob pushing back his chair. "So what are you going to make for the main course for the big dinner?" he asked, returning his book to the shelf.

"Good question. But I haven't decided yet." It was an important decision. The main course—traditionally meat or chicken—is what tends to be remembered after a meal is long over.

In my experience, however, it's often overrated; you're usually so full and your taste buds so exhausted by the time the main course arrives that a finely prepared meat dish is almost wasted on the diner. I certainly didn't want *that* to happen at the Ruth dinner. So I needed to make sure my earlier courses were small—a sort of tasting menu—and the main course interesting enough to hold its own against the earlier dishes.

I'd already settled on fish—fin fish, rather than shellfish—to follow the salad, but the question was, what kind? Because Santa Cruz sits right on the Monterey Bay, all sorts of fresh seafood is available in our town year-round, so I had a wealth of varieties to choose from. My plan was to do all the shopping before driving down to my parents' house, as there wouldn't be time between my arriving in LA and the big event.

"What kind of fish do you think I should serve for the Ruth dinner?" I asked Robin one evening at cocktail hour.

"I don't much care," she replied. "Whatever you want—as long as it's not too fishy tasting." Although she adores sushi, Robin's never been big on cooked fish, which tends to have a much stronger flavor than the raw variety. "Didn't you tell me that lean fish are milder than the fatty ones? So maybe one of those."

"Yeah, that's true. I'm sure you'd prefer something like halibut over salmon or mackerel."

"What kind of wine would you serve with halibut?" she asked. "Would it have to be a white?"

"Dang. Good point, it probably would. We don't want that." Neither Robin nor I are great fans of white wine, and we tend to agree with Robin's brother Russell, who likes to say, "The first obligation of a wine is to be red."

Now, I do enjoy a spicy Gewürztraminer or Riesling with Szechuan or Thai food, and I've been known to sip a sauvignon blanc whilst whipping up a batch of fettuccine Alfredo. But I definitely did *not* want to plan an entire dinner—particularly *this* dinner—without setting us all up for the magic that is a table full of smart people after several bottles of great red have been uncorked.

Okay, so I'd need a fish dish that could stand up to a red wine, even if it was a light one. *What if I prepared the fish in a robust, spicy style?* I'd been experimenting of late with searing fish steaks in a cast-iron skillet so that the outside turned nice and crispy while the inside remained juicy and rare. One popular dish cooked in this method is blackened fish, which is traditionally done with a Cajun dry rub of cumin, cayenne, garlic and onion powders, black pepper, and salt. But maybe that would be overkill on the spices. Did Ruth and Marty even like spicy food?

One brisk, windy afternoon after work while taking Rosie for a walk, as I watched the red and yellow leaves from a Japanese maple tree being tossed into a flurry, I had an idea: what about blackened ahi tuna, but with an Asian twist? I could coat the fish in a dry rub of brown sugar, sea salt, a little chili powder, and black sesame seeds and then sear the steaks in roasted sesame oil.

Yes. Ahi, with its ruby red flesh and meaty flavor would pair nicely with a light or medium-bodied red wine. Maybe I was finally getting there!

But then what would I serve for the starch? Rice would be the traditional choice of side for ahi tuna, but it seemed far too pedestrian for this elegant meal. I mused on this question, zipping up my jacket against the cold. *Something that can be made in advance so I won't have to be in the kitchen too much once the guests have arrived. How about soba noodles? They go well with ahi.* But then I thought about how easy it would be to overcook them, since they'd get mushy if they sat too long in the hot water waiting to be served. Not only that, but I had no clear vision of how to plate up the noodles so they would look attractive.

Wasabi popped into my head. *That's it*, I thought. *Wasabi mashed potatoes! Wasabi is a natural partner for tuna.* I could lay the tuna steaks over part of the potatoes, and a small serving of some vegetable could sit on the other third of the plate.

Perhaps fava beans. They're always a treat, and most restaurants don't serve them because they're so labor intensive. Each individual bean pod has to be individually shelled, then blanched and skinned—and only then are they ready to cook. I like to sauté them quickly in butter or olive oil with a little garlic or lemon zest and cracked black pepper. But then I remembered that the dinner would be in January, and fava beans don't come into season until several months later. *Damn*. This thing was like one long-running game of Tetris.

Returning home with Rosie, I scribbled my notes on a piece of paper. At least I now had a concept for all four of the savory courses: appetizer, soup, salad, and main course. The vegetable could wait. I also still needed to think about dessert, as well as something to nosh on during cocktails.

But I felt relieved to have come this far.

CHAPTER 4

But Will It Play in Peoria?

D minus two months.

Now that I finally had a rough outline of the menu for the dinner, my thoughts turned to the wines I'd serve with the various courses.

While in cooking school, I took a wine tasting class taught by an eccentric woman named Anita, who dressed only in burgundy-colored clothes. A couple of years later, I ran into her at the grocery store—she was wearing a burgundy sweater and matching wool slacks—and she invited me to join a "high-end" tasting group that met at her house once a month to try expensive new-release as well as "library" (i.e., aged) wines. The idea was that for $50 to $70 you could taste six or seven different wines that might cost that much or more for a single bottle.

The first event I attended was of aged California cabernet sauvignons, which were the only "good" wines I knew much about. A box of tasting glasses tucked under one arm, I knocked at the door of Anita's Victorian-era home and then gasped as she let me into her living room.[14] I was surrounded on all sides by

14. At the start, Robin chose not to attend these tastings, though she did eventually join the group.

wooden cases of wine stacked halfway to the ceiling. Additional cases and single bottles sat on all the tables and chairs. It was like being in one of those houses where a weird old lady keeps thousands of yellowed newspapers stacked against all the walls or has dozens of cats lying all over the furniture and carpet. But in this house there wasn't a cat or newspaper in sight; there was wine, wine everywhere.

When I stopped to stare, Anita just laughed and said, "That's nothing; you should see how many more I have underneath the house in my wine cellar."

There were eight of us at that night, tightly packed around Anita's small dining room table and surrounded by yet more boxes of wine. As I unwrapped my glasses, I told Anita of my love of big, full-bodied cabs. She smiled and replied in a knowing voice, "Oh, just you wait. You'll soon come to love pinots best. They're the most complex and interesting wines." The others in the group nodded their heads gravely in agreement.

Anita poured wine number one into her first glass and passed the bottle around for the rest of us to follow suit. After all six wines had been poured, we swirled our glasses to release the aromas and smelled each one in turn. Anita had passed out sheets of paper for our tasting comments, and several people immediately began writing copious notes.

The wines we drank that night were unlike any I had ever tried: Caymus, Château Montelena, Diamond Creek, Heitz . . . *Okay*, I thought afterward, *pinot noir may be good, but how could you possibly match those amazing wines?* (She ended up being right, though: I have come to love pinots and French Burgundies the best.[15])

---

15. A team of researchers has now mapped the genome of the pinot noir grape, and found that it has more genes in its DNA than does the human genome. Over 100 of them are dedicated to producing tannins and terpenes (which create flavor)—double that of any other plant.

The wine tastings were always blind. Anita had made cloth bags to cover the bottles, and after trying all the wines, we would vote on them, ranking them in order of least-to-most favorite. Anita would then compile the results using some mysterious mathematical formula known only to her—sometimes there would have to be a run-off between two wines, which would always set off a flurry of quick, frantic sips and requests for more wine—and then she would announce the group rankings, unveiling each one in turn.

At first I was a bit nervous and shy at these events, surrounded as I was by this group of knowledgeable wine aficionados. But then after several tastings, a woman named Sandy and I noticed that we often voted the same way, which led to an immediate bond between us. Sandy and I especially loved it when we both ended up ranking the wines in the exact same order as the group's average. I had told her about a law school friend, Lee from Peoria, who boasted that the expression, "If it plays in Peoria, it'll play anywhere" is actually true—that big companies really do test new products in Peoria because, supposedly, the city's demographics are similar to those of the country at large. ("McDonald's first test-marketed the Big Mac in Peoria," Lee once told me with pride.)

So whenever either Sandy's or my vote was the same as the group ranking, we'd exclaim with glee, "I'm Peoria!" By this time of the night, of course, after we'd all sipped through the better part of six or seven bottles of wine, the noise and rowdiness level of the group had always risen quite a bit, so one would have to shout to be heard over the din.

This bonding over a shared taste in wines and "being Peoria" eventually led to a friendship, and Robin and I started socializing with Sandy and her husband Tom outside of Anita's tastings. Sandy and Tom are extremely knowledgeable about wine and have an enormous cellar in their home, full of exotic bottles from all over the world. Since I love to cook, we therefore started a tradition of having joint dinners: I'd be in charge of preparing the meal and would tell Sandy the menu in advance, and she would bring the wines she thought would pair well with the different courses.

When it came time to try out some of the recipes I was thinking of using for the Ruth dinner, it therefore only seemed natural to invite Sandy and Tom over to help select the wines for the meal, as well as giving thumbs up or down to the dishes. I told Sandy I'd be making a roasted butternut squash soup and a baby spinach salad, and she said she'd think about appropriate varietals. For the main course, I decided to make my short ribs braised in Coke and dark beer, even though I knew I couldn't make them for the dinner with the Ginsburgs. But I had a hankering for beef—and the great wine I knew Sandy would bring to go with it—and I figured I could try out the blackened ahi some other time.

The night before our dinner party, I made the soup. The recipe I'd clipped was one of Thomas Keller's, the owner and head chef of the famed French Laundry in the Napa Valley. It called for cutting off the neck of the squash before roasting the rest and then simmer this piece in the soup, unroasted—to maintain the neck's bright color and fresh flavor, I figured. In addition, the recipe included leeks, carrots, and a bit of honey, which struck me as intriguing, since most butternut squash soups simply include onions, celery, and potatoes. But the clincher for me was that the soup was finished with brown butter, stirred in right before service, which sounded particularly yummy.

Sandy brought two different wines to try with the soup and the salad: a Hartford Court chardonnay from the Sonoma coast, and a Kim Crawford sauvignon blanc from New Zealand. Neither of us is usually all that fond of chardonnay, but we had discussed it beforehand and decided that the strong flavors of the butternut squash soup might match better with a chard than a sauv blanc.

I served the soup, which I'd garnished with chopped walnuts over a spiral of crème fraîche piped out of a squirt bottle, and Sandy poured us all a taste of both wines. We tried the sauvignon blanc first and found it to be typical for New Zealand, with its fairly aggressive flavors.

"I get pineapple with a tinge of tart grapefruit," Sandy commented.

"Hmmm," I murmured, frowning and swirling my glass in an attempt to unlock the same elusive aromas from my wine. Then we tried the chardonnay, which was much more citrus driven than the sauvignon blanc.

After sipping the soup and the two wines in turn for several more moments, Sandy and I looked at each other: definitely the chard, we agreed. It let the soup shine, while the sauvignon blanc seemed to fight it. Robin and Tom concurred.

"But what about the soup itself?" I prompted them. "What do you think of the recipe?" More sips and rolling of soup about the tongue, as if it were a fine wine.

"Too sweet," volunteered Robin.

This was a bit surprising, given her fondness for sweet food. But Sandy and Tom nodded their heads as well, and I found that I had to agree. It *was* too sweet. Too much honey, in particular. In fact, I decided, I didn't really like the honey in the soup at all; it made it too much like those sugary-sweet yam dishes some folks serve at Thanksgiving.

"I guess maybe I shouldn't serve it at the Ruth dinner," I said with a slow sigh.

Robin shook her head. "No, I bet you can fix it. You're really good at that—tweaking recipes till they're perfect."

"I dunno . . ." Kind and supportive as this comment was, all I could focus on at that moment was my disappointment at the failed soup course.

"I think all you need to do is omit the honey," Sandy piped up. "'Cause the basic recipe seems really great."

The others voiced their support of this idea.

"I suppose I could cut down on the number of carrots, too," I said, "since they're naturally pretty sweet. And I could use more leeks, to bump up the savory-vegetable flavor." I was warming to the idea. "If I do that, I bet the soup will be way better."

"Atta girl." Robin slapped me on the back. "And I sure don't mind trying it again once you adjust the recipe."

"Thanks, hon. Glad you've finally gotten over your earlier squash overdose."

Our soup and wine homework completed, the conversation now turned to the honored guests who would be consuming them in only two months' time. "So I know Ruth Ginsburg is famous for being on the Supreme Court an' all," Tom said, refilling our glasses and then topping off his own, "but you said something earlier about her and the ACLU. Did she work for them before she became a judge?"

I nodded and took a sip of chardonnay to wash down my mouthful of crusty baguette. "She did. And I have to say, in the legal world she's as famous for her successes back then on behalf of women's rights as she is for her opinions as a justice on the Supreme Court." Setting down my glass, I leaned forward. "I've been reading up on her—you know, in preparation for this dinner—and did you know that between 1971 and 1979, Ginsburg took part in *thirty-four* sex discrimination cases for the ACLU that made it to the US Supreme Court? And not only that, but she argued six of them herself, and won five of those six."

"Wow," Tom said. "Impressive."

"No kidding. Of course, I studied a lot of those cases when I was in law school—it was still pretty new law back then—but it wasn't till I started thinking about this dinner, about getting the chance to spend a whole evening with her, that it truly hit me, the import of what she'd done. 'Cause really, when you think about it, Ruth Ginsburg is pretty much responsible for all sorts of rights and opportunities that I always just took for granted—you know, having grown up after a lot of the fight had already been won."

"I'm old enough that I sure remember the time before that, and it was not fun," Sandy said with a shake of the head, then raised her glass in salute. "So thank you Ruth Ginsburg."

"But what's really interesting is *how* she was able to win all those cases," I went on after clinking glasses with Sandy. "She knew those old geezers on the Supreme Court would be a hard sell, so she avoided cases with hot-button issues that screamed 'women's lib!' and looked instead for ones to bring involving mundane, unsexy issues. You know, like social security and tax law. Things that would appeal to the sensibilities of the old men on the Court—and to middle America."

"You mean Peoria?" Sandy asked with a laugh.

"Exactly!" I said. "She knew she'd never be able to win the struggle for women's rights until it could play in Peoria."

INTERLUDE

In the spring of 1970, just a few months before that summer law conference in Pescara, Italy, Professor Ginsburg taught her first course on women and the law at Rutgers. Several women law students had come to her to request the class, and Ginsburg responded by reading every law review article and federal decision on the subject—a task that took less than a month, given the dearth of writing in this area of the law.

As she learned more and more about the arbitrary distinctions regarding men and women that existed in federal statutes and regulations, she began to wonder, how could people have been putting up with them for so long? How could *she* have been doing so? It was as if her consciousness had finally been awakened.

Then, in the fall of that same year, these concerns were transformed into action. It was her tax attorney husband, Marty, who (according to him, anyway) was the catalyst for the gender equality litigation that would be Ruth Bader Ginsburg's prime focus for the next ten years. He was in his home office one night reading new tax law rulings when he came across one that piqued his interest. Walking next door to the adjacent office, he handed the case to his wife. "You need to read this," he said and, ignoring her "I don't read tax cases" rejoinder, returned to his study.

Within five minutes, Ruth rushed into his office, beaming. "Let's take it!" she exclaimed.

They did. And in so doing, changed history.

The Tax Court ruling involved a traveling salesman whose eighty-nine-year-old mother lived with him and who paid someone to care for her when he was away on business. If Mr. Moritz had been a widowed or divorced man, or any woman no matter her status, he would have been entitled to a $600 dependent care deduction under the relevant statute of the Internal Revenue Code. But because he was a single man, he had been denied the deduction.

Ruth immediately recognized that this was the perfect case to raise the issue of gender equality. With the judicial benches filled almost entirely with stodgy, white men—who tended to view laws premised on gender-based stereotypes as being for the benefit of the "gentler sex"—she needed cases demonstrating that arbitrary distinctions based on sex hurt both men and women.

Moreover, the canny professor knew she risked alienating her audience of judges if she came across as some kind of "flaming feminist." Better to keep it simple and arcane—to avoid the complex or intimidating and educate the courts slowly and incrementally. What better way to begin that education than to present the story of a mild-mannered caregiver of an elderly mother who had been denied a tax deduction solely because he was a man?

And once they prevailed on this case (which they did[16]), the precedent would be set, laying the path toward, as Ginsburg termed it, "the constitutional principle of the equal citizenship stature of men and women."

• • •

I ate the last of my soup and got up to finish preparing the next course while Robin, Sandy, and Tom scraped their bowls clean and started to discuss what to do about the wimpy, non-visionary, Democratic National Party.[17] Our house is designed with the kitchen open to the dining room, so I'm able to still be in on the conversation around the dinner table when I'm busy cooking. But even though I heard what they were saying, I didn't have an answer to that question, so I focused on a surprise last-minute addition I'd made to the menu.

Our local grocery store had featured fresh sushi-grade ahi on sale the day before, and I'd decided to buy a little in order to test the difficulty and tastiness of my intended main course for the Ruth dinner. I'd already coated the fish with the dry rub—sea salt, chili powder, brown sugar, wasabi

16. For you legal beagles out there, the published opinion in the appeal filed by the Ginsburgs is *Moritz v. Commissioner of Internal Revenue*, 469 F.2d 466 (10th Cir. 1972). On losing at the appellate level, the government petitioned for certiorari, but the Supreme Court denied review, thus affirming the 10th Circuit's decision on behalf of Mr. Moritz.
17. Remember, this was 2005, the year after the Kerry-Edwards presidential slate.

powder, and black sesame seeds—so all I had to do was add a second coating of the seasonings while the sesame oil was heating in my cast-iron skillet and then sear the tuna quickly so it was still raw in the middle but nicely blackened on the outside.

"Huh? What's this?" Robin asked as I set the plates down. There was a small triangle of fish on each plate, with a tiny pile of *gari*—pickled ginger—nestled next to it.

"Just think of it as an *amuse-bouche*, but in the wrong order," I said. "I'm thinking of serving it as the main course at the big dinner."

"But I didn't bring a wine for this," Sandy said, attacking her plate with relish.

"I know. It was a last-minute addition. But tell me what you think of it, and what sort of wine you think it should be paired with."

There was a brief silence—unusual for this group—while we all chewed and contemplated. "Also too sweet," Robin declared after a bit. More grunts of agreement from Sandy and Tom.

I tasted it again. Yes, definitely too much brown sugar. "Damn," I said. "Two for two thumbs down so far."

"Hey, that's why you're testing the dishes out on us guinea pigs," said Robin. "And they'll all be great once you adjust the recipes a bit."

"Yeah, you're right. Better tonight than at the actual dinner," I said. Then at the sound of Sandy's bark of laughter, I added, "Not that this isn't an actual dinner, of course. But I do like the combination of spicy and sweet, and the crunch of the sesame seeds with the ahi."

Tom forked up the last of the tuna on his plate and licked the utensil clean. "Me, too. I'd definitely order this again."

"So, I'm thinking of serving it with wasabi mashed potatoes. What do you think?"

Yes, they all agreed; that would pair well with the ahi.

"But what about the wine?"

"I think you might have to go with a white," Tom said.

"Huh-uh." I shook my head. "No way. We have to have a red wine for the main course. I think it would stand up to a light one. Maybe a Châteauneuf du Pape or a Rhône?"

Sandy took another taste. "Yeah, that might work," she agreed. "But it shouldn't be too big."

I stood up to serve the salads, which I'd prepared in advance and put in the fridge to keep chilled. There were four separate composed salads, each with a base of baby spinach leaves and topped with rounds of blood oranges and red onion overlapping each other. Over this I had crumbled bleu cheese and sprinkled dried cranberries and pine nuts.

I brought the dressing—my "house" dijonnaise—to the table in a small pitcher to let people dress their own salads. One thing I was unsure about was what to do regarding the salad dressing at the Ruth dinner. On one hand, it's always best to toss a salad with the dressing before serving it so it's evenly coated over all the greens. But you have to wait until immediately before service to toss a salad with the dressing; dress it too early, and you'll end up with a plate of limp and wilted leaves. A problem therefore arises with composed salads: you have to either toss the entire salad and then compose the individual plates immediately before service—which requires a lot of last-minute labor—or compose them in advance and drizzle the dressing over the salads right before serving them—which doesn't taste as good. Quite the dilemma.

I was also concerned about the blood oranges. The ones I used that night in late-November for the meal with Sandy and Tom were pretty much the last of the fruit on our tree from the previous season. There were new ones on the branches, but even though oranges are a winter fruit, I was worried they might not ripen in time for the dinner in late January.

After tasting the salad, Sandy, Tom, and Robin all pronounced it to be splendid, agreeing that it would be a good palate cleanser before the main course. Thank goodness for that.

We discussed the question of wine and decided it would be best to simply let folks keep drinking the chardonnay left over from the soup course. Wine doesn't really go with salad in general, since the high acidity of the vinegar in the dressing clashes with the low acid and the alcohol in the wine (vinegar is, after all, merely wine with its alcohol converted to acid). But if anyone did want to sip their wine during the salad course, we figured a chardonnay would hold its own as well as any white.

I smiled in satisfaction as I cut a section of blood orange and speared it along with a slice of red onion, then popped them into my mouth. *Yes*. The menu was coming together.

CHAPTER 5

The Holy Grail and Other Dinnerware

D minus six weeks.

In mid-December, Robin and I drove down to Los Angeles for the weekend to go with my parents to hear Plácido Domingo in Richard Wagner's *Parsifal* at the LA Opera.

Robin adores Wagner's operas, which, she says, "give musical voice" to her deepest feelings. In particular, she's captivated by the way he is able to communicate the essence of humanity through his sublime music, taking the listener inside the thoughts and brains of his characters to convey their most profound emotions.

But it's also the stories he tells. One of the primary themes running throughout Wagner's work is the protagonist fighting against the odds, against the world. And what is more, unlike virtually every other opera composer, Wagner often makes his *women* the heroic characters. Just think of Brünnhilde and her brave and selfless acts of redemption. Or Isolde, Sieglinde, and Senta—tough, proactive women all, and the instigators of the action and drama in the operas. And because Wagner always wrote his own libretti, these strong female protagonists are truly his own creations.

Throughout her own life, Robin has consistently found herself running up against the status quo in terms of being a woman in a man's world. One of her most vivid memories of early childhood is being told to put her shirt back on when she was up in a tree, playing with the neighborhood boys.

"But *Mom*," she protested, "Tarzan doesn't *wear* a shirt!"

"I'm sorry Robin, but girls have to wear shirts."

"But the boys don't have their shirts on. It's not *fair*!"

And in adulthood she has consistently pursued jobs that are typically male-dominated: working as a union electrician, where she would often find herself the sole woman on-site amidst hundreds of male construction workers, and later, acting as the first woman facilities manager at UCSC.

Robin acknowledges that many—if not most—women have neither the predisposition nor the predilection to work in these traditionally male fields. But, she contends, she and those other women who *do* have the desire to pursue such careers ought to be given a fair chance to show they're able to do so without always first having to run the gauntlet to prove they can. As Robin sees it, this is what feminism is all about.

This philosophy was of course shared by Ruth Bader Ginsburg, who entered Harvard Law School at a time when women were still *personae non gratae* (and weren't admitted at all to the business school), and who only secured her first legal job after graduation because of that near-blackmail on her behalf by Gerry Gunther. Yet the young attorney persisted in her dream and, like the young knight Parsifal, never gave up her quest for that Holy Grail of women's rights. And not only did Ginsburg continue in this struggle for gender equality, she ended up being instrumental—both as an advocate and later as a jurist—in ultimately making it the law of the land.

Robin was thus especially eager, she'd told me, to see the justice again at the upcoming dinner because she wanted to thank her for making her life—and the lives of other women like her—so much easier.

INTERLUDE

When Ruth Ginsburg enrolled in Harvard Law School in 1956, she was one of nine women out of a class of five hundred.[18] There were no dorm rooms for women; they had to find digs off campus. And although there were two classroom buildings, only one had a women's bathroom, and that was in the basement. So if you were a woman taking a class—or worse, an exam—in the building without a women's bathroom, the justice later recounted, you had to make a mad dash if you needed to use the restroom.

The professors were, of course, all men in those days and loath to call on their women students. Except, that is, on "Ladies' Day," which some of them would hold, when they would call *only* on the women, asking humiliating questions. Not surprisingly, Ruth and the other female students felt as if all eyes were on them in class and as if they didn't belong.

Nevertheless, the bright and hard-working Ruth Ginsburg was one of two women who made the Harvard Law Review during her second year as a law student.[19] Her work for the prestigious journal was made much harder, however, by virtue of her sex. At the time, women were barred from one of the reading rooms in Lamont

---

18. Coincidentally, the first year that HLS admitted women was 1950, my father's class at the law school. Dad later returned to Harvard for a year as a teaching fellow, during RBG's second year there.
19. This is an institution peculiar to law schools, in which the top students are chosen to edit legal articles written by law professors and learn the craft of scholarly writing themselves. Being selected for law review is pretty much mandated for those students who desire judicial clerkships or careers as law professors.

Library—a room that housed periodicals the law review members needed to check for citations contained in the Law Review articles. One late night, the future-justice frantically begged the guard to grab a journal she needed for a cite-check while she stood at the door, but he refused her request.

Justice Ginsburg has told many times the story of Dean Griswold inviting the nine women law students to dinner and then asking how they justified occupying a seat at the law school that could have been filled by a man. Ruth was so flustered that she gave an answer she didn't truly believe—that she wanted to know more about what her husband did (Marty was a year ahead of her at the law school), so she could be a sympathetic and understanding wife.

But what's not so commonly known is that the dean, years later, claimed that he had not asked this question to be unkind. Rather, he explained, there were still doubting Thomases on the HLS faculty who thought it unwise to admit women, and he simply wanted to be armed with stories from the women themselves so he could satisfy his colleagues that they would make good use of their law degrees.

That some folks might be dubious about this later explanation is understandable. It is, after all, a rather convenient excuse for what these days is seen as incredibly sexist behavior. But an interaction between the dean and Ruth Ginsburg many years later suggests that he might truly have been the advocate for his female students' rights that he later claimed to be.

It concerned that first lawsuit then-Professor Ginsburg had brought as an advocate for gender equality—the case on behalf of the man denied a tax deduction for the care of his elderly mother, solely because he was a man. Ruth was at this time actively searching for laws she might challenge in court on the grounds that they differentiated solely on the basis of sex, and Charles Moritz's facts made for the perfect first case.

After she and Marty had won at the Tenth Circuit Court of Appeals, the Government petitioned the Supreme Court for review, arguing that the decision cast a cloud of unconstitutionality over hundreds of other federal statutes that similarly differentiated on the basis of sex.

At the time, before the advent of personal computers, it would have been virtually impossible for anyone to prove the existence of all these laws and thereby prove or dispute this claim. But the Government—via the Department of Defense's mainframe computer—had such power, and the Solicitor General used it to generate a list of all the regulations and statutes that treated men and women differently. This list was attached as Exhibit E to the Government's petition to the Supreme Court.

The Solicitor General lost his petition, and the Ginsburgs thus ended up winning their first case. But, in many ways, the most significant aspect of the *Moritz* lawsuit was the Government's Exhibit E. For this list of laws proved invaluable to the advocate Ruth Bader Ginsburg, providing her with, in effect, a "hit list" of laws to go after in the future. Which she famously did, with tremendous success.

So who was that Solicitor General? None other than Ruth's former Harvard Law School dean, Erwin Griswold. And to her dying day, the justice suspected the list he appended to the *Moritz* brief was an intentional gift to her.

• • •

Saturday night after the *Parsifal* performance, still giggling about the giant doughnut that had come floating down from the fly space to settle onstage (presumably to evoke King Arthur's round table),[20] Robin and I had a nightcap of bourbon-rocks before retiring. And it turned out to be a good thing we fortified ourselves in this manner, as it proved to be a chilly December night in my parents' damp, ill-heated, 1920s-era home.

But notwithstanding the disappointing *Parsifal*, the weekend was far from a loss. Since my parents' house was where the Ruth dinner would be held, I was looking forward to examining all their china, glassware, silver, pots and pans, and other culinary accoutrements prior to the event to see what I might use and what I might need to supplement from my own kitchen.

The morning after our frigid night, Robin and I were both up early. It was a warm, glorious Southern California winter's day, complete with sun shining and birds singing. My mom had awakened even earlier, and as Robin, my dad, and I were drinking our coffee and reading the *LA Times*, she came in the side door from her morning run.

"I was going to go through your dishes this morning before we leave to see what we might use for the dinner," I told Mom as she stood puffing and panting and catching her breath in the kitchen. "You wanna do it with me?"

"Oh yes! That sounds fun! Wait for me to change before you start."

While my mother rushed upstairs to shower, I rummaged around for a pad of paper and a pen and jotted down each course I was thinking of having, then drew columns for the

---

20. Our Wagner experience in LA ended up being somewhat of a disappointment. First, Plácido Domingo was sick and did not sing the role of Parsifal. In addition, we found the Robert Wilson sets and stage direction—replete with heavy-handed symbolism and lacking any emotion—to be distracting and utterly inappropriate for Wagner's ethereal story of an ingénue's journey towards an understanding of compassionate love.

china, stemware, and silver that would be needed for each. Once Mom came back down, I showed her my list and told her about the different dishes I was contemplating.

"Mmmmm!" she responded enthusiastically. Mom loved food as much as I did. I undoubtedly acquired this trait from her side of the family, as my father could take or leave most foods—other than dark chocolate, for which he always had a great passion.

"All right. Let's start at the beginning," I said to Mom.

"A very good plaaaace, to start," Robin sang from the breakfast room in her best Maria von Trapp voice. Mom and I chuckled. Our family used to perform and videotape ourselves in musicals every Christmas, and one year we had done *The Sound of Music*, featuring Robin—who at the time bore a striking resemblance to Julie Andrews—in the leading role of Maria.

"Okay," I continued after the musical interlude. "I was thinking we should have Champagne when the Ginsburgs first arrive. I don't know if they like to drink cocktails or not, but I figure bubbly is always safe; everyone likes that. And it's classy. And we won't get too drunk, which could be a problem if we started the evening with highballs. Whatd'ya think?"

Mom, a great fan of Champagne, readily agreed. I remember her telling me right before I started college, as a piece of whimsical maternal advice, "If you wear white to a party, always drink either martinis or Champagne. That way, if you spill on your clothes, it won't show." I've not always followed this wise counsel and often suffered the consequences.

"We should probably have something to nosh on with the Champagne, no?"

"Yeah," said Mom. "But nothing too filling. I can see it's going to be a rather large dinner." She nodded toward the list of courses in my hand.

"How about salted nuts?"

"Dad can't eat nuts because of his diverticulitis. So we should probably have something else, too."

"Oh yeah, I forgot. Hmmm. I'll have to think about it. But we don't need to decide that now. What kind of dishes do you have for things like nuts?"

My mother had been a potter for over forty years, and my parents' house was chock full of her ceramic artwork—including an intricate replica of Saint Basil's cathedral in Moscow, lava-inspired sculptures with jet-black outsides and fiery-red insides, and a sculpture of a demure young lady eating a bright pink ice cream cone. I knew she had an abundance of ceramic serving bowls, made both by her and the others in her pottery group.

Mom pulled a few small bowls out for my inspection. As I was pondering which would be best for nuts or other snack-type food, she told me she also had several silver serving dishes that had been given to her and my dad as wedding presents back in 1950. "Some of them I've never actually used," she admitted.

"Well, I think this is the perfect opportunity to do so, don't you?"

My mother smiled.

"Okay, what about the glasses? Do you have any champagne flutes?"

"We're pretty light in that department," Mom confessed. I followed her into the breakfast room. Robin moved to the other side of the table, taking her coffee and the newspaper with her, to allow us to gain access to the built-in cupboard that housed most of my parents' stemware. Inside were a dozen "*coupe*," or shallow bowl style champagne glasses, the kind that were popular in the '50s when my parents no doubt acquired them. It is widely reported that this style was modeled after the shape of Marie Antoinette's breasts, but I Googled this rumor and unfortunately, it appears to be false.

I shook my head. "I think we should use flutes; they retain the bubbles a lot longer."

Some folks get downright obsessive about the bubbles in Champagne. Anita and Sandy from my wine group, for example, have used a diamond drill to make a tiny scratch in the bottom of each of their crystal flutes so the bubbles have a rough spot to catch onto and float straight up in a line from the scratch. This trick reduces the number and frequency of the bubbles and makes the Champagne retain its fizz much longer than in unaltered glasses.

Mom pointed out some of her flute glasses, but we pulled them out and found that there were only two each of different styles. "No problem," I said. "I'll just bring down ours. We have some not terribly expensive, but passable, crystal flutes."

One course down. I put a check mark on my list. "Okay. What kind of soup bowls do you have?"

"There's the Syracuse china." Mom indicated the shelf below the champagne glasses, which held a set of plain white dishes and bowls. I pulled one of the bowls out to examine it. It was fairly wide but also somewhat shallow—just right for what I had in mind. The bowls had enough surface area to make a good "palate" for the garnishes but were not so deep that it would take a large serving of soup to make them appear full.

"Oh look—and we can use these matching white dinner plates as the base plates for the soup." I took one from the shelf and set the bowl on it to make sure the sizes worked together. "Perfect." After jotting more notes down on my sheet of paper, I consulted the list for the next courses.

"I think we should use Jane's plates for the entrée," Mom said, displaying a large dinner plate made by her pottery teacher many years earlier. Jane Heald had studied with Bernard Leach, a famous British potter who had studied in Japan, and her hand-thrown ceramics are exquisite. Made of light gray stoneware with flecks of brown, the plate my mom handed me bore a thin circle of reddish brown on the outer edge, another on the inner lip, and a third near the center. In the middle were several graceful strokes in the same reddish-brown color that looked like sheaves of wheat or wisps of dried grass.

"It has almost a Japanese feel to it," I said. "So it'll pair wonderfully with the blackened ahi with wasabi mashed potatoes." I studied Jane's plate, envisioning how it would look on the big night, and then Mom and I grinned at each other. It felt like we were two little kids playing "grown-ups," and I could tell my mother was thinking exactly the same thing.

I didn't know whether the Ginsburgs would even notice the china and glassware I used for the meal, but sitting there in the sunny breakfast room that winter morning, I realized it didn't really matter. The dinner had now grown far beyond a mere party for an honored guest. And as Mom and I giggled and reminisced about the celebrations and holidays when we'd last used this gravy boat and that crystal decanter, it hit me that although I'd be doing the lion's share of the work, the Ruth dinner had truly turned into a joint project. It had become a source of unity and shared jokes between my parents, Robin, and me—and of pride in what it meant to be a part of our family.

With a smile, I set the plate back on top of the others.

Mom next pulled out two heavy wooden boxes lined with burgundy velvet and opened them to reveal the Gorham Chantilly silverware my parents had been given as wedding presents. I picked up a salad fork, admiring the elegant design and the letter K in delicate script on the handle. "Nice. It's so civilized to use real silver."

"It'll need polishing," Mom said. "I don't always bother with it when we have guests, but for *this* dinner . . ." I replaced the fork, and she closed the boxes. "And we can use Nana's handmade lace tablecloth, the one I always use for Christmas. But I don't have any white napkins. Do you?"

"Sure—I have the white linen napkins that you gave me a few years ago."

"Oh, yeah. I forgot. Wasn't that nice of me," Mom said with a laugh. "So what else do we need?"

"Lemme see . . ." I consulted my list. "Oh, we should look at your other glasses. I'll bring down the stemware for the wine, but what do you have in the way of water glasses?"

"Let's have a look." Mom walked into the kitchen and opened the cupboard to reveal a set of chunky highball glasses, which didn't seem quite right. But they reminded me . . .

"I know," I said, and headed for the dining room.

Right after my parents were married, one of the first items of furniture they purchased was a two-piece matching china cabinet and bar. Mom didn't consider the set to be all that nice looking, but Dad thought the bar was the cat's meow. This was the era, after all, when putting a Sinatra album on the hi-fi and mixing up a shaker of martinis was as cool as cool can be. (Robin and I happen to think that's still true.) The bar has a cupboard on the bottom for storing the liquor bottles, and the top front pulls down like an old-fashioned secretary desk to make a table, revealing a full set of bar glasses lit up by an internal light.

I pulled the top door down—the light still worked after all these years—and there was a set of six tall highball glasses with gold-leaf rims. And unlike on the lowball glasses in the same set, which had been used for innumerable whiskey and sodas over the years, the gold on the highball glasses had not rubbed off, and they still looked brand spanking new. "*Voilà*," I exclaimed triumphantly, holding one up for Mom to see.

"Ha! I forgot we had those." She took the highball glass in her hand and looked inside the bar at the rest of the set, smiling at the memory. "Dad will be happy we're using these," she said, and gently set the glass back in its place.

CHAPTER 6

Scallops for a Chef Supreme

D minus five weeks.

I started shopping for the Ruth dinner the week after Christmas. While at Safeway, I noticed their sparkling wines were on sale for New Year's Eve and that the Veuve Clicquot yellow label was only $30 a bottle. I'd decided to serve this Champagne—aka "the Widow"—for the pre-dinner aperitif, as I adore its dry, lightly citrusy taste. Ever since our wine group had ranked the non-vintage Veuve Clicquot higher than several other Champagnes that cost three times as much, it had become Robin's and my wine of choice when we wanted a good, but not ridiculously expensive Champagne.

No reason I couldn't buy it now, I decided, and snagged two bottles and added them to my groceries. It seemed highly appropriate—in a celebratory kind of way—that the first thing I would buy would be the bubbly.

Wheeling my cart around the store, I next stopped at the seafood counter and saw that they also had large sea scallops on sale for New Year's Eve at half price: $10 a pound. I bent down to inspect them closer. They were IQF—individually quick frozen—which is a common way that restaurants purchase seafood. Although IQF generally costs more by the pound than block-frozen seafood because the water content is higher, it's convenient because you can thaw exactly how many you want to use and leave the rest in the freezer.

As long as it's frozen right away and kept at a temperature well below zero degrees Fahrenheit, most seafood actually bears up exceedingly well in the deep freeze. It's common for sushi grade fish, for example, to be "blast" frozen onboard ship right after it's caught. When I was at the Tsukiji Fish Market in Tokyo years earlier, I saw thousands of whole frozen bluefin tuna (which can fetch as much as $20,000 *each*) stacked up and ready to be auctioned off to restaurant buyers.

Nevertheless, I wasn't sure I wanted to buy the scallops yet. The dinner was still over a month away and, since my freezer wasn't nearly as cold as the sub-zero temperatures used by commercial seafood purveyors, I didn't know how well any scallops would hold up that long. I started explaining my dilemma to the sympathetic seafood counter clerk, when he stopped me and said, "Why don't I just give you a rain check? That way you can wait until closer to your dinner but get the same price."

"Really? You can do that?"

"Sure. How much do you want?"

"Ummm . . ." How much *did* I want? As he saw me agonizing over this question, he added helpfully: "You don't have to buy it all just 'cause I write it down."

"Oh. Okay. How about two pounds, then." I figured at that great price I might as well buy extra for Robin and me. He wrote up the rain check, and I carefully placed the receipt in my wallet. "And, what the heck," I said. "Go ahead and give me six of the scallops now; I think I'll use them for a dinner this weekend." Why not try out the scallop recipe for Robin's and my New Year's Eve meal? That way I could make sure that the frozen variety really did taste all right before buying them for the Ruth dinner.

I also wrote Martin Ginsburg again that week. Although I had pretty much planned the menu, I was concerned that maybe either he or Justice Ginsburg didn't like or couldn't tolerate spicy food and that the wasabi mashed potatoes and spicy blackened ahi would therefore be a bad idea. I certainly didn't want any of my guests gulping down glasses of water or bolting for the restroom during the evening.

Plus, I wanted to make sure they drank wine. I was fairly certain they weren't teetotalers, as I had read recently in the Metropolitan Diary section of the *New York Times* about Justice and Professor Ginsburg having been seen dancing and generally enjoying themselves at some sort of public event. I don't remember exactly what the column said, but I got the distinct impression from reading it that there was some wine or Champagne involved.

Nevertheless, I wanted to make sure. I sat down at the computer and composed an email message to Professor Ginsburg:

I've now planned the menu, but have two more queries: (1) How do you two feel about wasabi (I was thinking of using it in one of the dishes); and (2) are you wine drinkers?

Happy New Year!
Leslie

Once again, he wrote me right back:

(1) Fine with me and I believe with Ruth too. (2) Whenever we possibly can. Happy New Year to you too. Marty

Marty. He signed it Marty! How fabulous was that! And I laughed out loud when I read his response to number two. A man after my own heart.

I would definitely need to think seriously about what wines to serve.

INTERLUDE

"Mommy does the thinking and Daddy does the cooking," is how the young Jane Ginsburg (now a professor of intellectual property at Columbia Law School) once described the roles of her parents.

Martin Ginsburg always told the story as this: In September of 1954, right after the newlywed couple had moved to the army base at Fort Sill, Oklahoma so he could pay his two-year dues for having been in the ROTC in college, Ruth presented her husband with a tuna casserole for dinner. More like "dinosaur" than tuna, however, was Marty's take on the meal. His response was to set about learning to cook.

The Ginsburgs had received a copy of *The Escoffier Cookbook* as a wedding gift—no doubt intended for the new bride—and after teaching all day at the base artillery school, Marty would spend his evenings working his way through the culinary treatise. Having briefly been a chemistry major at Cornell, he soon discovered a knack for the detailed formulae set down by Georges Auguste Escoffier, the chef credited with modernizing French haute cuisine. A lifelong passion was thus born during that stint on the bleak Oklahoma plains.

Though Ruth continued to cook for the family on a day-to-day basis, frozen vegetables and lumps of tasteless meat tended to be her menu du jour. Finally, in 1980—by caveat of her children as well as her husband—she was banished permanently from the kitchen. Marty henceforth took over all cooking duties and ultimately became as celebrated for his culinary prowess as he was for being one of the preeminent tax attorneys in the United States.[21]

Marty took great pleasure in preparing lavish dishes for the triannual Supreme Court spouses luncheons (only the second man to ever have such a role), and invitations to dinner parties at the couple's elegant Watergate digs became more sought-after than seats at the high court's oral arguments.

And he equally relished making sure his wife, once she'd gotten "that good job" (as he called it) in Washington, was well fed. Though not at all interested in cooking, Ruth certainly enjoyed fine food. Her travel diaries record numerous memorable culinary events such as "excellent" mussels, duck dinners, and "elegant" meals at legendary restaurants around the world.

But when working, she was not inclined to stop and take nourishment, so Marty would call and urge her to come home to dinner, offering this sage advice: "You have to eat one meal a day and should go to sleep sometimes." (The justice was also well known for her late nights at the Court.)

Moreover, as with her unhurried and deliberate manner of speaking, Ruth tended to eat slowly, taking time to savor each bite. So it could be a while, if you were waiting for that nourishment to occur. Another favorite joke of Marty's was that it was fortuitous that Bill Clinton hadn't invited his future justice to lunch at the White House as he had Steven Breyer (whom he'd considered for the Court before RBG), for if he had done so, they'd still be there eating.

---

21. The story goes, however, that—notwithstanding his day gig as tax attorney and professor—it was his wife who handled the family's personal finances. Thus, when Bill Clinton's tax people showed up at the Ginsburg residence to vet Ruth as Supreme Court nominee, Marty's role was limited to making lunch for the crowd.

Night after night, for thirty years, Marty prepared the family dinners. Even after becoming so ill with metastatic cancer that he himself could not eat, nor barely stand because of the pain, he would prepare dinner for Ruth. Because, as their daughter Jane explained, "It was ever a joy to discuss the law over dinner with Mother while ensuring that she ate well and with pleasure."

In 2011, a year after Marty's death, the spouses of the Supreme Court justices collaborated with the Supreme Court Historical Society to publish a book of Marty's favorite recipes. This tribute to the talented and generous man is fittingly entitled *Chef Supreme*.

• • •

Like the Ginsburgs, Robin and I have also, over the course of our almost four-decade relationship, carved out separate domestic roles that we play. I believe this is the key to a lasting partnership: having a division of labor that both parties regard as equal and fair. For example, I detest doing house repairs such as plumbing, electrical work, and carpentry, nor could I perform them in any competent manner were I to try. Robin, however, learned these skills in the years she worked in the trades, and this has therefore become her domain.

On the other hand, Robin has little interest in the culinary arts—other than eating, of course. So it makes sense that I've become the cook in the family and do all the menu planning and grocery shopping. Robin does wash the dishes, for which I am eternally grateful.

In this respect, I see a parallel between myself and Martin Ginsburg. For although the law was clearly a vitally important part of his life, he had the need for a more tangible form of creative expression, as well. Experimenting in the kitchen satisfied this desire in him in the same way that cooking—as well as music, art, and writing—has for me.

But there was a key difference between us, too: Unlike Marty, for whom cooking remained ever secondary to his vocation as a professor and attorney, the longer I worked in the law, the more the job became eclipsed by my need for an expressive outlet. And increasingly, I found myself fantasizing about taking a leave of absence from work or, better yet, quitting entirely and spending my days doing music or art . . . or perhaps even trying my hand at the Great American Novel.

But the idea of actually making such a mammoth change in my life filled me with unease. It wasn't simply the question of whether or not we could afford it, but the deeper, far more disturbing concern that leaving the law would signify some kind of failure on my part. What would others think? What would my *father* think?

So I continued on, racking up those billable hours, paralyzed by my own fear.

• • •

Although I had yet to come up with a way to remedy this fundamental conflict within myself, at least the upcoming Ruth dinner gave me something creative to focus on for the time being. And that focus had now become increasingly concentrated, as there was less than a month to go.

The night before New Year's Eve, Robin had a bridge date at our friends Robert and Steve's house, and we'd both been invited over to eat beforehand. Having heard Robin brag to Robert over the phone about how I was going to be cooking dinner for Ruth Bader Ginsburg, I was ready for the usual onslaught of questions about the meal. But since Robert was a caterer, I was in truth quite eager to hear what he thought of the menu I was contemplating for the grand event.

Robert's mother—the type of woman my Grammy would have described as a "pistol"—was in town from the East Coast and would be cooking, and Robin and I were looking forward to an evening of her sarcastic sense of humor and hearty Italian fare. I would not, however, be staying for the bridge-playing after dinner, as I am not a fan of the game.

This fact has long been a source of great disappointment for Robin, who adores bridge (and recently attained the status of Bronze Life Master). Her frustration stems from the fact that the two of us actually met playing bridge. It was a blind date set up by a mutual friend who liked to play cards, and when he suggested a game of bridge for the evening, I replied, "Sure. My mom taught us kids to play when we were little, so I bet I can get up to speed pretty quickly."

And I did truly enjoy that evening, not only because I met Robin—which clearly worked out well—but also because of the bridge itself. As Robin likes to say about that first meeting, "It seemed like the perfect match. Not only did Leslie seem really fun and smart (I was weeks away from starting Stanford Law School at the time), but she *played bridge*! What could be better than that?"

Alas, it turned out not to be as she had hoped. Although I continued to play bridge on occasion with law school pals and Robin, the more I played, the more self-competitive and angsty I became about the game. It all came to a head one day at Robin's parents' house, when I burst into tears upon finding myself blocked from the board as I played my hand. And that was the last time I played.

But my other, more fundamental issue with bridge is that it makes my brain hurt. I realized some time ago that being a research attorney is not unlike playing bridge: In both pursuits, you must focus all your attention on minute details, while at the same time holding elusive, complicated patterns in your head, all in pursuit of the grand final prize. In bridge, it's cracking the puzzle of which cards your opponents hold, then employing the correct strategy to claim as many of them as you can. And in the law, the prize is unearthing elusive published cases that contain facts and law similar to your own, then devising a perfect analogy based on the case law to prove you should prevail.

This sort of intensive concentration can be euphoric, especially for folks who find the underlying subject fascinating. Such is the case with Robin with bridge, as it was for my father—and Ruth Bader Ginsburg—with regard to the law. But it's never been true for me. With both bridge and legal research, it always simply seemed that I was having to think really, *really* hard about something that ultimately, I found to be not terribly compelling. Exhausting, yet with little accompanying gratification.

All of this to say that as soon as we finished eating at Robert and Steve's, I was going to skedaddle on home and leave the bridge-playing to the bridge players.

I hadn't even made it through the door that night before Robert started peppering me with questions about the Ruth dinner:

> "So how come you're cooking for her?" (I provided an abbreviated history of my dad and Justice Ginsburg.)
>
> "Are you nervous?" ("Yes, but I'm trying not to think about that.")
>
> "When is it?" ("Less than four weeks." *Gulp.*)

Then, between bites of his mother's cheesy lasagna, he asked what I was going to cook for the meal.

"Well," I began, "Justice Ginsburg doesn't eat red meat, but she loves fish and shellfish, so the dinner will be heavy on seafood." I described the roasted butternut squash soup and the garnishes I was thinking of preparing, and he nodded.

"That's good for a winter menu," he said approvingly.

I then told him about the baby spinach salad with blood oranges from my garden ("if they ripen in time," I added) and the ahi and wasabi mashed potatoes.

"That sounds great, but don't use wasabi in both the potatoes and on the fish. You should never use the same ingredient twice in the same course."

Okay . . . I thought. *Does that go for garlic?* If so, I've been in violation of a basic tenet of cooking probably thousands of times.

"And I'm thinking of doing a scallop recipe with a ginger-lime cream sauce."

"How many scallops will you serve?" Robert asked.

"I dunno, just a couple I imagine, since we're gonna have a lot of other food."

"Because it's hard to make two scallops look good on the plate," he said. "You can't lean one on the other, 'cause it'll slide off, and two next to each other look funny. Since three would be too many, in my experience it's best to have just one large one for an appetizer course like you're doing."

Dang! There were so many little things to consider that I'd given no thought to. I tried to remember just how big the scallops were that I had seen at the store but couldn't recall exactly. No matter what size they were, though, the idea of only one scallop on the plate seemed pretty skimpy to me.

"But you know," Robert continued, "those big scallops you see for sale—they're really just pieces of fish cut to look like scallops. The real scallops are the little ones."

"Huh?" I looked at him incredulously. "I don't remember that from cooking school." We had learned about scallops, and I was sure I would have remembered something like that if it were true.

But Robert was a professional caterer, and it had been a while since I'd taken those cooking classes. And besides, I was a guest in his home, so I didn't press the point, even though it sounded just plain wrong. After all, how many times had I eaten huge scallops in fancy restaurants? No way were those places serving fish disguised as the real thing. *Or were they*? Could those scallops I'd put on my raincheck really just be big discs of compressed fish? I made a mental note to look it up, just in case. Because I certainly didn't want to be serving *fake* scallops to the Ginsburgs.

After dinner, I left the bridge players to their game, kissing Robin goodbye and telling her as I always do, "I hope you bid and make a grand slam!"

Once home, I headed straight for my *Larousse Gastronomique* and perused the entry on scallops. Nothing about fake scallops being made with fish or about big versus small ones. But I did learn why scallops are called *coquilles Saint-Jacques* in French: they used to be found in great numbers on the coast of Galicia in Spain where their shells served as emblems for medieval pilgrims who had reached Santiago de Compostella, the Shrine of Saint James (*Saint-Jacques*, in French).

Next I tried my old text from cooking school, *Professional Cooking* by Wayne Gisslen. *Aha!* This treatise informed me that there are two varieties of scallops: bay scallops, which are small (32 to 40 of them per pound), with a delicate flavor and texture; and sea scallops, which are larger (10 to 15 per pound) and, though not so delicate as bay scallops, still tender unless overcooked.

So the big scallops really were scallops: sea scallops.[22] As long as I didn't overcook them, I could serve them with confidence. But I definitely needed a practice run. *Right*, I

22. I've since learned that circular pieces of skate and ray are sometimes sold as sea scallop substitutes, but the practice is illegal if they are passed off as actually being scallops; they have to be marketed as skate or ray, or "faux" scallops.

decided. *I'll try out the recipe with ginger-lime sauce tomorrow for our New Year's Eve dinner.*

Reshelving my cooking text, I went out to our wine cellar in the garage to fetch some bubbly to put in the fridge, to go with the scallops and help ring in the new year. A new year that would bring with it—in four short weeks—the culmination of all my stressing and obsessing over the past eight months.

CHAPTER 7

A Ranger, a Jurist, and Elvis Walk Into a Bar

D minus four weeks.

Staring out the kitchen window at the black clouds overhead, I zipped up my fleece sweater and shivered. I'd gotten home from my afternoon bike ride in the nick of time, as the sky looked about to open up into a deluge.

"What do you say about heading down to the Mall for a New Year's Eve drink before dinner?" I asked Robin. "Unless you want to stay in 'cause of the weather, that is."

"No, that sounds great," she said. "I don't mind a little rain."

The Pacific Garden Mall, a shop- and restaurant-lined street in downtown Santa Cruz, is the cultural heart of our city. The sushi bars and pizza joints do brisk business, and the sidewalks are full of all sorts of characters: moms with strollers, accordion and cello players busking for spare change, hipsters hanging out in front of the vinyl record store, magicians doing card tricks, parents visiting their college kids, families down for the weekend to visit the Boardwalk. It's a wonderful place to walk around and people-watch.

As Robin and I strolled from our car to Pacific Avenue, we passed Soif, a wine bar and restaurant that served delicious food and an ever-changing selection of wines to taste by the glass. Attached to the restaurant was a retail store offering a host of varietals and vintages from all over the world.

"Hey, let's go in and check out what they have at the store," I said to Robin. "I was thinking today during my bike ride that maybe I should serve some local wines at the dinner, which I bet the Ginsburgs have never tasted. Don't you think it would be great to show off to them what a terrific grape-growing and wine-making region we live in?"[23]

As we were wandering through the stacks of cases and shelves of wine on display, a young woman asked if she could help. "Actually, you can," I said. "I'm interested in getting some local wines for a dinner party. I'm going to serve blackened ahi with a sort of spicy dry rub and need a locally produced red to go with it. I figure it'll have to be somewhat light but full bodied enough to hold its own against the spices. I was thinking of maybe the Bonny Doon Old Telegram . . ."

"Oh no, that's a very big wine—lots of fruit and tannin. It would overwhelm the fish."

"Ah . . ." I had remembered it as being more of a lighter, Rhône-style, wine. "Well, what about their Cigare Volant," I asked. "It's not so big, is it?"

"Right. It's lighter, but still has lots of complexity. Yes, I think it would go well with ahi." She showed me the 2001 Cigare Volant, which they were selling for $20—a great price.

Bonny Doon Vineyard was started by Randall Grahm. A UCSC graduate, he went on to obtain a degree in viticulture from UC Davis and subsequently founded a winery up in Bonny Doon, an area in the Santa Cruz Mountains just north of Santa Cruz. Noted primarily for his Côtes du Rhône-style

23. The Santa Cruz Mountains were named a viticultural appellation back in 1981.

wines, Randall soon became known as "the Rhône Ranger" by wine writers, as well as something of a celebrity in the wine world.

Not only are his wines interesting and great tasting, his marketing style is a hoot. He has an irreverent sense of humor, which comes through in the descriptions of his wines and in his publicity and promotion. Take, for example, the label for his Cardinal Zin,[24] which features an illustration by Ralph Steadman—the same guy who did the drawings for Hunter S. Thompson—and which contains a reference to all seven of the deadly sins (one of which is tricky to find). Randall isn't interested in placating the wine-snob culture that predominates in many parts of the wine world, which is why he's been a great proponent of the screw cap on wine bottles and now uses it even on some of his high-end wines. I'm all in favor of this trend. No more struggling with stubborn corks, and no more corked wines. Hallelujah!

Le Cigare Volant is Randall's take on a Châteauneuf-du-Pape, and on its label is a picture of a flying saucer, or as the French would say, *un cigare volant*—a flying cigar. Randall's description of the wine from his 2006 website reflects his lighthearted marketing style:

> *The 2001 is a chiaroscuro of light, vibrant, fruity and floral notes contrasted against a denser, darker, almost inscrutable core the likes of which has not been seen in preceding Cigares. The first wafts of aroma benignly suggest cooked raspberry preserves, licorice whips, and garrigue. There is something nearly sinister in the wine upon closer inspection, though, mirroring our flying machine on the label in its menacing arboreal concealment.*

---

24. Randall has since sold the Cardinal Zin label, so—although it's the same wine with the same packaging—it's no longer produced by Bonny Doon Vineyard.

As I smiled at the flying cigar on the bottle I was holding, I tried to remember back to when I'd last tried the wine, but as it had been several years, I couldn't remember exactly what it tasted like. "Thanks," I said to the salesclerk, "but I want to try it before buying any for my dinner party. Are you pouring it next door?"

"No," she said. "And I should warn you that today's the last day we'll be open for a few weeks. The wine bar and the store are both going to be closed for vacation."

"Okay. Thanks for the warning."

I should have, of course, simply purchased the bottle to take home and try out. But I didn't; my propensity towards indecision struck once again. Instead, I put it back on the shelf, and Robin and I walked outside.

It was now five o'clock. Cocktail hour. "Let's go have that drink," said Robin. We headed back to Pacific Avenue and went into Costa Brava, a Latin American restaurant with an old-fashioned, classic bar and Picasso-inspired line drawings on the walls.[25] Taking two seats at the still fairly empty bar, we were greeted by the bartender.

Josh was a cyclist and looked the part: lank and wiry, pure muscle. One night several months earlier when Robin I were marveling at his lack of body fat, Robin had told him, "If you were a woman, you wouldn't have a period." Josh had laughed, causing the tendons in his neck to stand at attention.

Laying two cocktail napkins before us that New Year's Eve, he asked with a toothy grin, "What'll it be, ladies?"

Robin picked up the wine list. "Uh, give me a sec," she said, squinting at the small print.

"Sure thing." He left us to make an order of mojitos, the bar specialty.

"Hey, look!" Robin pointed at the sheet of paper. "They've got the Cigare Volant." When Josh came back to take our order,

---

25. It's now, alas, closed.

she asked if they had it by the glass. Then, in a mock-boastful voice she added, "Leslie's cooking dinner for Supreme Court Justice Ruth Bader Ginsburg and is thinking of serving the Cigare Volant with the main course."

"Wow," he responded, raising his eyebrows. "That's pretty amazing. What's the occasion?"

I told him a brief history and a little about the menu for the dinner. "And I have inside intel that she and her husband are fond of wine," I said, "so I thought it would be great to serve her something from around here. You know, since she probably only knows the big-name areas in California like Napa and Sonoma. It'll be my way to show off our own fabulous Santa Cruz wines to those big kids out on the East Coast."

"Man, that is *so* awesome." Josh paused a beat, and I could see him come to a decision. "We don't actually have the Cigare listed by the glass, but I'll open a bottle for you."

"Really? I don't want to get you in trouble."

"No, it's fine. It'll be easy to sell the rest of the bottle. And that way I can have a taste too," he said with a smile. "One or two glasses?"

"Two," said Robin.

Josh went to fetch the bottle, then reached up and removed two globe-shaped wine glasses from the rack above the bar and placed them before us. As he opened the Cigare Volant—yes, it had a screw cap—he asked what our plans were for New Year's Eve.

"I'm going to try out the scallop recipe for the dinner with Justice Ginsburg tonight," I told him. "So we'll probably just have a drink here and then head home."

"Yep. I doubt I'll even make it to midnight," Robin added. "We're pretty boring."

After pouring our wine, Josh poured a small taste for himself. We clinked our glasses, then gently swirled the wine and inhaled the aroma. *Nice*. There was that *garrigue*—the herbal nose that wines from the south of France often exhibit. I took a sip. *Yum!* I always love the black pepper notes that Grenache brings to Rhône style wines, but this was more complex than many of the other Rhônes I was used to drinking, with lots of berry and earthy flavors. At the same time, however, it was soft—not too tannic, and easy to drink.

"This will go great with the ahi, don't you think?"

Robin nodded as she finished swallowing.

"Oh!" I set down my glass and slid off the bar stool. "I should run over to Soif and buy a couple of bottles before the shop closes. Be right back."

The wine store was still open, and in no time, I was back in the bar with my purchase. "Okay, that's done," I said as I set the parcel on the floor under my stool and lifted my glass once more. "Thank goodness you dropped Ruth's name, or we wouldn't have been able to taste this fabulous wine."

"Yep," Robin agreed. "It's funny how excited people get about meeting celebrities—even when it's not even *them* who's doing the meeting, but just someone they know. I mean, no way would Josh have offered to open the bottle if I'd told him you were hosting a dinner for say, I dunno . . . Fred Ebey at your law firm."

"Ha! So true. Nothing like being pals with a famous person to open a few doors—and bottles of wine, as well." I raised my glass in a toast: "To celebrities, the new year, and the dinner!"

INTERLUDE

As a teenager, Kiki Bader spent her summers at Camp Che-Na-Wah in the Adirondacks. The quiet but socially-active girl—who twirled baton for her high school pep squad and was treasurer of the "Go-Getters," as well as editor of the school newspaper—was popular with her fellow campers and before long was designated camp rabbi. No one at Camp Che-Na-Wah, however, would likely have guessed that the girl they knew as Kiki would end up the icon she later became. Yet the shy teenager's time at that camp in fact played a part in her later transformation into "the Notorious RBG."

Fast-forward twenty-plus years. The now-Professor Ginsburg is busy at work in her Rutgers University office when there is a knock at the door. Who is standing there, but a friend of hers from Che-Na-Wah—a boy four years her senior who'd worked as a dining hall waiter at the camp—Mel Wulf, now the national legal director for the ACLU, come to say hello.

It was the fall of 1970, and Ruth and Marty had just decided to jointly take on the Charles Moritz case. The timing of Wulf's visit could not have been more perfect.

After a months-long bout of arm-twisting—not to mention a Gilbert and Sullivan-inspired letter to Mel, harking back to their old summer camp's productions—Ruth eventually convinced the legal director that the ACLU should lend its support to the *Moritz* case, both in legal assistance and funding. This collaboration in turn led to RBG's co-writing a brief with Mel Wulf, her first before the nation's highest court. It was what Ruth would later come to call "the mother brief."

Reed v. Reed was the first constitutional sex-discrimination case since 1961 to make it all the way to the US Supreme Court, and that 1961 case had not been a success.[26] So *Reed* was a big deal. Like *Moritz*, it concerned a law that differentiated solely on the basis of sex, this time giving preference to men, with regard to who should be the administrator of an estate. Ruth didn't get to argue the case before the Court, but her brief was a winner.

Several months after her victory in *Reed*, life changed dramatically for Ruth Bader Ginsburg. She accepted an offer from Columbia University to become their first female tenure-track law professor, and shortly afterward was asked by the ACLU to co-found and be the first director for their brand-new Women's Rights Project.

Armed with the hit list of discriminatory laws so conveniently provided by Solicitor General Erwin Griswold, the WRP went to work, focusing on six core areas of inequality between the sexes: employment, government aid, reproductive control, university admissions policies, government training programs, and credit/finance. Their ultimate goal was to elevate gender-based classifications under the law to the same high standard used in cases concerning race—that of "strict scrutiny."

To the dismay of Professor Ginsburg, however, she never achieved this goal while working as an advocate for the ACLU. But in 1996—as Justice Ginsburg—she ultimately attained what most legal scholars consider to be its legal equivalent and in the process became perhaps the biggest celebrity the Supreme Court has ever known.

---

26. The citation for *Reed* is 404 US 71 (1971). The 1961 case (*Hoyt v. Florida*, 368 US 57) involved a woman convicted by an all-male jury of murdering her husband. The Supreme Court denied her claim that the system whereby women had to volunteer in order to serve on juries was unconstitutional.

• • •

As soon as we got home from Costa Brava I set to work making dinner, and Robin opened the bottle of J that had been chilling in the fridge. "You know, we seem to have only five of our crystal flutes left," she said, filling our glasses with the bubbly. "Last time we used them, I broke one while doing the dishes." Robin shrugged, then took a seat at one of the stools across from me at our kitchen island. "I guess I shouldn't try to wash breakables while tipsy."

We'd originally had a dozen of the flutes, but over the years their numbers had dwindled. It's those annoying fragile stems—they're not designed to survive clumsy drinkers. We have the same problem with our martini glasses.

"Well, the dinner is a good excuse to buy some more, then." I tasted the J, a California sparkling wine that had beaten out several far more expensive French Champagnes in one of Anita's blind tastings. "Mmmm." Setting the glass on the kitchen counter, I continued mincing the shallots for the ginger-lime cream sauce, then stopped mid-chop and turned back toward Robin. "Hey," I said, "I bet there'll be a lot of sales on champagne glasses right after the new year."

Pleased with this revelation, I returned to the preparation of my sauce. Once the mixture was simmering on the stove, I picked up my champagne glass again. "Ya wanna put on some music?"

"Sure, babe." Robin stood and walked over to the jazz and lounge-singer section of our CD collection and bent to peer at the titles. After a bit, the crooning voice of Ella Fitzgerald came over the speakers. "I keep thinking about Josh opening that wine for us tonight because of my name-dropping," she said once settled back at the kitchen bar, "and it got me wondering: Do you suppose famous people also get excited about meeting other celebrities? Or is it just us peanut gallery types who get all starstruck?"

"Well, I read that the Beatles were pretty starstruck when

they met Elvis, and they were pretty damn famous at the time. So yeah, I think they definitely can. But I doubt it's anything like what us regular folks go through." I tried to project how I was going to feel when Ruth Ginsburg actually showed up at my parents' house for dinner next month; the exercise generated more anxiety than excitement.

"It probably depends on who it is," I went on. "You know, who's the awe-or and who's the awe-ee, and how awed they in fact are by the other person."

Robin laughed. "You mean to tell me Ruth Ginsburg probably wouldn't fawn over Elvis if she met him?"

"If she met him *now* I bet she'd be impressed. Or more likely run away in terror that she was being stalked by a ghost." I stirred my sauce, then set down the wooden spoon. "But yeah, you do have to wonder if there's anyone she'd get all nervous about meeting. She strikes me as someone who wouldn't give a fig about celebrity. Unless maybe it was John Marshall or Oliver Wendell Holmes come back from the dead, and even then, only if she could pick their brain about constitutional law."

The sauce had now reduced by half, so I added a tiny bit of lime zest and the heavy whipping cream and let it simmer a couple more minutes before tasting it. "Hmmm." I smacked my lips. "Here, you try," I said, offering a spoonful across the range top to Robin. "Think it needs anything?"

"Too tart," was her conclusion, accompanied by a severe face scrunch. I had suspected this reaction, as she doesn't tend to like things that are very acidic. Robin is what is called a "supertaster." This may sound like a good thing, but it's actually more of a curse, because supertasters, as I learned in cooking school, are people with taste buds exceedingly sensitive to certain flavors, especially sour and bitter. As a result, foods that may seem delicious to the rest of us—like lemon meringue pie or pickles (sour), or arugula or beer (bitter)—make her face pucker up like the winner of a gurning contest.

But I agreed with her assessment of the ginger-lime sauce. It did need some sort of sweetening and less lime juice. I couldn't take any lime out, of course, but I hadn't used all the cream, so I added more, as well as some additional wine and clam juice and a little sugar. I let this simmer for a few minutes, and then we tasted it again.

"Much better," Robin proclaimed.

"Yeah," I agreed, and jotted down a note on the recipe.

While we listened to Ella and sipped a second glass of bubbly, I prepared a Caesar salad to go with the scallops. I usually cheat and make a dressing in advance, rather than mixing it in the bowl along with the romaine lettuce as is traditional. But I *always* include coddled eggs. It's simply not a Caesar salad if there isn't runny egg yolk and white in it, which is truly the most important part of the dressing, to my mind.

When everything was ready for the salad, I finished the sauce by adding chunks of butter piece-by-piece and stirring until they were incorporated, which thickens and enrichens the sauce. Clearly, this is *not* a dish for anyone on a diet. But it was New Year's Eve. What better time to splurge on calories?

Next, I pulled my cast-iron skillet from the rack above the stove and got the scallops sizzling in butter over a high flame, then used a spoon to place the eggs in the simmering water to start the coddling. Watching my scallops with an eagle eye, I flipped them over as soon as they'd browned and let them cook for only another thirty seconds before removing them from the pan. I then lay them gently on top of the pool of sauce I'd spooned onto two plates and sprinkled lime zest on top for a delicate garnish.

While Robin took our scallops out to the dining room table, I scooped the egg out of the shells and tossed it, as well as the rest of the salad ingredients, with the lettuce leaves.

Robin filled our glasses once more, killing the bottle of J, and we sat down to our feast.

"These plates are wrong," I said before I'd taken one bite. I had used two of the darkest colors of my small Fiestaware plates—dark orange and turquoise—but the creamy-white sauce didn't look right on them. Standing up again, I took a white plate from the cupboard and spooned some sauce on it, and we both stared at the dish. "White on white doesn't work either. It needs some contrast."

I sat back down at the table. "*Zut*. Those off-white plates my mom has won't be any good for this dish either." Frowning, I tapped my fingers on the tabletop. "I guess I'm just going to have to buy some plates that will work. Maybe black ones, like the plates we used for appetizers in cooking school."

Robin, meanwhile, had tasted the scallops. "Oh, yum," she declared. "These are great!"

"Really? Not too limey?" I cut a slice for myself, dunked it in the sauce, and popped the piece in my mouth. The scallop was nice and tender, barely cooked in the center, but crispy on the outside. And I loved how the sweetness of the ginger and cream—and sugar—in the sauce complemented the tart lime and savory shallots and clam juice.

A wave of relief passed over me. This course was a winner.

CHAPTER 8

In Pursuit of Perfection

D minus three weeks.

For six years I'd been singing alto with the Symphonic Chorus at Cabrillo College, and during the first week of January, we started up rehearsals again. During the winter term, we'd be performing Bach's *Mass* in B minor and, given the length and complexity of the work, would be meeting three times a week—Tuesday and Thursday nights and Saturday mornings.

I knew it was crazy to take on such a time-consuming activity at this period of my life. In addition to the scheduled rehearsals, I would of course also have to put in serious practice time on my own in order to learn my part. Plus, I still had a ton of preparation to do for the Ruth dinner: planning and logistics, shopping for plates and glasses and food, advance cooking, as well as organizing and packing everything up for the trip to LA.

Oh yeah, and there was my job, which I was doing my best not to think about unless physically present at the firm.

So it wasn't the best timing for the Bach. But I'd always wanted to sing the B minor *Mass* and had sworn I wouldn't miss the chance when it arose; I therefore wasn't going to let some dinner party get in the way of it. Or so I told myself.

After I got home from our first Saturday morning chorus rehearsal, Robin suggested we head over to Macy's to look for champagne flutes and plates for the scallops in ginger-lime cream sauce. As soon as we stepped off the escalator at the kitchen supplies, china, and stemware level, my eyes were drawn to a display of medium-sized square plates, in flat black. There was a Japanese feel to them, curving slightly upwards at the four corners. And they were on sale—only eight bucks each. *They'd be perfect for the scallops!*

I started grabbing plates and stacking them in my arms, furtively glancing over my shoulder lest someone else should come up from behind and attempt to secure them before I. One, two, three, four, five . . . Just five? No. *This couldn't be happening.* I needed six for the dinner, and preferred to get eight, for future parties. I looked under the table to see if there was any overstock stashed down there. No such luck. *Damn!* The sale, which I had previously considered a blessing, now became a curse: If they had not been such a bargain, no way would they have already been down to only five.

Clutching my stack of five plates, I wandered around searching for a salesclerk. Robin came to my aid and collared a young man, who consulted his cash register/computer to see if there were any more of them in the storeroom. "Five," he announced to us. "It says we only have five of them."

"Yep, that's right. Here they are." With a sigh, I set the five precious plates down on the counter. If only there had been one more . . .

Seeing my crestfallen expression, he turned back to the computer and started typing again. "Lemme check the nearby stores for you." He tapped at the keyboard for a minute or two, frowning and murmuring to himself while I fidgeted. The clerk looked up with a smile. "Bingo! Fifteen in Salinas, thirty-two in San Jose, and . . . fifty-three in Monterey." He handed me the print-out with a flourish, and I beamed back.

"We'll be in Monterey next weekend anyway, for Gaby's bistro dinner," Robin said, taking the paper from me to examine it. "Let's get the plates on the way there."

"You don't think they'll sell out in a week?"

"C'mon, they have *fifty-three* of them." She waved the sheet for emphasis, then handed it back to me. Robin can be rather absentminded—especially about keeping track of small pieces of paper—so I'm the one in the relationship generally assigned to hold on to parking stubs, concert tickets, validation cards, and the like. "Let's go check out their champagne glasses," she said, and headed off towards the stemware. I reluctantly returned the five black plates to their display and followed after her.

There were a variety of styles, from Waterford crystal at $50 apiece to simple glass flutes for under $10. I picked up one of these latter glasses and ran a finger over the lip—much too thick. A wine glass needs to have a thin edge so it feels delicate on the mouth as you take sips.

"Hey, Les!" I heard from several aisles away. I carefully replaced the glass and went over to where Robin stood. She was holding a champagne flute triumphantly in her hand.

"Oh, wow." I took it from her. "That's our pattern, isn't it?"

"Yep. And look, they're on sale." Our pattern—of which we only had the five left—isn't terribly fancy. The glasses were clearly made in a mold and are heavier than fine Riedel ware. But they *are* crystal and have a nice shape. And most importantly, they have a thin lip and a delicate stem.

"But there's a slight problem." Robin looked down at the shelf.

"What?" I asked. I followed her gaze. "Oh." There were no more of the glasses; Robin had the only one in her hand. "We're jinxed!"

"We could just get the one," Robin said. "We only need six for the dinner."

"Yeah, but what if one breaks in transit? I was planning on bringing down a couple extra, just in case. They're so fragile, with the thin stems." I looked at the lone glass in Robin's hand and stamped my foot in frustration. "Damn, damn, *damn*! Plus, it seems silly to buy any more of this pattern unless we can get more of them. We really should have at least ten, don't you think? You know, for future breakage?"

"Maybe the other stores have these, too," she suggested.

We checked with the saleslady, but none of the other stores in our area had more than a couple of them. However, she told us, we could order them from their online catalogue and receive them within a week.

Empty-handed, we walked to the car. "Well, *that* was a useless outing," I grumbled.

"No it wasn't," said Robin. "We now know where we can get the black plates, and I can order the champagne glasses online today."

"Hrumph," I responded, not convinced that the glasses would truly arrive in time for the dinner.

"What time is it?" Robin asked.

"Three-fifteen."

"Let's go check out some white wines for the dinner," she said. "A little wine tasting is just the ticket to cure what ails ya."

• • •

Since we'd decided at the dinner party with Sandy and Tom that a chardonnay would go well with the soup and salad courses, Robin and I headed downtown to Storrs Winery, which is known for its chards.

"Let's see what happens when we drop the 'Ruth Ginsburg' name, here," Robin whispered as she opened the door to the tasting room. We made our way to the bar, where she immediately informed Jim, the fellow pouring, that we wanted to try out wines for a dinner I was going to cook for Justice Ginsburg.

"Really?" It took him a moment to realize we weren't pulling his leg, at which point he asked what I'd come to think of as "the usual questions": How did I know the justice? Where would the dinner be held? What would I be preparing for the meal?

As I was providing my usual responses, the couple standing next to us at the counter listened in. "Who are you cooking for?" the woman asked.

"She's going to cook dinner for Justice Ginsburg," said Jim. "Isn't that amazing?"

"Who's that?" she asked.

Robin and I looked at each other. *Is she kidding?* we wondered.

"You know, the *Supreme Court* justice," her companion answered quickly, glancing at me with an embarrassed expression and shrugging his shoulders.

"Oh . . ." she said, and trailed off.

So maybe the RBG card doesn't play quite as well with everyone.

Robin and I turned to the task at hand. "Which wines would you like to taste?" Jim asked.

"I've decided to serve a chard for the white wine at the dinner," I said. "Which ones are you pouring today?"

"Only two, the Santa Cruz Mountains and the Ben Lomond Mountain. But for you—and for Justice Ginsburg," he replied, "I'm happy to open the other two to taste. I think it would be awesome if you served a Storrs wine to the justice."

"Great!" I flashed a knowing smile at Robin.

The Santa Cruz Mountains was perfectly fine, but a bit too simple, I thought, to stand up to the butternut squash soup. It required something a little more complex. The Ben Lomond Mountain, on the other hand, was big and full of tropical fruit, with lots of toasty oak and that buttery flavor that comes from malolactic fermentation. Too much for what I wanted. And the Meyley was similar to the Ben Lomond, heavy on the vanilla and butter, though it did have a fair amount of acid to balance out the oak.

But when I tried the Storrs Christie chardonnay, I felt like Goldilocks tasting the baby bear's porridge. *This is just right*, I thought as I swished it around my mouth. A good balance of oak and acid with a bit of pear or even pineapple, but not too overbearing. And a hint of vanilla and butter, but much more subtle than the Ben Lomond and Meyley.

"I think the Christie is the one. Whad'ya think?" I asked Robin.

"Sure. It's fine." Robin's even less of a white wine drinker than I am, so I couldn't expect her to be overly enthusiastic, but she agreed that it would pair nicely with the first few courses of the dinner.

Of course, we had to try the reds too. We tasted several pinots and zinfandels and a couple other varietals. Jim queried me more about the dinner and joined us in sipping some of the wines.

"Are you nervous about hosting a party for Justice Ginsburg?" he asked. "I've heard she's kind of . . ."

"Taciturn?" I finished, and he laughed. "Yeah, that's true. We know from experience she's not what you'd call the life of the party when it comes to chitchat. She much prefers law talk to small talk."

Jim nodded. "So I've heard. But you mentioned earlier that you're a lawyer, so you can do law talk with her."

I shuddered, imagining what would happen if the justice engaged me in a discussion of some detailed issue of federal jurisdiction. "Oh, God, I'd probably be so nervous I'd confuse due process with due diligence," I said. "No, I think I'll leave the law talk to my dad. But that's one reason we're here to buy wine for the dinner. I'm hoping the Christie will calm my nerves."

INTERLUDE

While an undergraduate at Cornell, Kiki Bader took a European literature class from an as yet unknown Russian émigré named Vladimir Nabokov,[27] a man she credits with changing the way she read and the way she wrote. Nabokov was deeply drawn to the sound of language, and the professor instilled in his young student the value of syntax—how crucial the placement of each word could be to conveying a message.

The justice was always quick to acknowledge Nabokov's influence on her writing style. Whenever she drafted an opinion she would think of him, asking herself, "Can I say this in fewer words? Is there another way to write it so the meaning will come across with greater clarity?"

In a culture not known for its brevity—Supreme Court opinions can run well over a hundred pages—RBG made every effort to keep her opinions to under twenty. And the justice had little tolerance for jargon or legalese when plain English would work just as well.[28] Her law clerks, who generally prepared the first drafts of her opinions, were used to getting their pages back from her, covered in cross-outs and edits. "Get it right and keep it tight," was Ruth's motto.

Her goal was to make the writing that came out of her chambers as intelligible as possible, a task made difficult by the often esoteric and complicated subject matter. In particular, she strove to make the opening paragraphs of her opinions comprehensible to the general public, as she was well aware that few people other than those in the legal profession will read past those first few sentences.

---

27. The year after Ruth graduated from Cornell, Nabokov's tragicomic novel, Lolita, would shoot him to fame—and notoriety.
28. She's not alone. I still remember one of my law professors at Stanford, Robert Weisberg, telling us that the verb "use" was always a better choice in writing than its pretentious cousin, "utilize."

This desire for precision and clarity is no doubt what caused her speech to come across as stilted and halting. The justice would often pause several seconds—what can seem like an interminable amount of time, in casual conversation—before replying to a comment or question. Some of her clerks, who learned to follow the "five Mississippi rule" to make sure she was done talking, have termed this trait a "tolerance for conversation silence."

But given how important language and word choice were to Ruth Bader Ginsburg, it should come as no surprise that she was as thoughtful about selecting the perfect spoken words as she was when putting them on paper.

• • •

The champagne glasses Robin ordered arrived the following Wednesday, well within the promised one-week's delivery time. One less thing to worry about. I unwrapped them just enough to ensure they weren't broken, then rewrapped eight (two extra, in case of accidents) and replaced them in the shipping box, ready for the trip down south for the dinner.

On Friday I called Macy's in Monterey to make sure they still had enough of the square black plates in stock. I'd told my mom the good news about the plates, and she had asked me to get her eight of them too, if they had enough. The Macy's clerk informed me that the computer still showed there to be fifty-three in stock. *Thank goodness.*

The following night we were invited to dinner at the house of our friend Gaby, a gregarious, chain-smoking, Brazilian woman who has now settled in Northern California with her Brazilian husband Carlos. Gaby, whom I'd met through Slow Food, had apprenticed as a cook with Paul Bocuse in Lyon and loved to show off her cooking skills by hosting fabulous bistro dinners once a month at her Pacific Grove home. Tonight would be *cassoulet*, one of my favorite country-French dishes.

Robin and I stopped at Macy's in Monterey before Gaby's dinner. Quickly locating the china department, I looked for but didn't find the coveted square black plates. "Oh, those are in the *housewares* department," a saleswoman told me when I asked about them. "This is *fine* china."

Robin and I snickered as we left the counter. "*Oh là là*," I said *sotto voce*. "Zis is ze fine china department."

Once in the correct plebeian section, we found the plates right away. There were dozens of them, and I started to make a stack of the sixteen I needed. But then I stopped. "Wait. These are different from the ones we saw last week."

"Huh?" Robin picked one up and examined it. "They look the same to me."

"No. These are much shinier; the others were a flat black. And look." I pointed to a blob of glaze in the shape of a drip. "These have lots of imperfections. It's almost as if they were seconds."

I could tell that Robin was starting to get annoyed. They were just *plates*, after all. I've thought about this since—why something so seemingly insignificant as plates was so very important to me—and have come up with a theory. Although I have a degree in culinary arts and adore cooking and all things food-related, I've never had any desire to be a chef or run a restaurant or catering company. For me, cooking is purely a creative outlet, something that provides artistic and sensory pleasure. If I worked as a cook, it would become a job—a drudgery.

But this dinner for the Ginsburgs was like play-acting at running a restaurant or being a chef. And it was likely the most important food event I'd ever host; I wanted to get it absolutely right. And that included not simply the meal itself but also the table arrangement—the glasses, plates, silverware, and linens. I knew my mom would understand.

After all, I rationalized, Ruth Bader Ginsburg's lifelong pursuit of perfection was well known. And given the justice's attention to detail regarding her work and her manner of speech—not to mention her manner of dress—she would surely take note of the presentation of the dinner that I served to her.

But that wasn't the sole reason for my preoccupation. Even if my honored guests paid no heed whatsoever to the sort of dishes they ate from that night, it was important to *me*. For I knew this would be an evening I'd replay over and over again in my head for years to come.

And I wanted that memory to be perfect.

I held two of the square black plates up side by side. "Huh. How weird. This one is like the ones we saw last week. See? It's got a flatter finish than the other." But there were only three of the flat black plates. I took one of each kind of plate to the cashier and explained the issue. "So, do you have any more of these"—I held up the flat black one—"in the storeroom?"

"I'm not sure. Let me call Bill." She got on the intercom, and after a minute a middle-aged man with a pronounced limp hobbled up and asked politely how he could help us. I showed him the difference between the two plates and asked if there were any more of the flat black ones in the storeroom. He looked from one to the other and scratched his head.

"Yeah, they are different. That's odd." Bill disappeared into the stockroom, then reappeared a few minutes later, pushing a cart piled high with square black plates. "I brought out as many as I could find, so you could pick which ones you wanted," he said.

"Wow. Thanks!" I started to sift through the plates. It was a good thing we had given ourselves lots of time for this detour on the way to Gaby and Carlos's house, as it turned out that many of the plates—the flat black ones too—had defects, so I had to go through them one by one. I found eight plates that seemed pretty much perfect and set them aside in a stack.

"Great, now for eight more for Mom." But by now the pickins had been reduced, and it was harder to find plates that met my admittedly high standard. As I held one up next to another and eyed them critically, I became self-conscious that both Robin and Bill were watching me. I tried to hurry my pace.

"Right," I said finally. "These will do." I set the two stacks of eight on the counter, and Bill started to ring them up.

"Just keep the best ones for yourself," Robin said. "No way will your mom care as much as you do." Did I detect a slight eye roll there?

"But then I'll need to take them *all* down to LA. It would be stupid to spend all this time picking through them and then not use the best ones for the dinner."

"Don't worry," Robin countered, trying to maintain a semblance of patience. "We'll have a car. There'll be lots of room."

Okay. I am now willing to admit—well after the fact—that perhaps my concerns were more than a little over-the-top. Even I don't much notice the flat vs. shiny finish on those black plates anymore. But what can I say? At the time, swept up as I was in the tsunami of The Dinner, it seemed *vitally* important.

• • •

Gaby's bistro dinner was marvelous, as usual. She always started us off with some exquisite cocktail—on that rainy night it was a martini *aux pommes* (vodka and apple liqueur)—while everyone hung out in the living room and schmoozed before the meal. Robin and I tended to arrive around seven, when the dinners technically began, but this being a Brazilian household, to be on time was to be early. Gaby never minded when we were the first to arrive, however, as this gave us a chance to catch up on gossip and help her find her missing shoes before the others arrived. Plus, she knew I was always happy to be put to work in the kitchen for last minute help, if necessary.

Robin and I would then stand around, chatting and sipping our drinks and greeting the other guests—who had learned there was no need for punctuality—as they drifted in. As is customary in Latin American culture, dinner starts late at Gaby and Carlos's house, so we were often a bit tipsy by the time we'd finally eat. Accustomed to dining at ten or eleven in her native country, Gaby no doubt considers even an eight-thirty start to be terribly barbaric, but she reluctantly acceded to the demands of her adopted culture and—as one did with children at home—would feed the Yanks early.

It was close to nine by the time we sat down to dinner that night and, having consumed two apple martinis but no lunch, I was ready to eat. After an *amuse-bouche* of wasabi foam, the first course was served: a mini fritter of rice and mozzarella *di bufula*. The melted, creamy cheese encased in the crispy, batter-encrusted rice was simply divine, and had I not known that there were four more courses to come, I would have sneaked into the kitchen and covertly gobbled down several more.

I was glad I restrained myself, as the salad course was one of my favorites: *frisée aux lardons*, a salad popular in the *bouchons* (small bistro-type establishments) of Lyon. Each plate had a base of frisée lettuce and other mixed greens tossed with a delicate vinaigrette and was topped with *pancetta*, homemade croutons, and a softly-poached egg. I eagerly broke the egg open with my fork, and the yolk dribbled down and mixed with the greens. Heaven!

The third course was vichyssoise. This potato-and-leek soup is traditionally served cold, but being a stormy night in the dead of winter, Gaby chose to serve it warm. According to legend, vichyssoise was invented in the summer of 1917 by Louis Diat, the head chef at the Ritz-Carlton Hotel in New

York City, who was inspired by the potato-and-leek soup his mother and grandmother used to make and by his memories of how he and his brother would cool off the soup in the summertime by pouring cold milk into their bowls. He named it *Crème Vichyssoise Glacée* after the town where he was born, so the story goes.

Next came the cassoulet, the reason I'd been so excited to attend this dinner. I love anything with white beans in it and especially adore this traditional stew from the southwest of France. Cassoulet takes its name from the *cassole*, a type of clay casserole pot in which the stew is traditionally cooked. It is purportedly traditional to deglaze the pot from the previous cassoulet in order to provide a base for the next one, which has led to stories—not unlike those about sourdough bread—of a single original cassoulet being extended for years or even decades.

Cassoulet is exceedingly labor-intensive to make properly and often disappointing in restaurants, so I was thrilled when I found out it would be on the January bistro dinner menu. Gaby's cassoulet had two of my other favorite ingredients as well: fatty pork-sausage and a fall-off-the-bone tender inside/crispy outside duck *confit* that Gaby had slow-cooked in the oven at a low temperature for ten hours the night before.

As soon as everyone had been served the main course, Gaby rushed out of the kitchen to announce that we had to eat the crispy part of the duck first, before it got mushy from sitting in the stew. Robin, alas, impatient to begin, had already stirred hers and allowed the duck to sink into the soggy depths. Dismayed, she apologized to Gaby, who lovingly but reproachfully rapped her knuckles, and then ordered me to give Robin a taste of my crispy skin. I willingly obliged, and we both declared it to be superb.

Nevertheless, I made a mental note: *Don't prepare anything for the Ruth dinner that requires instructions or that might result in any sort of embarrassment to your guests.* Then again, I thought, Ruth and Marty would undoubtedly know *not* to stir their crispy confit into their cassoulet.

I didn't really have room for it, but dessert was a rich raspberry-lemongrass trifle with gobs of custard and whipped cream. Luckily, it was served on the sideboard, and we were allowed to help ourselves, so I was able to take just a tiny portion. Had it not been for all that cream, I would have forgone it altogether, but when cream is involved, so am I!

After the dessert had been served, Gaby sat down next to me, exhausted from all her work, but eager, as always, to talk. She opened the window next to her and lit a cigarette. Waving her hand to encourage the smoke to blow outside and ignoring Robin—who immediately shivered and put on her jacket—Gaby turned to face me.

"Okay," she said in her thick Brazilian accent. "Tell me all about your dinner for the judge."

Once again, I recounted the menu, a process that was now starting to become automatic. She nodded thoughtfully as I described each course, requesting more details now and again.

"What kind of garnish are you going to use for the soup?" she asked.

"A swirl of crème fraîche and chopped walnuts."

"You might want to sprinkle on a few drops of roasted walnut oil, too," Gaby said. "It floats prettily on top of the soup and gives a nice, shimmery effect."

"Oooo, good idea. Thanks!"

I then told her about the blackened ahi and wasabi mashed potatoes, and she again nodded. "Yes, I like it," she said, tapping the ashes off her cigarette into the bushes outside the window. "What about dessert?"

"I'm not yet sure what I'm going to do for that," I answered slowly. "I'm actually thinking of maybe just buying something from a fancy *pâtisserie* down in LA."

Gaby clucked in disapproval at this idea, but I paid her no heed.

I'm not keen on baking. It requires an exactitude for which I have little patience: measuring and weighing ingredients, as well as precise temperature control. (It's for this reason that baking recipes are referred to as "formulae" by bakers, not "recipes.") I much prefer the kind of seat-of-the-pants cooking where you mix the ingredients until they look or feel right, then taste what you've got and decide what it needs, add that to the pot, and taste it again. Of course, a good baker can experiment to a certain extent with the formula and change things around, but you need to be far more experienced than I to do so.

"Do you need any help with the cooking?" Gaby asked when I'd finished recounting the menu.

"No, I have it all under control."

This was, I admit, a show of bravado. I didn't feel *out* of control, but truth be told, I was nervous as hell. Still, there was no way I was going to accept help from Gaby—or from anyone else besides Robin, Mom, or Dad. Because ever since that revelation I'd had in my parents' breakfast room, I'd been keenly aware of how important it was to me to keep the preparations for this dinner within our own small circle.

This was a family affair.

Gaby stubbed out her cigarette and stood. "So are you excited?" she asked.

I thought for a moment. "Yeah," I responded, "I guess I am."

And then, as soon as the words were out of my mouth, I recognized the absurdity of the situation. I'd been so preoccupied with all the planning and details of the dinner and so nervous about making a fool of myself in front of the justice that I hadn't allowed myself to feel *excited* about the momentous event.

"When is it, exactly?" she asked.

I swallowed. "Um . . . two weeks from tonight."

CHAPTER 9

Parties, Preparations, and The Marshal Plan

D minus eight days.

The final week before the big day was jam-packed with activities, most of which had nothing to do with the dinner. On Friday night was my law firm's annual party. This was originally to have been a Christmas celebration, but because of everyone's hectic schedules around the holidays, it had been postponed until January.

Although these affairs traditionally involve lots of drinking, I judiciously limited myself to only two glasses of wine. I tended to get hung over easily—another bummer about getting old that they don't tell you about—and since I had another party to attend the next day, I didn't want to wake up green about the gills. But it was good fun to socialize with everyone at the firm outside of work. Although I'd been growing ever more unhappy with the job itself, I did still enjoy the company of the staff and my fellow attorneys.

The next night, Robin and I were invited to dinner at our friends Sandra and Whalen's house, along with two other guests, Jim and Joy. We'd met Jim and Joy on several occasions in Manhattan, the last time being when they'd hosted a memorable celebration at their enormous West Village loft in honor of Sandra and Whalen's recent wedding.

One of the guests at the party had been the actress Cynthia Nixon. This was at the height of the original *Sex and the City* craze, and even though neither Robin nor I were yet familiar with the show (we're now great fans), we certainly knew who she was and quickly became aware that we had a celebrity in our midst—a celebrity whose photograph, we realized in the days following, was plastered all over the subway walls in *Sex and the City* ads.

"What is *she* doing here?" we wondered aloud, utterly baffled at why Cynthia Nixon would be at a party celebrating Sandra and Whalen's wedding—especially given that the happy couple were, like us, merely visitors to New York from California. What connection could the three possibly have with each other?

And then, as Robin and I surreptitiously gawked at the famous actress from across the room, we noticed something else completely bizarre: Cynthia was accompanied by an entourage of six young women, all of whom immediately set off our gaydar like the clanging of a fire engine's bell. *What the hell?*

Watching the women laugh and share jokes, the two of us tried to make sense of what we were seeing. This was well before Cynthia came out publicly, so the disconnect at seeing her with a gaggle of lesbians was severe.[29]

---

29. We learned later that night from Sandra that Cynthia had recently gotten involved with Sandra's niece, Christine. I'm guessing this was one of the first times the two were seen together at a (quasi) public event. Cynthia and Christine are now happily married.

Flustered at this apparent revelation we were being made privy to—not to mention nonplussed simply to be at a party with such a famous actress—neither Robin nor I ever alluded to the fact that Cynthia was a celebrity (and also *queer*?), even though we chatted with her quite a bit over the course of the evening. Before long, however, avoiding the topic of her stardom became exceedingly awkward, and we vowed afterward that if the same thing ever happened again, we would act more naturally and talk to the person about their fame and their life.

Robin and I now refer to this as "the Cynthia Nixon rule." (The irony, of course, was that the whole evening—with us and other party guests trying to act all cool and collected in the presence of a famous actress—was just like a *Sex and the City* plot.)

As a result of this unforgettable experience, when Robin and I attended that dinner at Sandra and Whalen's house several years later, the four of us quickly dissolved into giggles as we discussed the whole "Cynthia Nixon affair" over a scrumptious meal of braised pork roast with applesauce made of apples from Whalen's own trees. Then afterwards, Sandra entertained us by playing the bass sax, an instrument that stands almost six feet tall. I still smile when I think of that scene: the slender, elegant, seventy-something-year-old Sandra dwarfed by that monstrous saxophone, eyes closed in concentration, booming out a jazz tune in the lowest register known to mankind.

The next day, Sunday, I found time for a task I'd been meaning to get to for several weeks. Growing ever more nervous about the potential dinner conversation with the Ginsburgs, I'd vowed to read up on the current term's cases for the US Supreme Court—the cases already argued, as well as those to be heard after the winter break. Although the justice obviously couldn't speak about her views regarding the outcome of the cases, I knew from my experience in her chambers that she might choose to discuss them in general terms. If she did, I wanted to be prepared.

Scanning through the list of cases and their descriptions on the Cornell Law School website, I saw that there were many hot-button issues on the docket this term. The Court had already heard a case brought by a group of law schools, contending that a federal law mandating the withholding of federal funds from universities that deny military recruiters access to their campuses violates the law schools' First Amendment right by compelling them to disseminate a message—discrimination against gays—with which they disagree. (Yes, that sentence was a bit long-winded, but I thought I'd give you a glimpse of the way lawyers write. The Court ultimately held no; the law does not violate the First Amendment.)

Also interesting to me was that in February, the Supreme Court was to hear a case involving the inheritance rights of Anna Nicole Smith, the former strip-club dancer who had married 86-year-old oil tycoon and Texas billionaire J. Howard Marshall II. Granted, the issues presented by the case weren't all that sexy—it involved federal jurisdiction questions of probate and bankruptcy law—but I still found it amusing to imagine Ms. Smith vamping her way into the Supreme Court the day her case was argued. I later read that, although the media were excluded from attending oral argument, it was indeed quite a circus on the courthouse steps that day. (The Court eventually held for Vickie Lynn Marshall—aka Ms. Smith—and Justice Ginsburg penned the opinion.)

In addition, I learned from the Cornell website that the Court had already heard oral arguments in several abortion cases, one involving parental consent and two regarding whether picketing and blocking access to abortion clinics violates the RICO Act.[30]

Oh, boy, I thought as I logged off my computer. Given what I knew Ruth Ginsburg's feelings to be about *Roe v. Wade* and the political movement it sparked on the right, she was sure to be mighty nervous about how those decisions would go later on in the term.

INTERLUDE

From that very first case she and Marty took on together back in 1970, Ruth Ginsburg's strategy in the fight for gender equality was always consistent: go slowly, taking incremental steps to avoid jumping too far ahead of national sentiment. To her mind, it was necessary that social change first gain support within the populace and the legislature, and only then should the courts act. Otherwise, there would be a risk of backlash, a turning of the legislative tide in the opposite direction. As stated by Ginsburg at her Supreme Court confirmation hearing (quoting Benjamin Cardozo), "Justice is not to be taken by storm. She is to be wooed by slow advances."

A primary component of RBG's plan of action, founded on deeply felt judicial philosophy, was the meticulous selection of cases to bring before the courts. And as an advocate, Professor Ginsburg seemed to have an uncanny knowledge of which fight to pick and at what time. As noted earlier, at the beginning of her career, for example—before the concept of women's equality was even on the radar of most Americans, least of all the conservative judiciary—she chose lawsuits involving men who had been denied benefits

30. The parental consent case was ultimately punted back to the lower court, and the Supreme Court held that the anti-abortionists' activities do not constitute "extortion" under federal law, and thus do not fall under RICO.

routinely granted women. These cases were unintimidating to the Court and generally had little financial impact on the government and therefore easily won. But the standard of scrutiny articulated for gender discrimination could then be applied equally to both sexes.

Then along came *Roe v. Wade* in 1973, brought by two recent University of Texas law grads to challenge their state's antiabortion law, which banned all procedures except those necessary to save the life of the mother.[31] Neither Ginsburg nor her Women's Rights Project were involved in the litigation, and RBG later famously expressed her dismay at the strategy of bringing the case at that time, and the resulting opinion. For in her eyes, *Roe v. Wade* was a perfect example of the harm that comes from using the courts to lead, rather than follow, social change.

In *Roe*, the Supreme Court not only struck down the Texas antiabortion law but went on to set forth an elaborate trimester scheme that displaced virtually every state abortion law then in force. Ginsburg believed, however, that it would have been far better if the Court had invalidated the state laws one at a time, rather than issuing the broad ruling they did. In this way, as she saw it, the political and social momentum for liberalization of abortions that was already occurring could have continued naturally. But instead, the *Roe* decision precipitated a forceful political backlash.

Not surprisingly, this theory has its critics, who argue that the social momentum for abortion rights had already stalled before *Roe*, and thus the decision was necessary. And ironically, the most vocal of the naysayers were some of RBG's feminist colleagues, who used the statements she'd made regarding *Roe* to oppose her candidacy for Supreme Court justice.

---

31. The citation is 410 US 113 (1973). A lesser-known companion case, *Doe v. Bolton*, 410 US 179 (1973), was also decided the same day.

• • •

In those last weeks leading up to the dinner, my father and I had again been corresponding about how to handle the issue of the marshals. Dad had written Justice Ginsburg's assistant Linda to query, among other things, regarding what had become almost an obsession with us: *should we feed the marshals?* (I kept seeing an image of Yogi Bear, Acme hammer in hand, pounding into the ground a sign that read, *Don't Feed the Marshals.*[32]) Linda had responded—as had Martin Ginsburg when I asked him the same question—that whatever we wanted to do would be fine. In other words, we really shouldn't worry about it.

Undeterred, however, we continued to obsess. Dad emailed me:

> *I'm not thrilled about the idea of the marshals at a table for eight, but it does seem odd to make them sit outside in the car while we are eating, no?*

I wrote back that of course we wouldn't seat them at the table with us, but maybe the best thing would be to let them hang out in the den (a room in my folks' house with a library and TV and easy chairs), and I could set up a buffet of soup and salad for them. After all, although we didn't *need* to feed the marshals, it seemed like the gracious thing to do. That appeared to appease my dad, and I heard nothing more from him on the subject for another week.

Then, in mid-January, he emailed me again, in a message with the subject-line: *Marshals to the right of us*:

---

32. And yes, I do recognize that's an amalgam of both the *Road Runner* and *Yogi Bear* cartoon shows.

> *The head marshal phoned back and left a message that there would be four—count 'em four—marshals accompanying the Ginsburgs on Saturday night. Four in the den seems like a lot to me . . . It strikes me that they might come in two cars, so that two could eat while the other two defended us against Al Qaeda, and then they could swap places. Anyway, I think this is something that you and Mom ought to discuss.*

I responded saying not to worry; I'd plan on making lots of extra soup and salad, and we could get some French bread too, so it wouldn't matter how many marshals there were. *But four does seem excessive*, I agreed. *We, or your neighborhood, must be especially suspect . . .*

Dad also forwarded me his recent email correspondence with Ruth regarding her upcoming talk at UCLA, as well as their other scheduled events that weekend. I could see that she and Marty (and my mom and dad) had a very busy few days planned.

Friday afternoon there was to be a Q&A session with Justice Ginsburg at the UCLA law school, to which Robin and I were invited. They'd decided to do a Q&A rather than a lecture to let the law students have a more interactive experience with the justice. This, however, was now being moved to a large auditorium in a building next door to the law school because of the popularity of the event, and they were going to have a lottery for tickets for the students, as well as a closed-circuit TV in a big law school classroom for those who weren't lucky enough to get a seat for the live event.

After the Q&A there would be a reception for Justice Ginsburg at the law school dean's residence, which my parents would be attending. It was to be a small affair, Dad told me, limited to law school mucky-mucks and other VIPs, so Robin and I unfortunately weren't invited. Instead, we'd return to my folks' house after the Q&A, and I figured I'd get a head start on preparing for the dinner the following night.

Saturday afternoon, my parents were going to take the Ginsburgs to the LA County Museum of Art (LACMA), which Ruth had told Dad she'd never seen and would like to visit. Before this, they would have an early lunch at a restaurant near the museum. Saturday night would be the dinner I was cooking, *chez* Mom and Dad. And finally, on Sunday, my parents had tickets to *Madame Butterfly* at the LA Opera and had acquired two more seats for the Ginsburgs to join them.

When you're dealing with a Supreme Court justice, however, it seems nothing is simple. A week before the dinner, my mom emailed to tell me that the Saturday lunch and LACMA visit had ballooned from just the four of them to eleven people; two friends of the Ginsburgs were joining the activities, as well as five other people. Add to that, of course, the four US marshals. Quite an entourage. As a result, Mom and Dad had decided to bow out of the daytime Saturday events as it all sounded too exhausting, and that way they'd be home to help me with the dinner, if needed. In addition, Mom wrote me, the seating had been changed for the opera:

> *Dad and I already had matinee tickets . . . so Dad just changed ours for four together in the same section—the Loge, which ranks pretty good on view, and very good on acoustics. Well. When the opera folk finally got it together and realized who our "Guests" were (they were most discreet over the phone), they couldn't have these dignitaries sitting in peasant seats, so they have moved us to the center of the front row of the Founders' Circle—I think this is where Fergie and Andy sat—and a reserved table in the Founders' Lounge during intermission, so we can have a glass of bubbly. I don't know about the marshals, but that's*

not our problem. The acoustics in the FC are terrible, except for the front row—it's all filled with overstuffed chairs.

Mom also told me that a Sunday morning visit to the Disney Hall—the (then) new concert hall with superb acoustics designed by Frank Gehry where the LA Philharmonic performs—was now in the works. Although it wasn't open on Sunday mornings, someone was planning a private tour for the Ginsburgs and my parents, complete with a solo violinist to perform for them. *After all*, Mom wrote, *the hall must be Heard as well as Seen.*

It sure pays to have friends in high places, I wrote back, more than a little envious that I couldn't join them.

Meanwhile, my mother and I were also corresponding about the tableware. Mom had the unenviable task of washing the dishes and water glasses to rid them of years of accumulated dust as well as polishing all the silver. *There are plates and bowls all over the kitchen waiting to be dried and put back on the shelves*, she wrote.

Several days later she emailed me again: *I'm taking a break from polishing the silver—gadzooks we have a lot!* She told me that the white Syracuse china was clean and ready to go, and that the pink and white Printemps china we'd be using for dessert and coffee was all done but for the luncheon plates and that she'd do the gold-rimmed glassware after finishing the silver.

And I've been encouraging the camellias to bloom, she added. *One is currently covered with big pink and white buds, which would make a good see-over display for the table . . . It's getting to be exciting!*

I received another message from Mom a couple days after this, informing me that she was polishing four candlesticks for the dinner table. This was good, as I hadn't even thought about candles, which would be a lovely addition. She then told me she would dig out and polish a silver tray for the dessert. I had finally settled on buying a selection of pastries from a *pâtisserie* for the dinner, since I knew I couldn't make anything as artful or tasty as a professional. Besides, I rationalized, lots of fancy restaurants buy their desserts from other establishments that specialize in such items. Why shouldn't I? I therefore put Mom and Robin to work researching pastry shops in the West LA area.

Mom also asked if we'd like to be invited to the reception for Ruth at the dean's house after the Q&A session at the Law School. *It turns out there is room for you after all, if you'd like to go.*

We would indeed, I wrote back. *That sounds terrific! And I'll have plenty of time to cook the next day.*

It was starting to become very real.

CHAPTER 10

Final Count Down

D minus five days.

Concentrating on work was becoming near impossible. On Monday morning, I tried to focus on my current legal research issue: was a release signed by a woman taking a class at a health club sufficient to protect the gym from liability for injuries caused by one of its employees dropping a barbell on her as she did stretching exercises on the floor? (As is often the case in the law, the answer turned out to be "maybe.")

After that, I started on my next project, drafting a motion to change the venue of a trial from Los Angeles, where the plaintiff lived, to Monterey, where the accident had occurred. But visions of scallops, champagne flutes, and RBG's oversize, black-frame glasses kept dancing in my head.

Restless, I got up from my chair in the law library, where I'd been looking up the venue statutes, and walked down the hall to my office to retrieve my daily midmorning snack—half a peanut butter and jelly sandwich. But a little icon of an envelope on my computer beckoned me, so I sat down to check the new email.

It was from my father, forwarding a message he'd just received from Justice Ginsburg: *May I take 20 minutes at the start of the student session to speak of Chief Justice Rehnquist and*

Justice O'Connor? (The Chief Justice had recently passed away at this time, and Justice O'Connor had just announced she was stepping down from the Supreme Court.) Dad had added a note to me, above the justice's message: *I answered, "Yes, absolutely."*

Leaning back in my chair, I stared out the window at the law firm parking lot, my heart rate having just shot up some twenty beats per minute. *Okay, so now I'm supposed to go back to the mundane world of change of venue statutes after reading an email from a Supreme Court justice?* Yeah, right.

I had no choice, however, so I forced myself to concentrate on work. Two hours later, I printed out my motion and shut off the computer. Walking to my car, I inhaled with relish the brisk, fresh air and did my best to shake the tort liability case law from my head. *How much better it would be to spend my days writing something other than law*, I mused as I started the engine. To have the luxury to get up in the morning and work on a novel over your morning coffee instead of having to rush out of the house to get a start on legal research? How great would that be?

A murder mystery. Now that *would be a fun thing to spend my days writing.* With a smile, I pulled out of the parking lot and left the law firm behind. *If only.*

• • •

I had several stops to make on my way home. First on the list was the produce stand, to check out vegetables and garnishes for the dinner. As it was the dead of winter, I had no edible flowers blooming in my garden other than nasturtiums, whose blossoms don't travel well. I'd learned in cooking school that one should never use inedible items for garnishes, even if you know they won't be consumed,[33] and was therefore hoping they'd have some appropriate flowers for sale.

---

33. If you include beverages, I don't always follow this rule, since I will occasionally garnish cocktails with decidedly inedible paper umbrellas and plastic monkeys.

No such luck. But they did have nice looking snow peas. I'd still been pondering what vegetable to serve with the ahi tuna, and when I saw those peas, I realized they'd be the perfect match for the fish, both texture- and flavor-wise. And, it occurred to me as I gazed at the bin, they could be arranged on the plate in a sort of wave shape, which would tie in with the Japanese and seafood themes. I picked one up, snapped it in two, and popped half into my mouth. Yes, crunchy and full of flavor.

"Will you have new snow peas on Thursday, or will they be the same as these?" I asked the woman at the cash register.

"Oh, we'll get new ones in by then," she said.

Good. That's what I'd use, then.

Wandering down the aisle as I chewed the other half of the pea, I noticed a display of various kinds of sprouts. In addition to the usual mung bean and alfalfa variety, there was a box of pea sprouts. I scooped up a handful and examined the threads. They had long, pale green stems, with a cluster of tiny dark green leaves at the end. "Cool!" I said to no one in particular. These would be a perfect garnish for the ahi, snow pea, and wasabi mashed potato course. But I wouldn't buy them yet. I'd come back and get them on Thursday when I picked up the snow peas.

Pleased with the results at the produce store, I walked next door to The Fish Lady to check out their ahi. There was a gorgeous chunk in the display case—ruby red and firm looking. "How often do you get your ahi in?" I asked.

"It comes in fresh every morning."

"Terrific. I'll come back Thursday, then. I need some for Saturday night. It'll keep okay till then, won't it?"

"Sure. Just keep it nice and cold, and it should be fine for two days."

Next stop was the Santa Cruz Coffee Roasting Company for a pound of Steve's Smooth French Roast beans for the dinner, then on to the grocery store. After snagging a couple of butternut squash for the soup I'd be making on Wednesday night, I headed to the fish counter to check out their scallop situation. I still had my rain check for sea scallops at $10 a pound, but I'd been checking every week and there hadn't been any scallops for sale, so I was starting to get worried. I told the young man at the butcher case about my rain check and asked if they'd be getting a scallop delivery that week.

"You know," he said in a low voice, glancing quickly from side to side, "the scallops we sell here at the fish counter—they're the same as the ones in the frozen meat case, which are ten dollars a pound without being on sale."

"What? I don't understand."

"C'mere." He led me over to the large freezer at the end of the frozen vegetable aisle, reached in, and pulled out a two-pound sack of IQF sea scallops. "See? Nineteen ninety-nine a bag. We just open these up and sell them at the fish counter."

"But you sell them for twenty dollars a pound over there, unless they're on sale. You mean you sell the *exact same* scallops for twice the price?" I was aghast. How could they do such a thing? Was it even legal? But of course they could; they could sell them for whatever amount they wanted. And we naïve customers paid the price—literally.

"Well," the young man went on, "we used to get bags of frozen scallops from our distributor, which we'd put in our display case, but not anymore. So ever since we started stocking these retail bags here—which was pretty recently—we've just been opening them up and selling the scallops for the old price. We sometimes do the same thing with the shrimp, too. Here." He handed me the bag.

As I stood there incredulous, mouth agape, staring at the bag of frozen scallops in my hands, he added: "Plus, you have to buy two full pounds to get this price." The butcher nodded toward the freezer. "At the counter you can buy as few as you want."

I thanked him for making me privy to this information and, shaking my head, dropped the bag of frozen sea scallops into my basket. When I got home, I opened the package. It was a good thing it held a lot more scallops than I needed, as they were all different sizes, from rather small (though not as tiny as bay scallops) to enormous. I picked out the six largest of the bunch for use at the dinner—I'd decided to take Robert's advice and serve just one large scallop per person—and placed them in a zippered baggie. Still shaking my head in disbelief, I stashed both bags in the freezer.

• • •

I had the first of several anxiety dreams that night. In it, I was hosting a never-ending dinner party where things kept going amiss: the food wasn't ready; there weren't enough places at the table; I couldn't remember what the next course was supposed to be. And although I kept managing to wake up and roust myself from this frustrating scenario, every time I went back to sleep, I continued with the same dream, like some interminable soap opera.

My anxieties were creeping into my waking life as well. For instance, I was becoming consumed with nervousness over my blood oranges. Usually by January we have scads of them on our tree, some already starting to turn a fiery red where they face the sun. But this year there were only a few that looked close to ripe, and of these, only a couple had even started to change color. What would I do if the blood-red fruit—which were to be the focal point of my salad for the Ruth dinner—weren't ripe enough by then?

So, in a sort of parallel anxiety dance with my mother who was at the same time encouraging her camellias down in Southern California to bloom in time for the weekend, I'd been going out into our backyard every day and staring down the blood orange tree, willing the fruit to ripen.

I was also worried that I was catching a cold. Since childhood I've had a tendency to get sick as a result of stress. I can't remember a Christmas vacation during college—which always came right after final exams—when I didn't come home with a flu or cold. And I'd often get sick the week before a chorus concert, when my life would become hectic from the crazy schedule of working during the days and then having long rehearsals every night.

Sure enough, the week before the dinner I'd started getting the telltale signs: a slight throbbing in my ear, pressure in my sinuses, and the beginnings of a sore throat. As a result, I'd been ingesting massive amounts of echinacea, goldenseal, and vitamin C. (I'm not convinced that these substances actually have any effect on a body, but I *do* believe in the power of the placebo. And since belief is the causative factor in a placebo, and since I do think there's a chance that echinacea *might* help prevent a cold, I figure, how can it hurt?)

• • •

Wednesday—D minus three days.

I was, thank goodness, not sick, though I was still worried about a mild aching in my left ear. At my law firm, I tried to concentrate on the work I'd begun the day before: a motion for summary judgment (i.e., to have the case dismissed prior to trial) based on the statutory immunity of a father whose daughter, after getting drunk on alcohol he had purchased for her, had been involved in a car crash, killing another person. It wouldn't have been a pleasant project under any circumstances, but this morning my brain was rebelling at the combined unhappy facts of the case and tedium of the task.

I could chalk this up partly to anxiety and excitement about the upcoming weekend, but I knew it was also the ever-increasing feeling that I had to make some kind of change in my life. Although I no longer suffered those black mornings I'd once experienced, my workdays still seemed to drag on and on, and I'd frequently find myself checking my watch to see if it was yet time to go home. Such was the case that Wednesday morning—three days before my dinner with RBG.

The irony, of course, was not lost on me that I was about to spend an evening with perhaps the most celebrated attorney in all the land, yet here I was, bitching and moaning about a few hours of unpleasant legal research. Ruth Bader Ginsburg—who, over her years as attorney and jurist, had burned countless gallons of midnight oil researching subjects equally as tedious and heartbreaking—had surely never complained about her work.

But we're different, my internal voice responded in protest. *She loves the law. It's a passion for her, a vocation. It's her life.* For me, on the other hand, much as I'd attempted to convince myself otherwise, my work as a research attorney would always be simply a job.

Why, oh why couldn't I find a vocation I *truly* loved—as much as Ruth did the law?

I was still musing on this quandary as I made several stops after work that day to buy groceries for the dinner. After swinging by Staff of Life for salad ingredients and crème fraîche for the soup, I drove to Trader Joe's, where I snagged a cart and pulled my shopping list out of my bag. First the snack food aisle. I'd decided on cashews and Japanese rice crackers with seaweed and wasabi peas to have with the Champagne, as a hint of the main course to come. I also needed pine nuts for the salad.

The rice crackers and pine nuts were easy, but oh my, were there a lot of different varieties of cashews! I stared at the rack, trying to choose which I wanted: raw or roasted, salted or unsalted, flavored or plain, huge ones or small ones. *Roasted and salted, definitely*. I may be from health-conscious Santa Cruz, but I've never much cared for raw or unsalted nuts. *And plain, so the flavor of the nut can stand out, unhindered.* And although the large cashews were impressive, I finally decided to go with the small ones, given their higher nut-to-salt surface area.

Okay, that decision took five minutes. Hopefully I could be a bit more decisive with the rest of my ingredients.

On to the cheese section, via the produce where I grabbed two bags of prewashed baby spinach. I quickly spotted the Gorgonzola and added it to my cart. Next, a bottle of echinacea as a precaution against the cold I still feared was coming on.

The last item was fizzy water. I knew this wasn't by any means a vitally important part of the dinner, but nevertheless, I stood staring at the shelf for several minutes. Ruth would notice every detail of the meal, I felt sure, and I wanted it all to be perfect—even the water. I studied the options: Crystal Geyser (too mundane); Blú Italy (too nauseating a name); Pellegrino (maybe); Gerolsteiner . . . I stopped there.

At the time, I'd recently started following the professional cycling peloton, and Gerolsteiner was the team for whom one of my favorite cyclists, Levi Leipheimer, rode. Not only that, but he was one of the favorites to win the inaugural Tour of California bike race the following month. It seemed like a sign. Grabbing two bottles, I set them down with satisfaction next to the cashews.

My final stop was Safeway, where I picked up ingredients for the ginger-lime sauce, soup, and wasabi mashed potatoes. Once home, after putting the food away and taking Rosie for her afternoon walk, I sat down to make a list of what I needed to do that evening: whisk up the salad dressing, prepare the soup, choose my clothes for the weekend, and pack all the wine glasses.

I started with the glasses. First I wiped them down with a soft cotton cloth to ensure they were clean and spot-free. I normally wouldn't be so fastidious for a dinner party, but once again, my overriding thought was: *What will Ruth think?* No way did I want her noticing water marks on her glass when she should instead be appreciating the complexity of the wine's vintage.

Next, I brought in from the garage a stack of newspapers from the recycling bin and two cardboard boxes. Robin came home from work at this point and commented, "We're only six, you know. You've got eight glasses each."

"I know. But I'm bringing extra in case any break on the trip down or once we get there."

She rolled her eyes. "Whatever."

After crumpling newspaper sheets to make a soft nest on the bottom of the boxes, I wrapped each glass and set it inside, taking care to have more crushed paper on all the edges, in case the box got knocked around in transit. Even though the boxes were enormous, the sixteen glasses—for both white and red wine—barely fit into the two of them because of the massive amount of paper I'd used.

That task complete, Robin set the table, and we had a quick dinner before she had to head off for her bridge game at Robert's house. Since we'd be leaving for LA in two days time, I was doing my best to use up all the leftovers in the fridge, so dinner that night was a green salad mixed with steamed broccoli, stir-fried veggies, chunks of roast chicken, and diced baked potato. Quite tasty, it turned out.

Once we'd eaten, Robin washed our plates and set them in the dish drainer, then grabbed her wallet and keys and kissed me goodbye. "I hope you bid and make a grand slam!" I called out as she climbed into her car. After watching her drive off, I walked back into the kitchen and took a deep breath. Now to get to work cooking; the dinner was finally starting in earnest.

First—doing my best to think of this prep work as no different from any other I'd ever done—I got the butternut squash baking, its oiled halves face down over sprigs of sage from my garden. Next, I whipped up a batch of my Dijon vinaigrette salad dressing.

I then returned to the soup, sautéing leeks, carrots, onions, and garlic, then adding chicken stock and a *bouquet garni* and setting the pot over a low fire. When the squash in the oven was fully roasted, I removed the skin, added the bright orange flesh to the soup, and left it to simmer for another half hour to allow the flavors to blend.

Just enough time to decide on my clothing for the big weekend ahead.

INTERLUDE

Ruth Bader Ginsburg was a snappy dresser, no question. And given that her father, Nathan Bader, worked throughout her childhood in the garment district of Manhattan—first as a furrier and later as a haberdasher—this acute fashion sense should not be a surprise.

Photos of Kiki during high school and college display a perfectly coiffed young woman, often in cashmere and pearls or sporting a crisp button-down blouse accented with a delicate brooch. In later days, the justice tended toward more exotic garb, such as brocaded shawls and colorfully threaded silk robes, often acquired on her frequent travels about the globe. And instead of the simple pearls or brooches of her youth, Ruth came to favor bold pendants and dangling earrings to set off her natty attire. Not to mention knit gloves, and even the odd turban. And, of course, the myriad oversize eyeglasses that later became a trademark for the diminutive justice.

So renowned was RBG for her sense of style that she was named one of *Glamour* magazine's Women of the Year in 2012. An impressive achievement for someone in a profession where conformity of dress—enforced by the requirement of a uniform, black robe—is the norm.

But of course even in this regard, the justice was an outlier. More than for her large glasses and pulled-back hair, RBG is probably best known for the lace ruffles and frilly collars she would wear over her black judicial robe. This practice started when she first took her place on the bench of the Supreme Court. Noting that the justices' robes were designed with men in mind, with a notch in the front to show off their shirt collar and tie knot, she and Sandra Day O'Connor—the only other woman then on the high court—decided they needed something to dress up their robes. Hence was born the tradition of the jabot, inspired by the decorative collars and frills used in English and French courts.

The closet in Ruth's chambers held a variety of jabots in different styles, some gifts, some purchased abroad, and one from the Met Opera gift shop. Most were regular-court-day jabots, but two had special significance. On those rare days when she got to announce the majority opinion, the justice would wear the collar given to her by her clerks: an elegant, crocheted piece ornamented with what appear to be golden eyes peering out from atop a dusty rose background and accented by gold trim and dangling cut-glass beads.

But for dissents, RBG got downright steam-punk, arming herself with a black velvet number studded with shiny bling. This bib-style jabot—reminiscent of a collar Jeanne d'Arc might have draped over her chain mail—came from the gift bag Ruth received as one of *Glamour*'s Women of the Year. She immediately deemed it "fitting for dissent."

Fitting indeed.

• • •

With a frown, I stood gazing into my closet as I considered the events I'd need to dress for this weekend. Three: the Friday afternoon Q&A session with Justice Ginsburg at the law school, the reception afterwards at the dean's house, and the dinner at my parents' house the next night. But, I realized as I thought about it, I wouldn't be able to change clothes between the law school talk and the reception, so that was really only two outfits I'd need.

Settling on one's clothing for a fancy occasion is never an easy task, and for someone as indecisive as I, this was a particularly daunting decision. Like Robin, I've never been comfortable in skirts or dresses, so I didn't have that favorite "little black cocktail dress" as a go-to item. *So what to wear?*

Finally deciding that business attire would work for the Friday activities, I pulled out a pair of dark brown pleated slacks, a green floral-patterned blouse, and an olive blazer.

And I'd wear Grammy's pearls.

My dad's mother Pauline was in her twenties in the late 1920s, and I have a picture of her wearing a long strand of faux—but "good" faux—pearls. In the photograph, she's standing with her friend Belle Conlan (I'm named—via my dad's middle name—after Belle's husband, Les) in front of a house in West Los Angeles, and they're both wearing cloche hats and low-waisted flapper dresses. Grammy has a beaded purse in her hands, and around both their necks the two young women sport identical strands of pearls knotted in the middle, one end looped tightly around their necks and the other end hanging down almost to their waists.

Grammy would have been mighty pleased to know I'd be wearing her pearls to meet the justice.

Now the outfit for the dinner—which was a much harder call. It needed to be somewhat elegant (though there was no way I could hope to match the stylish RBG), but at the same time, it should be something I could cook in, as there would be quite a bit of last-minute work to be done between courses. I could, of course, always wear an apron while in the kitchen, but what if I forgot to remove it when I came back to the table? No, that would be too embarrassing for words.

After several minutes' hard thought, I finally settled on the black stretchy—i.e., comfy—pants I often wear out to dinner or to the opera, and a long-sleeved pale yellow button-down shirt, topped by a vest of Italian make that I'd scored several years earlier at a thrift store in Manhattan (the same visit during which Robin and I had met Cynthia Nixon).

Finding "fancy" clothes when you're a woman who's uncomfortable in skirts and dresses and other so-called "feminine" attire can be tricky. I've solved this problem by adopting vests as my go-to dress clothes and now have a collection in a variety of styles: silk, brocade, embroidery, satin, knit, and wool. The vest from the New York thrift store that I chose for the Ruth dinner is one of my favorite items of clothing. It has a deep burgundy background with a subtle feather pattern in black, and in the foreground are rows of golden feathers. Very classy, notwithstanding its humble origins. And I'd wear my dressy black flats (not that I own anything *but* flats) both days for the shoes.

My clothing determined, I returned to the pot simmering on the stove, fished out the *bouquet garni*, and turned off the burner to let the soup cool down. Then, happy for a moment's rest, I plopped down on the couch in the living room to read a chapter of *Double Shot*, the latest Diane Mott Davidson mystery, which my mom had recommended to me.

Once the soup had cooled, I blended it into a purée and then took an anxious taste. Although I'd omitted the honey altogether, cut down the amount of carrots by half, and added extra leeks, I was still a tad nervous it might be too sweet. But no.

Other than needing a little salt, it seemed fine. With a satisfied smile, I took another taste. It wasn't just fine; it was *delicious.*

Yes! I could do this.

The clouds had been accumulating all day, and it was now beginning to rain. After decanting the soup into three large containers and stowing it in the fridge, I stood at the kitchen window to stare out at the water running across the terra cotta tiles in our back patio. With a yawn, I checked the clock on the wall—almost eleven o'clock. I was exhausted, but wondered whether I'd be able to sleep.

CHAPTER 11

Busy Bees and Celebrities

Thursday—D minus two days.

It took a while, but I did eventually fall asleep, only to have another anxiety dream. This time it was about a mysterious person who was trying to track me down for some unexplained offense. Trespass? Or perhaps stealing a bag of Cheetos? I wasn't sure, but I kept managing to elude him on my bike, even though I knew the right thing to do would be to turn myself into the authorities. Although it was icy cold in the house, I woke up covered in sweat.

On that last day at the office before leaving for the Ruth weekend, the law firm was abuzz about my impending encounter with Justice Ginsburg. As I was fetching my morning coffee, I was joined at the coffee station by Bob and the senior partner, Fred.

"I'm sure you have room for one more at your dinner," Fred said. "So how about I come down and join you?"

"I don't know why she'd invite *you*," Bob countered. "A Republican? Invited to a dinner with Justice Ginsburg?"

With a wink, he headed back towards his office laughing softly to himself.

Everyone asked me about the menu I'd chosen, and I'd now recounted it so many times that my telling had become rote:

> Champagnewithcashewsandricecrackers, seared scallopswithagingerlimecreamsauce [breath], butternutsquashsoupwithbrownbutterandacrème fraîchegarnish [breath], babyspinachsaladwith bloodorangesredonionandpinenutswithadijon vinaigrette [breath], andblackenedahiwithwasabi mashedpotatoesandsnowpeas [gasp].

"Mind you, that's the abbreviated version," I'd add.

Luckily, I had only some legal research to do that day, as I'm not sure I would have been able to focus enough to actually compose anything. Distracted as I was, however, I did manage to bill almost six hours before I could stand it no longer and cut out.

I had two errands to run after work. First I went back to the produce store and bought my snow peas and pea sprouts. Then I headed next door to The Fish Lady for the tuna. My eyes were drawn immediately to a huge chunk of glistening red fish.

"That's the ahi, isn't it?"

"Yep. Fresh caught this morning, and that's the last of it."

"Great. I need enough for six steaks, and that looks like plenty." I gazed at the fish in the case. "So what kind of tuna is ahi, anyway? I've heard that it's bigeye, but I've also heard that it's yellowfin."

"Well, I think this here is bigeye, 'cause when we get yellowfin in, we sell it as yellowfin tuna. But both this and the yellowfin we sell are sushi grade tuna. I think you're right, though—that they're both called ahi. So, how much did you say you wanted?"

"I need six steaks, but they need to be really nice, 'cause, well . . ." I paused. Part of me wanted to crow about my renowned dinner guest—and see if name-dropping would result in any perks here at the fish store. But the other part of me was becoming slightly embarrassed by the idea of continually bragging about how I'd be hobnobbing with such a celebrity as RBG.

The braggart in me won out: "I'm actually going to be serving the fish at a dinner I'm cooking this weekend for Supreme Court Justice Ruth Ginsburg."

The man behind the counter raised his eyebrows. "*Really*? Wow." And then he looked at me again, this time as if really seeing me for the first time. Pulling the ahi out of the case, he set it on the scale. "It's a little under five pounds, this piece."

"Well I won't need that much, especially since we're having lots of other courses. But how many pounds do you think I should buy to get six medium-size steaks from the center?"

He cocked his head and studied the fish for a moment. "How 'bout I cut off this small end, and you take this piece here." He demonstrated with his finger where he suggested cutting the fish, and I tried to envision the size that six steaks cut from the center remaining piece would be.

"Yeah, I think that would work." It would be far better to have too much than too little, and I could always freeze any extra for later use.

"And I tell you what. Since it's for Justice *Ginsburg*, I'll knock a buck a pound off the price."

"Oh, you don't need to do that," I said, chuckling to myself.

"No, really, I want to. I think it's great that she's gonna eat our fish."

"That's so sweet. Thank you!"

He cut the tuna and held it aloft for approval, then wrapped it in plastic and set the chunk on the register scale. "Fifty-four eighty-five. Let's just call it fifty even—for the justice." He folded the fish into a sheet of white butcher paper and rang up fifty dollars.

"Well, thanks again." I paid and took the parcel from him, then smiled and waved as I walked out the door.

I couldn't wait to tell Robin about this latest example of RBG-induced benefits. *What would happen*, I wondered, *if I said I was cooking for some* super-*celebrity like, say, Mick Jagger?* But then, of course, they wouldn't believe me. No, I decided, a Supreme Court justice was the perfect amount of celebrity for name-dropping—famous, but believable. And way more impressive than some ol' rock star.

Once home, I unwrapped the fish and patted it dry with a paper towel, placed it on a folded paper towel on a plate as my fisherman friend Dylan had taught me to do, then laid the plate on a bowl of ice. I then covered the whole thing in plastic wrap and set it in the fridge. I'd replace the paper towel when it got soaked and replenish the ice as it melted. This is the best way to keep fish fresh for a few days, Dylan says, as the folded paper towel absorbs all the liquid released by the fish, instead of having the fish sit in it.[34] I gather it has something to do with the ammonia in the fish juice, which hastens the process of its going bad. He used to work on a fishing boat, so I trust him about such matters.

That done, I checked the time. I had several hours before I needed to leave for chorus rehearsal, and there was no other prep work for the dinner I could do right now. But I was so antsy about the upcoming weekend that I had to do something. A brisk bike ride seemed just the thing to burn off some of my anxiety.

Pedaling off toward the ocean on my vintage red-and-black Motobecane, I rode down the coast to the entrance to the wharf, then turned around and pumped back up the hill to

---

34. It also works to put the fish on a tray with drainage holes in it and place this on a tray full of ice, which is what restaurants do (but most folks don't have such items at home).

West Cliff Drive. After completing a full circuit of the winding road that hugs the coastline, I returned home, out of breath but less agitated than before.

After showering and packing my suitcase for the weekend, I headed—with some trepidation—out to the back patio to pick my blood oranges. I'd purposely avoided looking at the tree for the past several days, hoping that unwatched, the fruit might somehow more quickly ripen. I was therefore ecstatic to discover that quite a few had started turning red and looked as if they'd be fine. I picked nine and brought them inside. Cutting one open to check its color, I saw that it was a bright red inside. I tasted it: tart but full of flavor.

Whew.

Next I quickly prepared a couple quesadillas for Robin's and my dinner.

"So, how are you doing?" she asked as we ate. "You nervous?"

"Yeah. But I'm finally getting excited about it all, too. Although it's kind of hard to tell the two apart. My body feels like it's got an electrical current shooting through it full blast."

"Not surprising. But I know it's going to be a great success. They're gonna love all the amazing food you're making."

"I hope . . ."

Robin reached out to squeeze my hand. "Well, I'm sure singing tonight will help calm your nerves. Is there anything you need me to do while you're at rehearsal?"

"No, I'm good. But thanks."

And for the first time since embarking on this project, I truly believed those words as I spoke them. For notwithstanding the nervous flutter in my stomach, I finally felt confident and prepared.

Gulping down my last bite, I took the plate to the sink, then grabbed my B minor *Mass* score, jacket, wallet, and car keys. "Gotta get going," I said, kissing Robin goodbye. "J. S. Bach calls."

INTERLUDE

With regard to nonlegal matters, Justice Ginsburg was as renowned for her love of music—particularly opera—as she was for the frilly lace collars she'd sport over her black judicial robe. The personal items in her chambers at the Supreme Court demonstrated this passion. Scattered about the bookshelves sat framed photographs of her favorite sopranos and tenors (as well as the one Robin and I had seen of herself and Justice Scalia on stage as supernumeraries in the Strauss opera, *Adriadne auf Naxos*), and she kept a small stereo in her office so she could listen to music as she worked.

The justice was a well-known figure backstage at the Washington National Opera—she and Marty chose the Watergate as their abode largely because of its proximity to the Kennedy Center, which houses the opera company—and had been a guest one time on the opera show during the Metropolitan Opera's Saturday radio broadcast.[35] She even once hired a law clerk, at least in part, because she was so pleased to see that his writing sample concerned the use of contract law in Wagner's *Ring* cycle.

This love of music began early. Kiki Bader studied piano starting at age eight and later played cello in her high school orchestra. Though she never moved up from the last row of cellos, she always claimed she was happy simply be a part of the ensemble.

Her mother took Kiki to her first opera when she was eleven (an abbreviated version of Ponchielli's *La Gioconda*, for children), and by high school Kiki was hooked: she started traveling from Brooklyn to Manhattan as often as possible to see operas at the New York City Center, buying seats in the last row of the top balcony.

---

35. It's worth noting that while on this show, Justice Ginsburg was asked what she would recommend as a first opera for someone to see, and remarked that she would definitely *not* recommend Wagner's *Parsifal*. Having now seen it at the LA Opera, I agree that is a rather daunting work, but I can certainly think of far more difficult first operas than that one.

Marty shared this passion for music—no doubt one of the things that initially attracted the couple to one another. His grandfather had been a mechanic in an opera house in Odessa, Russia (now Ukraine) and passed along his appreciation for the art form to Marty's mother, who listened every week to the Met's Saturday broadcasts.

When Marty was stationed at Fort Sill during his two-year stint in the Army, he and Ruth would drive four hours to Dallas to attend the traveling performances put on by the Metropolitan Opera, and the couple would check out records from the base library to listen to at home. Once back in New York, they started sharing the box Marty's mother had at the Met.

In 2011, Harvard University conferred upon Justice Ginsburg an honorary degree (because she had transferred from Harvard to Columbia for her third year of law school to be with Marty, the university had refused her a degree at that time). To her utter delight, one of her fellow recipients was Plácido Domingo. As the justice was being presented with her certificate, the celebrated tenor stood up and serenaded her, having set the ending portion of the conferral to music. "It was one of the greatest moments of my life," she later gushed.

Justice Ginsburg has stated that if she could have chosen any career—and if she'd had the talent to do so—she would have been a great diva: a Renata Tibaldi, a Beverly Sills, or a Marilyn Horne. But, alas, her grade school music teacher ranked her "a sparrow, not a robin." So, she liked to say, she would sing in two places: in the shower and in her dreams.

• • •

After warming us up with scales, "bumble-bee" arpeggios, and group back rubs, our choral director, Cheryl Anderson, began rehearsal that night with the *Credo*, the second movement of the Bach B minor *Mass*. And it was all going fine until we got to the words "*visibilium omnium et invisibilium*," at which point I came down with a serious attack of the giggles.

Robin and I had recently watched the Christopher Guest movie, *Best in Show*, which features a wacky scene where a yuppie couple misplace their Weimaraner's stuffed bumble bee toy while grooming the dog for the show and become hysterical. "It's not in the crate!" the Parker Posey character screams. "If she doesn't get it, she's gonna *flip out*! Go to the hotel and *get busy bee*! Run! *Run*!"

Well, each time I sang "*visibili*" that night—which happens several times in quick succession—I kept thinking "busy bee," and had to focus intently to keep from bursting out laughing. Unfortunately, however, try as I might to control myself, I couldn't help letting loose with several snorts and giggles, drawing confused expressions from my fellow altos and a stern look from Cheryl. Since the choral director was well aware of my upcoming Big Weekend, however, I imagine she chalked it up to what it was—pent-up nervous tension choosing this inappropriate moment to escape.

Once we turned to the last movement, I was able to get serious again. We'd sung only the first few pages when the director cut us off. "Don't rush the eighth-notes," she said. "It should be solemn. But joyous at the same time." As she talked us through the music, I followed along in my score, and then Cheryl summed up this final portion of Bach's sublime *Mass*: "We are *happy*, having built the world!" She stopped speaking, and I looked up to see tears streaking down her cheeks.

After a moment, during which many of us chorus members in turn wiped our own eyes, we continued on. And although it took great concentration to sing the difficult piece,

I found that as we made our way through the *Osanna*, the *Benedictus*, the *Agnus Dei*, and finally the *Dona Nobis Pacem*, my mind was calm, serene. The music had stilled the internal noise—the constant chatter in my brain telling me I had to do this, do that, get ready for the momentous event that would be taking place in two days' time.

Johann Sebastian Bach had performed a near-miracle: for the first time in weeks, I was able to forget about the Ruth dinner and simply be in the *moment*.

• • •

It was foggy as I walked to my car after rehearsal, the kind that settles over you, covering your clothes with a fine layer of mist. Such pea-soup fog is unusual for Santa Cruz, but tonight it was so thick on the freeway that I could see only about thirty feet ahead of me, and I—as well as all the other drivers on the road, thank goodness—crept cautiously along at a snail's pace. *Great*, I thought, hands tightly gripping the steering wheel. *All I need is to be involved in a grisly car crash the night before I finally leave for my big weekend with Ruth.*

I arrived home unscathed, but to calm my nerves, I promptly poured myself a nightcap of a fine, aged dark rum that Laura had brought back from a recent trip to Martinique. Staring out the back door at the fog shrouding our blood orange tree, I did a few breathing exercises we'd learned in chorus: *in, out; iiiin, ouuuuut*. The house was quiet, with Robin and Rosie curled up in bed together sound asleep, and the only sound I could discern was the slow drip of water from a drain spout just outside the door.

As the rum performed its magic, my muscles relaxed and my heartbeat slowed to a normal rate. But my brain had begun to race once again; the serenity instilled by Bach had been short-lived. Tomorrow began the big adventure: seeing the celebrated RBG in the flesh at the Q&A and the dean's reception. And the very next day, I'd be cooking dinner for the justice and spending an *entire evening* in her presence. How could anyone's brain *not* race at such a thought?

But then, forty-eight hours from now, it would all be over, I realized with a pang. This wondrous journey would come to a close, and I'd return to the daily grind of billable hours and motions to compel, as if the entire experience had been but a dream.

No. Don't go there. Enjoy the moment.

Easier said than done. With a sigh, I turned from the window and set about organizing everything for Robin to pack into the car in the morning. Perhaps concentrating on the mundane would serve to once more quiet my mind.

First, I filled two boxes with two cast-iron skillets, various utensils, the coffee maker, Mom's eight square black plates (I'd decided it would be downright silly to bring mine down too), and my knife bag. Next, into a separate box, went all the food not requiring refrigeration: ginger root, bottled clam juice, pine nuts, walnuts, cashews, rice crackers, dried cranberries, roasted walnut oil, sesame oil, potatoes, spices for the ahi dry rub, wasabi powder, red onions, blood oranges, individually wrapped sugar cubes from France, and the coffee beans and filters.

This I carried out to the car and set on the back seat. I then pulled out the big cooler, to be filled in the morning. After placing the boxes of glasses and wine and bottled water on the kitchen floor next to the empty cooler, I threw two sleeping bags on top of them. We'd learned from our last visit to Santa Monica and were determined not to be cold at night on this trip. Last of all, I wheeled out my packed suitcase and set it next to Robin's.

After going over my list one final time, I plopped onto the couch to finish my rum. It was eleven-thirty. Only five and a half hours till I had to wake up for the drive to LA.

• • •

Friday—D minus thirty-seven hours.

The buzzing of the alarm clock would always bring rapturous joy to Rosie. Dogs love a routine, and welcoming the new day was one of her favorites. She knew she was supposed to wait until we showed signs of waking before bothering us, but she had apparently decided that lying with her head mere inches from our faces, staring intently to see if we'd opened our eyes, was within the rules. I always knew she was there, as I could feel her hot breath on my face and sense her eyeballs boring into my closed lids. Sometimes I'd open my eyes a crack to get a glimpse of her rapt gaze, but if she noticed this movement, it was all over, and the ritual of enthusiastic morning kisses would begin.

When the alarm went off, however, Rosie knew this meant wake-up time—eyes open or not—and she'd jump up and start barking and frantically licking us. So at five o'clock the next morning, Robin and I were wakened not only by the alarm but also by a dynamo of black and white fur and a hot tongue.

It was cold and pitch-black outside the window. Robin immediately jumped out of bed, but I allowed myself another quarter hour of dozing time, since she had said she'd pack the car. I lay under the warm eiderdown for those few luxurious minutes, then forced myself to climb out into the cold air.

By the time I made it to the kitchen, Robin had already loaded up the car and was in the dining room finishing her morning banana and bowl of granola. Rosie was sitting expectantly at her feet, waiting for the banana pieces that Robin would slip to her. As I sat down to look at the morning paper, Robin took her bowl to the sink and grabbed the leash, setting Rosie off on a new round of barking.

After a hasty review of the day's headlines, I consulted my list and got to work packing the food from the freezer and refrigerator. On top of a couple of packets of blue ice, I set the containers of soup in the cooler, surrounded by the half-and-half, cream, and crème fraîche. Above these went the frozen scallops, the ahi, the Gorgonzola cheese, the salad dressing, and the butter, which pretty much filled the container. The produce—the spinach, snow peas, and pea sprouts—would have to go into a brown paper bag.

I carried the cooler and bag of produce out to the garage and, when I opened the car door, was hit with an overpowering smell of coffee. *What the . . . ?* Oh yeah. I'd left the box of food containing the bag of coffee beans in the back seat overnight, not realizing how pungent it would become in the closed car. I saw that Robin had wisely moved the coffee beans to the trunk, but the intense aroma—akin to skunk or tuna fish—was still strong and was already starting to make me feel a little nauseated. I opened the garage door and all four car doors to get cross-drafts circulating.

Heading back inside, I did a last walk-through of all the rooms in the house to make sure I hadn't left anything behind. It all looked good, so I told Robin—who'd now returned from her walk—that we were cleared for takeoff. We called Rosie so we could say goodbye and give her a treat. But when she didn't come when called, we looked at each other and then laughed, both realizing where she was. Sure enough, the dog had jumped into the open car and was sitting expectantly in the front passenger seat.

"No, honey. You're not going." I coaxed her out of the car and back into the house, but she was none too happy, as she could surely tell we were leaving for a while. "Don't worry, Dylan will be here in a few hours to dog sit," I reassured her, but the sad look in her eyes remained. Unhappy as she was, though, she greedily accepted the dog biscuit I offered her, and gobbled it up before we even got out the door.

It was still dark as we headed out of Santa Cruz at six o'clock. The coffee smell had largely dissipated, but Robin screwed up her face as we got in the car. "Pew. I can't believe it's so strong, even after I moved it to the trunk."

"Yeah, sorry about that. My bad."

"It's all right. I'll just drink my coffee and pretend the smell's coming from that." She passed me the thermos, and I poured a cup and handed it to her. As she pulled out of the driveway, Robin sang the opening lines from "Born to Be Wild," her traditional start to any road trip.[36]

I was still sleepy, having tossed and turned most of the few hours that I'd spent in bed, and Robin encouraged me to nap if I could. This seemed like a wise idea, so I grabbed one of the sleeping bags and lowered my seat back as far as possible without bumping into the cooler behind it.

I managed to doze for about an hour and a half, and when I awoke we were on Highway 101, south of Salinas near Soledad. The sun was peeking over the hills to the east, and the sky had turned a deep purple-blue. Only a few of the brightest stars—or perhaps they were planets—were still visible.

"Wanna listen to some music?" I asked, bringing the seat back to its upright position.

"Sure. You pick."

I flipped through the CD holder, scanning the titles we'd brought along for the trip: Ella, Frank, Wagner, the Beatles, Roger and Hammerstein's *Cinderella* (the Julie Andrews version), Elvis Costello . . . "Would you mind listening to the B Minor *Mass*? It'd be good for me to get used to how it sounds for real, rather than just hearing the alto section."

"That's fine," Robin said. I inserted the disc and settled down to listen, snuggling once more into the sleeping bag I

---

36. I'd quote the famous lyrics from the Steppenwolf song—which many of you are no doubt humming to yourselves right about now—if not for the copyright law which prevents me from doing so.

still had wrapped around me. The stars disappeared as the sky brightened, changing from cobalt to a pale blue. It was going to be a gorgeous day.

At Paso Robles, we stopped for gas and a bathroom break and then took Highway 46 east—past the site of James Dean's fatal crash—to Lost Hills, where we got on Highway 5 heading south through the Central Valley. A little before eleven, at the base of the San Gabriel Mountains which separate the Central Valley and the Los Angeles basin, we stopped at a Jack-in-the-Box for lunch. This is Robin's favorite fast-food joint, and she always orders the exact same thing: two tacos with no sauce, onion rings, and a small Coke. I had a Jumbo Jack burger. I don't eat much fast food—maybe two or three times a year—as it's not healthy, either for me or for the agro-economy. But it *does* taste good. And, I figured, I likely wouldn't be eating again until the reception at the dean's residence that evening, so a big juicy burger seemed just the ticket.

We arrived at my parents' house in Santa Monica at eleven forty-five, which gave us over an hour before we had to leave for the law school. Dad was already at UCLA—lunching with Justice and Professor Ginsburg, other law professors, and various VIP types—but Mom was there to greet us. After helping Robin and me carry load after load from the car into the house, she stared in amazement at the amount of stuff piled on the kitchen floor.

"Yeah, I know," I said, reading her thoughts. "Good thing we're only six for dinner."

Mom and I stowed all the food that needed it in the fridge, and I also got the white wine, Champagne, and fizzy water chilling in the second refrigerator out in the Peacock Room—the converted garage that was my mom's art studio, which she'd named after a room in a once stately home our family had stayed at years earlier in Devon, England. Since we had the time, the three of us also started unpacking the glasses and plates I'd brought down. The breakfast room table already had stacks of dishes, ready for use at the dinner, and we quickly covered the rest of the table with my additions.

"Here are the plates I bought."

"Oh, goody." Mom watched eagerly as I removed the wrapping from the first of the packets of square black plates. "These are wonderful!" she exclaimed, picking a plate up and examining it with her potter's eye.

"These eight are yours. And after the dinner, when you use them at future parties, you can tell people that Ruth ate off them." I continued unwrapping the plates. "Of course," I added, "you won't actually know which one she used."

"Well," said Mom with a devilish grin, "perhaps we just need to make a secret mark on the bottom of the plate we give to her, then."[37]

---

37. Alas, in the heat of the moment, we failed to do this.

CHAPTER 12

Happily, A Woman's Voice May Do Some Good

D minus twenty-nine hours.

Robin drove us to UCLA, with my mother sitting shotgun, acting as navigator. Once on campus, Mom—who'd been a student there (she and Dad had met as undergraduates)—guided us through the confusing labyrinth of winding streets. "There's the lot," she said. "Turn left here."

We parked and headed for Dodd Hall, the auditorium next door to the law school. The lobby was teeming with people. As we walked past the students lining up to get into the hall, a woman at the door called out to my mom, "Hello, Smiley!" Mom greeted the woman—someone from the law school I didn't know—and asked what time they'd be letting us in.

"Not for about twenty minutes," was the answer, so we wandered outside and sat on a bench in the sun to wait.

When we returned they were letting people inside, and the woman Mom had spoken to earlier pointed out to us the reserved area at the front right of the room where we were to sit. After we sat down near the back of the section, the three of us made guesses as to who the other VIPs were. I scanned the crowd to see if any of them might be Marty, but since I had no idea what he looked like, this proved to be a futile exercise.

"I don't see any marshals," Robin said to me. I twisted around in my chair to see if I could spot anyone around the edges of the room who could be a US marshal, but no one seemed to fit the bill. Looking around the rest of the hall, I saw that, other than our small guest section, it was filled entirely with students, chattering amongst themselves excitedly.

Many of them had their enormous casebooks at their feet, and seeing these brought back memories of the fear and anxiety I'd felt as a first-year law student. It was good to be one of the "adults" now. I nodded at a young woman across the aisle from us who happened to catch my eye, then smiled to myself. Here I was on the "celebrity" side for a change, and no doubt the students were checking me out too, trying to guess who I might be. *How bizarre.* But then again, I mused, I *was* about to host a private dinner for the star of today's talk. Maybe that did make me a celebrity in my own right.

Finally there was a rustling of the curtain at the side of the stage. A youthful-looking man in a dark business suit walked out—"That's the dean," Mom whispered to me—followed by my father's slender figure and then by Justice Ginsburg. A thrill of excitement swept over me at the sight of the justice, along with a surge of pride at seeing Dad up there on stage with her.

My father wore a dark blue sports jacket and a colorful tie, which my mom had surely sewn for him. Back in the late '60s he'd started wearing his hair long and sporting "love beads" and bright neckties, and although the shoulder-length hair and beads were long gone, he was still known around the law school as the professor with the cool ties.

The justice was dressed in an elegant black suit with a subtle floral pattern woven into the fabric. On her collar was pinned a circular golden brooch inset with what looked to be diamonds in the shape of a star. She had dangling gold earrings and her hair was pulled tightly back in a bun, her signature look.

Dad walked to the far side of the stage and took a seat in one of the two chairs that had been set out for him and the dean. Justice Ginsburg sat down at a table next to the podium center stage and looked over at our section of the room. With a quick smile, she waved to someone a few rows ahead of us. I craned my neck, but from the back I could tell only that it was an older man in a suit. *That must be Marty*, I thought. How cute that she waved at him, given they had been together only moments before, at the luncheon.

The audience had quieted down briefly when the three of them walked out, but then quickly started applauding. The dean—Michael Schill[38]—walked to the podium, and the crowd hushed as he leaned into the microphone.

"Now I know how to get a room to be quiet when I walk in," he said, then turned and looked at Justice Ginsburg. "Do you have some time to spend here more often?" The audience and the justice laughed appropriately, and he continued. "My guess is that when Justice Ginsburg was where you are today, she didn't expect to be sitting on the Supreme Court." Behind him, the justice smiled. He then turned again and said to her, "You can disagree, if you knew this is where you were going all along." She maintained the same enigmatic smile, and I wondered if indeed she ever did think it was a possibility, even back in her law school days.

The dean then introduced my father, and he walked to the podium. After thanking the Ginsburgs for taking the time to come from Washington, DC to Los Angeles—even though they would be leaving for South Africa, in the opposite

---

38. Mike Schill is now president of Northwestern University.

direction, in a week—he stated: "Of the one hundred and eight men and two women who have served as Supreme Court justices, three would deserve a place in the Pantheon of American law—even if they had not been appointed to the bench—because of their contributions as advocates to the growth of the law. The three are: Louis Brandeis, Thurgood Marshall, and Ruth Bader Ginsburg."

Once the applause had died down, Dad spoke about Justice Ginsburg's impact as an advocate on the area of women's rights. "In nearly every sex discrimination case from the 1970s that appears in a casebook," he told us, "she either argued the case herself or filed an *amicus* brief." I thought about how exciting this information must be for the law students in the audience, many of whom were no doubt studying those very cases. He continued: "Her constant position—which the Court adopted—was that government could not justify treating men and women differently on the basis of assumptions about what she called 'the way women are.' "

Dad then concluded his introductory remarks: "Justice Ginsburg is an opera fan, and today is Mozart's two hundred and fiftieth birthday. Tomorrow, the Metropolitan Opera will perform one of his most popular operas: *Così Fan Tutte*—or, in English, 'that's the way all women are.' The idea still plays in the opera house, but it's a loser in the courthouse. For confirmation, you can ask the lawyers who represented Virginia Military Institute." A pause. Then: "I am *so* glad to be saying these words. Here, to talk with our students, is Justice Ruth Bader Ginsburg."

And that's when it hit me.

Up until this very moment—notwithstanding that I'd been stressing and obsessing for some nine months over this weekend's dinner—the fact that I was going to spend an evening in the presence of Supreme Court Justice Ruth Bader Ginsburg had existed in my brain as merely an "idea," a "construct." But now, seeing her before me on that stage as she smiled up at my father, listening to him recount how she had virtually singlehandedly changed the law of the land for the betterment of women, that "construct" became very real indeed. Tomorrow night, Justice and Professor Ginsburg, my mom and dad, Robin, and I were going to sit around my parents' dining room table drinking wine, eating food I'd prepared, and talking the whole night long. What an opportunity.

What an *honor*.

Hoping no one would notice, I wiped away the tears that had pooled up in my eyes, then joined the crowd in clapping as Justice Ginsburg rose from her seat.

Standing at the microphone, she looked even more petite than I remembered, as only her head and shoulders could be seen from behind the podium. The enthusiastic applause showed no signs of subsiding, so after a few moments, the justice smiled and motioned with her hands for us to stop. She pulled the gooseneck mic down to her height.

"It is a special pleasure to be here," she said after we had settled down. Her voice was soft, and I could detect traces of her years growing up in Brooklyn. "Ken, I think, has invited me every year for the last twenty years." She looked over at my dad, and he smiled and nodded in agreement. "When he wrote to me this time and said, 'This is my last year of teaching, so please come now,' I said yes . . . at once."

Justice Ginsburg began by speaking about the late Chief Justice Rehnquist, who had passed away the previous September, and then about Justice O'Connor, who had stepped down from the bench at the start of the Court's winter break, just four days earlier. Her deep affection for "the Chief," as she called him, was obvious from her remarks. He ranked among the fairest and most efficient of all the "bosses" she had had in her years in the legal profession, she told us: "While presiding over six of what I call 'prime dons' and two 'prima donnas,' he kept us in line and on time."

Among the Chief's many responsibilities, Justice Ginsburg explained, "He gave us our homework assignments," deciding who would write which opinion. "Yes, there was an occasional grumble," she admitted. "For example, from the justice assigned to write in a sloggy ERISA case. And ERISA—for those who are not in the lawyer's trade—I will tell you, is the acronym for the Employment Retirement Income Security Act, my candidate for the most dense piece of legislation Congress ever passed." Knowing laughter from the audience. "But, at the end of the term, there was general agreement among the eight associate justices that the distribution had been fair."

Part of the secret of Chief Justice Rehnquist's success, she noted, was that "the Chief had an irreverent sense of humor: he could deliver poker-faced lines that provoked smiles, sometimes even bursts of laughter." As an example, she recounted the story of how, when his nomination as Chief Justice was announced, a reporter had asked Rehnquist, "Do you consider it a culmination of a dream?" She then smiled as she told us his answer: "The soon-to-be Chief responded, 'I wouldn't call it that, but it's not every day when you're sixty-one years old and get a chance to have a new job.'"

Justice Ginsburg also explained the history behind the gold stripes on Chief Justice Rehnquist's robe, which I'd often wondered about: "Visitors to the Supreme Court during recent years could hardly miss noticing the Chief's self-designed robe," she told us, "copied from the Lord Chancellor's costume in a local theater company's summer production of Gilbert and Sullivan's *Iolanthe*. The robe has gleaming gold stripes, as does the robe of the United Kingdom's Lord Chancellor, but Chief Justice Rehnquist's version is less regal, resembling the stripes of a master sergeant more than those of a British lord."

"Well," she continued, "why did a man not given to sartorial splendor decide on such a costume? In his own words, he 'did not wish to be upstaged by the women.'" The justice allowed herself a quick smile before going on. "Justice O'Connor has several attractive neckpieces—collars from British gowns—and a pretty, frilly French *foulard*. And I wear British and French collars too, and sometimes a collar of French-Canadian design."

I chastised myself for having assumed that Justice Rehnquist had added the gold stripes out of a sense of self-importance. No, it was all in fun, even if it was a bit of an inside joke. I had also been curious about the frilly neckwear that Justices O'Connor and Ginsburg wore, so it was interesting to learn where they came from as well.

Justice Ginsburg spoke a little longer about "the Chief," and then moved on to her "dear colleague," Justice Sandra Day O'Connor, the first woman to sit on the nation's highest bench. She started by remarking that, in her view, Justice O'Connor "has done more to promote collegiality among the Court's members than any justice in the Court's history." She recounted her own story as an example:

"Her welcome when I became the junior justice is revealing. The Court has customs and habits one cannot find in the official rules. Justice O'Connor knew what it was like to learn the ropes on one's own. She told me what I needed to know—not in an intimidating dose—just enough to enable me to navigate safely my first days and weeks on the Court.

"At the end of the October 1993 sitting, I eagerly awaited my first opinion assignment, expecting—as the legend goes—that the brand-new justice would be slated for an uncontroversial unanimous opinion. When the list came around, I was dismayed. The Chief had given me an intricate—not at all easy—ERISA case on which the Court had divided six to three." The audience, surely recalling the justice's earlier comments about this "dense piece of legislation," laughed appreciatively.

"And Justice O'Connor was among the three. I sought her advice. It was simple: 'Just do it,' she said, 'and if you can, circulate your draft opinion before he makes the next set of assignments; otherwise, you will risk receiving another tedious case.' That advice typifies Justice O'Connor's approach to all things: Waste no time on anger, regret, or resentment. Just get the job done."

Justice Ginsburg also spoke of Justice O'Connor's ceaseless energy and her "extraordinary ability to manage her time." "As first woman on the Supreme Court, Justice O'Connor set a pace I could scarcely follow," she said, noting O'Connor's numerous visits to different colleges, countries, and bar and civic associations. "My secretaries once imagined that Justice O'Connor had a secret twin sister to share all her extracurricular appearances."

"Why would she spend her own precious personal time in such a manner?" Justice Ginsburg mused, and then provided the answer: "In her own words, 'For both men and women, the first step in getting power is to become visible to others and then to put on an impressive show. As women achieve power, the barriers will fall. As society sees what women can do, as *women* see what women can do, there will be more women out there doing things, and we will all be better off for it.'"

Justice Ginsburg recounted several other anecdotes about Justice O'Connor. We were told about the time she led the Olympic women's basketball team on a Supreme Court tour "that ended at the highest court in the land—the full basketball court on the building's top floor"—and how the team practiced for a few minutes and then passed the ball to Justice O'Connor. "She missed the first shot, but the second went straight through the hoop."

She also told us how "some advocates each term reveal that they have not fully adjusted to the presence of two women on the high court bench," as illustrated by the fact that during oral arguments certain "distinguished counsel" (including a Harvard Law School professor and more than one Solicitor General) would begin their responses to Justice Ginsburg's questions, "Well, Justice O'Connor . . ." "Sometimes when that happened," the Justice recalled, "Sandra would smile and crisply remind counsel, 'She's Justice Ginsburg; I'm Justice O'Connor.'"

Anticipating just such confusion, we learned, the National Association of Women Judges had T-shirts made up for the two of them when Justice Ginsburg first joined the Supreme Court. Justice O'Connor's read: "I'm Sandra," and Justice Ginsburg's read: "I'm Ruth."

To conclude her remarks about Sandra Day O'Connor, Justice Ginsburg spoke of the surprise appearance that her colleague made one night some seasons earlier in the Shakespeare Theatre's production of *Henry V*: "Playing the role that evening of Isabel, Queen of France, she spoke the famous line from the treaty scene: 'Happily, a woman's voice may do some good.' Indeed it may," Ginsburg said, "as Justice O'Connor has demonstrated so well in her nearly twenty-five years of service on the Supreme Court of the United States."

INTERLUDE

Most people likely have little problem understanding Justice Ginsburg's feelings of affection for her "Chief" and for Justice O'Connor, particularly after hearing how generous and warm the two were to the new justice when she first took her place on the high bench. And although over the years Rehnquist and O'Connor would often take the opposite side from RBG on cases, both the Chief and the Court's first female justice were relatively moderate conservatives compared to certain others on the Court.

But when told of her close friendship with Justice Antonin Scalia—by no means a moderate, nor generally considered to be "warm"—folks are often surprised. Here was a man, after all, who with his "strict constructionist" views, was about as far from RBG in judicial philosophy as imaginable.

Whereas Ginsburg always considered the US Constitution to be a living, evolving document that must be interpreted in accordance with modern conditions and societal changes, Scalia firmly believed that it requires a literal and narrow interpretation based solely on the intent of the Framers at the time of its drafting. As a result of this fundamental ideological difference, the pair frequently sparred on the Court, and Scalia's dissents to RBG's majority opinions were not always polite.

Nevertheless, dating back to the days when they were both on the DC Circuit Court, the two were good friends. They would attend operas together, and when abroad on judicial junkets would sometimes act as "shopping buddies" for each other. Not only that, but their two families famously celebrated each New Year's Eve together with a fabulous formal dinner at the Ginsburg's Watergate apartment (Maureen Scalia and Marty doing the cooking).

There are several possible reasons for this friendship. A shared love of opera didn't hurt, nor did the fact that "Nino" was one of the few people who could always make Ruth laugh. But the most basic explanation is likely that, although on the surface they appeared to have diametrically opposed legal philosophies, the two justices were in many respects very alike.

Ever since her stint in Sweden, RBG had taken a keen interest in legal procedure—the rules that dictate the manner in which cases are decided. The rules of procedure can severely limit the outcome in any given case, and they comprise the one area of the law that is completely neutral, since the rules always apply equally to both sides.

As a jurist, Ginsburg often turned to procedural issues as the basis for an opinion. It's a decidedly unsexy approach to determining cases, but one that works. For sometimes, as the justice has noted, you may have a terrific civil rights case, but the choice is to either to go down in defeat with an argument based on the merits or win on a procedural impediment on which the Court will agree.

Her choice to focus on process as opposed to substantive issues could make RBG seem a sort of apolitical liberal, but it also explains her ability to be on such good terms with a rampant conservative such as Justice Scalia. After all, it would have been difficult for him to carry much antagonism against someone who was so much more centered on procedure than on politics.

Perhaps the recent comic opera, *Scalia/Ginsburg*, by Derrick Wang best sums up their relationship. It opens with a "rage aria" by Scalia, in which he sings: "The Justices are blind! How can they possibly spout this—? The Constitution says absolutely nothing about this." But when he is imprisoned in a dark room as punishment for "excessive dissenting," Ginsburg comes to his rescue, entering through a glass ceiling.

Later, when Scalia is about to be banished as a result of his failure to remain silent upon being confronted with the decision in *Bush v. Gore*, Ruth once again comes to Nino's defense. "We serve justice together," she declares, "and that means we can speak with one voice." In a glorious denouement, the two friends then engage in a moving duet:

We are kindred.
We are nine . . .
Always one decision from charting the course we will steer . . .
For our future
Is unclear,
But one thing is constant—
The Constitution we revere.
We are stewards of this trust;
We uphold it as we must,
For the work of our Court is just
Begun . . .
And this is why we will see justice done:
We are different;
We are one.

• • •

It was now time for the Q&A session. Two microphones had been set up in the aisles, and students began lining up to wait their turn to ask a question of the justice.

The first one concerned the nomination process for Supreme Court justices, no doubt inspired by the recent confirmation hearings for Chief Justice Roberts and Justice Alito. Justice Ginsburg made it clear that she had little patience with the current process, which she believed had become primarily an opportunity for grandstanding by senators. When she'd been nominated to the Court, she told us, former Chief Justice Burger came to congratulate her and said, "Ruth, you know, when I was nominated in 1969 to be the Chief Justice of the United States, my hearing lasted exactly one hour."

Her response was: "Yes, Chief, and there is one word that explains the difference: television." The confirmation hearing, she told us, "is a marvelous opportunity for the senators to speak to their constituents to show how brilliant they are and how caring they are about what the voters want. So you are sitting there for four days in a row, mostly being talked through."

Later, another young man followed up on this topic, asking rather smugly about the Senate's "duty to advise and consent" on nominees to the Supreme Court, noting an "increasing pattern of the nominees' non-responsiveness."

"Do you know when hearings began for Supreme Court nominees?" the justice asked in response, like a teacher setting a trap for an unwary student. "You're contrasting a past that I don't recognize. But when did it begin?"

Oblivious, he fell into the trap head first: "Uh, I believe the 1880s . . ."

I heard a game show buzzer go off in my head. *Wrong!* Robin and I exchanged glances, stifling giggles. Justice Ginsburg corrected him in a lecturing tone: "The first judicial nominee who ever appeared before the Senate—Professor Karst will correct me if I'm wrong—was Felix Frankfurter,[39] and he appeared for something like a half hour. That was it. Nobody would have thought about asking the kind of questions that are being asked now."

The next student wondered if Justice Ginsburg thought the current policy regarding recusal of Supreme Court justices was sufficient. Although neither the student nor the justice referred to it, the flap two years earlier about Justice Scalia going hunting with Vice President Cheney, and Scalia's subsequent refusal to recuse himself from the Sierra Club's

39. The year was 1939.

case against Cheney, was clearly the unspoken subtext of the question.

Justice Ginsburg explained that the rule prohibits a federal judge from sitting on a case in which the judge, their spouse, or minor dependent child has a financial interest, however small. For instance, she told us, her son had been given a share of some oil stock at birth, and, after she was appointed to the DC Circuit Court of Appeals, she was able to escape sitting on federal Energy Regulation Commission cases until the stock was sold, about which she was quite happy.

She also noted that in her early years on the appellate court bench, attempts had been made by parties to get a Supreme Court justice recused by engaging, say, the justice's son's law firm to file an *amicus* brief in the case. The Court had since agreed, however, that unless the son could personally benefit from the decision, there should be no recusal. "Remember," she told us, "on the Supreme Court, a recusal means only eight judges—not a good number." Moreover, Justice Ginsburg reassured the audience, "I can think of no case where a colleague of mine should have recused him or herself and didn't."

Another student stepped up to the microphone and asked an elaborate question about the *Alameda Books* case,[40] which concerned the issue of whether a city zoning ordinance ran afoul of the First Amendment. "It sounds like a law school test question," the justice replied with a smile. "Except you didn't tell them what the case was about. So why don't you, for the benefit of the audience"—she waved her hand in our direction—"fill them in on that." She continued to smile as he awkwardly started to answer her question.

"The *Alameda Books* case involved . . . uh . . ."

"Adult bookstores," she jumped in.

---

40. The full name is *City of Los Angeles v. Alameda Books, Inc.*, 535 US 425 (2002).

"Adult bookstores, yeah," he mumbled. The audience, most of whom had studied the case, chuckled.

"That was a split decision," she reminded him. "The Court regarded this as a 'who decides' question. As my spouse says—and I agree—there are only two questions in the end in the law, and they keep repeating. One is, Who decides? and the other is, Where do you draw the line?"

In that case, Justice Ginsburg explained, the Court decided that the local town council, not the Supreme Court, decides. "But some of us [i.e., she and her fellow dissenters in the case] felt, well, there is this"—she walked away from the mic to retrieve a small book that she'd left on the table where she'd been sitting—"Constitution, that I carry around with me wherever I go." She held the pamphlet aloft for us to see. "And it's got a First Amendment in it. And we are supposed to be the guardians of that."

Based on the enthusiastic applause and stamping of feet that followed this comment, the vast majority of the audience agreed with her sentiment.

Several students next asked questions concerning the justice's personal experiences, about women breaking into predominantly male occupations and about balancing her personal and professional life. The justice noted that the legal profession was now far more open than it once was. "Think of the days when I started out. I graduated from law school in 1959, and I had good grades. There was not a firm in the entire city of New York that would employ me."

But she had advice for those feeling the effects of discrimination: "The way you deal with that is not to be angry, not to be resentful, but to say, 'I'm going to think of myself as a teacher to these people to show them that women and mothers can do the job as well as any others.' I tried to regard putdowns as opportunities to educate someone. And I think you take advantage of what you have. You have a law degree, and you use it to try to make the world a little better, first for your local community, whatever it is, and then perhaps for the larger society."

On the subject of balancing her personal and professional life, Justice Ginsburg offered this advice: "First, choose as your life partner someone who thinks your work is as important as his. That is a good starting point. Another: If you are going to have a family, realize that there is going to be a balance, and neither side is going to be perfect. But one thing we agreed on"—a glance towards our section—"was, unless there was something really special, you would come home for dinner every night and that would be our family time."

"Now," she said with a smile, "I will admit that coming home to Mommy's cooking was not always a delight for my children, so in my daughter's high school years she made the suggestion that Mommy really ought to turn the kitchen over to Daddy. And it has been his domain for the last twenty-five years; I have not cooked a meal since that time."

The crowd erupted into laughter and applause, and I jabbed Robin in the side with my elbow. "I can't wait to meet him," I whispered.

The most interesting question to me that afternoon was the one concerning the *Bush v. Gore* decision in December of 2000,[41] which halted the ballot recount in Florida and allowed George W. Bush to be certified as winner of Florida's electoral votes, thereby effectively handing him the presidential election. The student noted that the Supreme Court seemed to suffer a public opinion blow after the opinion was published and wondered if Justice Ginsburg would comment on the decision.

I too had been troubled by both the majority and dissenting opinions in that case, as they appeared to be, as we used

41. The citation is 531 US 98 (2000).

to say in law school, "result oriented," rather than based on precedent and rule of law. For example, Rehnquist—normally a strong proponent of states' rights—ruled to stop the vote count on equal protection grounds; and Ginsburg—normally a strong proponent of equal protection—opined in her dissent that the count should have been allowed to continue based on states' rights grounds.

Justice Ginsburg had this to say in response to the student's question: "You can speak from the point of view of the public. My concern was how the Court was going to work together. Well, first, it was an exhausting experience because the Court granted *cert.* on a Saturday afternoon. Briefs were filed on Sunday. Oral arguments on Monday. Decisions out on Tuesday. There were many sleepless nights for my law clerks and for me in that hard time.

"Very soon after that decision, we came back for our regular January sitting with our normal array of cases, and I can say that things were *almost* the same." The justice was choosing her words carefully, and she looked sad as she continued. "We approached that sitting . . . We came into the robing room as we do always, each justice shakes hands with every other. Things were *almost* the same."

There was a pause, and then: "That case—perhaps you've noticed—*Bush v. Gore* has never been cited by the Supreme Court again."

CHAPTER 13

Starry Night

D minus twenty-five hours.

We almost didn't make it to the reception at the dean's house. After the Q&A at the law school, the four of us climbed into my parents' Camry, leaving Robin's and my Corolla at UCLA to be picked up after the party. Then, heading south from campus, Dad turned left onto Wilshire Boulevard—directly into the path of a car coming north.

Robin, who was in the right side of the back seat and thus the one most in the line of fire, gasped and lunged towards me. The driver of the oncoming car did not slow down a whit—I don't know if he didn't notice us or was just being cocky—but luckily we completed our turn before he zipped through the intersection, missing us by mere feet.

Perhaps they were preoccupied with their own concerns regarding the momentous weekend before us. Or perhaps it was simply a matter of their advanced years—a possibility that made me a bit sad. But in any event, neither of my parents made any sign they'd noticed our near-death experience. Ignorance is bliss.

We parked around the corner from the entrance to the dean's building, eschewing the valet parking that was being offered, and Dad turned off the engine. Although we were right on time, we didn't want to be the first ones to arrive, so we sat in the car talking amongst ourselves for a few minutes.

Dad, who was not usually much of a gossip, was keyed up from having introduced Justice Ginsburg at the Q&A session and no doubt also excited about the upcoming reception like the rest of us, and so he was quite chatty. Robin and I took advantage of his state of mind and pumped him for information about the law school—who liked or disliked whom, the politics of deanship appointments, who was gay, and who'd had affairs with whom over the forty-plus years he had been teaching at UCLA. (Don't worry anyone; my lips are sealed.)

We also asked him who would be at the reception. Select faculty, big donors to the law school, and family and friends of the justice who lived in the area, he imagined, though he wasn't privy to the guest list. But there'd definitely be big donors, he said. That was of course, I realized, one of the primary reasons for the reception: as a reward for giving big bucks to the law school you're put on the "A list" and are invited to parties where you get to meet a Supreme Court justice.

But what were *we* doing here? As we climbed out of the car, Robin and I looked at each other. "We're certainly gonna be the odd ones out," Robin said to me as we followed my parents around the corner onto Wilshire Boulevard. "I wonder if there'll be anyone else here like us—mere hangers-on."

"Hey, man," I said. "I'm cooking dinner for the justice tomorrow night. That should count for something."

Mom and Dad stopped in front of a large pair of doors. "This is it," said Mom. "The dean lives on the ninth floor."

We entered an enormous lobby that looked like a hotel. A man at a reception desk looked up as we walked in. "The Schill residence?" he asked, guessing correctly.

"Yes, that's right," Dad said. "We know where it is."

I gawked at the statues and brocade-covered sofas, lagging behind my parents who headed across the plush carpet toward the elevator. As I was staring at an enormous gilt-framed mirror, Robin sidled up to me and jabbed her elbow in my side.

"Ow!" I frowned at her as we caught up with my folks and stopped at the elevator. "What?"

Mom and Dad were chatting with a couple of people who had come in right after us. One of them stuck her hand out towards me to shake.

"Hi, I'm Diane."

I tore my gaze from the opulent furnishings and turned towards the woman and extended my hand in return. My polite "I'm-about-to-meet-one-of-my-dad's-colleagues" smile froze on my lips as she took my hand in a firm grasp and I looked up at her for the first time. It took maybe only a fraction of a second to sort out the confusing information being absorbed by my brain, but it seemed like much longer. The face was familiar, but completely out of context.

It was Diane Keaton.

"H-hi . . . I'm Leslie, their daughter." I pointed feebly at my mom and dad.

Diane smiled—that *exact same* smile from the movies—and turned to Robin. "Hi. I'm glad to meet you." She extended her hand again.

"I'm *very* glad to meet *you.*" Robin took her hand and shook it with a grin. "I'm Robin, Leslie's partner."

Dad was chatting animatedly with another woman, who looked to be in her early forties and had shoulder-length blonde hair. He introduced her to us. "This is Ann Carlson, our associate dean."[42] Robin and I shook hands with Ann and then the elevator arrived.

42. In 2021, President Joe Biden appointed Ann—a celebrated professor of environmental law at UCLA—as chief counsel for the National Highway Traffic Safety Administration, part of the DOT. She has now been promoted to acting administrator of the NHTSA.

Dad later told me that as we had all started for the elevator, he'd called Ann back and asked her, "What was the name of that woman you just introduced to us?"

"Diane Keaton," she replied.

"*Woody Allen's* Diane Keaton?" Dad asked. "Previously, I mean . . ."

Ann smiled. "Yes," she said.

In the elevator, I stood at the back, next to Diane. She was about six inches taller than I and dressed all in black: black jacket and skirt, black fishnet stockings and heels, a black scarf with small white polka dots, and a black bowler hat. And blue-tinted granny glasses.

My heart was pounding, but remembering the "Cynthia Nixon rule," I got up the nerve to turn and talk to her. "Were you at the Q&A session with the justice this afternoon?" I asked.

"No, I couldn't come. I had to *work*," she answered with a bit of disgust.

"Oh. Too bad. It was really interesting." As I wondered what movie she was shooting, the elevator stopped and the doors slid open.

We poured out into the hall, Mom leading the way. It looked like a hotel hallway, with doors to the various residences along the walls, not at all like the usual California condo or apartment complex, where each unit has its own outdoor entrance.

I followed Diane Keaton as we turned left down the hall. "Oh! This is *so New York*!" she exclaimed, twirling around with her arms extended.

As I watched her spin and waltz down the hallway, all of a sudden—as if a switch had been thrown—my brain jumped into some other reality. I was *in* a movie, and there was Annie Hall, walking with me to the dean's reception. Except, there wouldn't be a reception at Dean Schill's condo in a movie, would there? And the Diane Keaton who was laughing gleefully as she tripped down the hallway wasn't a character in a movie; she was a flesh and blood real person, right there in front of me. It was more as if the movies had entered real life. The line between the movies and reality had become blurred.

I was light-headed, and my heart continued to pound. My perception was all out of whack, and the angles of the walls and floor seemed askew. I can only describe it as surreal, like Alice must have felt going down the rabbit hole. Or like a dream, where objects take on a distorted shape. Or like someone had spiked my lunch with LSD.

I followed Diane dizzily down the hall and through the door into the dean's living room, which was already starting to get crowded. Robin came up next to me. "What is she *doing* here?" she whispered loudly.

"I dunno; it's weird. I need a drink." I had spotted a bar set up across the room, and Robin followed me over to it. Although it was a full bar—including a very nice single barrel bourbon that caught my eye—we both asked for red wine. We hadn't eaten since our early lunch, and I knew the alcohol would go straight to my head.

Glasses in hand, we turned from the bar only to find Diane standing right behind us. She ordered a red wine too, and we all stood together at the bar sipping our drinks. I tried not to be too obvious, but I couldn't help staring at her. The actress had much longer legs and was more slender than I would have imagined from seeing her in her films.

After an awkward moment's silence, Robin turned and spoke to Diane. "Can I ask you a question?"

I was a little surprised by this forwardness on Robin's part. She's generally uncomfortable approaching public figures, as she's embarrassed by the idea of invading a person's privacy simply because they're famous. She's been known to walk away from me in mortification when I've gone up to talk to someone in a situation which she considered to be *Seinfeld*-ian "level jumping."

But we *were* at a cocktail party together, and Diane *was* standing right there with us, so I guess it made sense that she would feel okay about talking to the actress—especially given that Robin was no doubt also thinking about the "Cynthia Nixon rule." In addition, I knew Robin loved Diane Keaton. We actually had *Baby Boom* on our Netflix queue at that very moment, and had rented *Annie Hall* only a month earlier.

"You can ask me *anything*," Diane responded with a friendly smile and a twinkle in her eyes (at least so it seemed, behind those blue shades).

Wow. I watched Robin. What would she ask?

"Why did Nancy Meyers cut out that scene with Jack Nicholson singing '*La vie en rose*' at the karaoke bar in your movie?"

"How do you know about that?" Diane asked with a puzzled look.

"It's an 'extra' on the DVD."

"Really? I didn't know it was on there."

Robin told her about how we'd taken the movie with us to Paris the previous summer and watched it at night in bed on our laptop. "I can't understand why anyone would want to cut that scene," she said. "It made me cry when I first watched it. It still does, actually."

"I've *gotta* tell Jack you think so. That scene was really hard for him."

Robin glanced at me. I knew what she was thinking: *She's gonna tell Jack Nicholson about* me*?* "It wasn't just Jack's singing, though," Robin continued. "What really made that scene work was the cuts to your face. The emotion you showed without speaking any lines was incredibly moving."

"Really?" Diane said again, looking genuinely touched, perhaps even surprised. She turned her glass around in her hands and shrugged. "I don't know why she cut the scene; I guess she didn't think it would work in the movie."

We sipped our wine for a moment. "Since we're talking about that movie, I have a question," I said. "Does le Grand Colbert really have good roast chicken?" This is the restaurant the Diane Keaton character raves about and (spoiler alert) where Jack Nicholson goes to find her on her birthday only to discover she's having dinner with Keanu Reeves.

Diane laughed. "I have no idea what their food is like," she told us. "It's so crazy when you're filming a scene in a restaurant; you never get to try the food or see what it's really like on a normal day."[43]

We talked about Paris for a while longer, and then Diane left to go speak with some other people. I looked at my watch. "When do you think Ruth will show up?"

"Who knows?" Robin said, turning to check out two young men who'd just come through the front door. "She probably went back to her hotel to 'freshen up,' as they say. Plus, it's always best for the guest of honor to come fashionably late." She nodded toward the spread of food set out on the dean's dining room table. "Wanna grab something to eat?"

"Nah, I'm way too hyper to eat anything right now. But I could use another glass of wine."

We decided to mingle as we waited for the justice to arrive. Introducing ourselves to a couple standing near the bar, we learned that the man was an ex-law student who'd been in my father's Constitutional Law class in the late '60s. When Robin was told this, she said, "Ah ha! You must be donors."

The man smiled. "You are correct."

Robin accepted a piece of grilled chicken on a skewer proffered by one of the circulating servers and dipped it in a bowl of creamy avocado sauce. "That would be a good game, don't you think?" She got a gleam in her eye; Robin loves games. "To

---

43. On a recent trip back to Paris, Robin and I did finally dine at le Grand Colbert, and I can tell you that the roast chicken was indeed the best I've ever had at a restaurant: fall-off-the-bone tender and soaking in a pool of its own luscious juices.

guess whether the people here are faculty, donors, or friends of Ruth Ginsburg." She cast her eyes about the room. "That guy," she said, jabbing her skewer in the direction of a man with gray hair and an expensive looking suit. "Definitely a donor. And those two." She nodded towards a younger couple with a baby, "I bet one of them's a law professor."

As Robin said this, there was a commotion at the other side of the room, and we all turned to see what it was. "I think the Ginsburgs are here," the ex-student donor said.

It was indeed Justice and Professor Ginsburg. She was so tiny that the people who immediately crowded about as she entered blocked her almost completely from my view. But I was able to see Marty, who had glasses and thinning gray hair and was wearing a dark suit with a red tie. He was standing back a bit with a smile on his face, watching the guests swarm his wife.

The crowd parted and I finally got a good view of the justice. She had on the same outfit she'd worn to the Q&A session but had added a gold-colored shawl on top, which looked to be made of silk with metallic threads woven into the fabric. And she wore black net gloves. Very elegant.

I turned my attention to Marty, who'd now left the crowd and wandered over to the picture window overlooking West LA. My heart—which had only recently calmed down after seeing Diane Keaton—had started to thump once again at the sight of the justice and her husband, and I stood there a moment trying to get up the nerve to approach him. *Go on, do it. He's alone; now's your chance.*

"Professor Ginsburg?"

"Yes." He turned from the window. "How do you do?"

"Hi." We shook hands. "I'm Leslie Karst, the one who's been badgering you with emails about the dinner tomorrow night."

His face broke into a warm smile. "Oh, hello. I'm so glad to meet you. We're both very much looking forward to your dinner."

"As I am. And I think you'll be happy with the menu I've chosen." I gestured out the window. "Not a bad view, no?" My eyes had been immediately drawn to the Mormon temple, with the angel Moroni atop the spire illuminated from below. This church is something of a landmark in Los Angeles. The Mormons purchased the land for the temple from the Harold Lloyd Motion Picture Company in 1937, but construction was delayed—first by the depression and then the war—and the building was not completed until 1956, the year I was born.

For the first few years of my life, we lived on Selby Avenue in West LA, while my father was working as a young lawyer for Latham & Watkins. From a window in our house, you could see the golden statue of Moroni, and my mother had told my older brother, Dicky, its name. Though I was too young to remember it happening, it's become part of our family lore that Dicky would insist on being taken out into the backyard to say "Goodnight Moroni" every night before going to bed.

While Marty and I were gazing out over the twinkling lights of West Los Angeles, some acquaintances of his came over to talk with him. Knowing I'd get a chance to converse with the professor all I wanted the following night, I excused myself and wandered over to join my parents.

Dad introduced me to the couple he and my mother were chatting with: Mark Greenberg, a member of the UCLA law faculty who had clerked for Justice Ginsburg, and his English wife Andrea Ashworth, an author. After exchanging a few pleasantries, I asked my father if he knew why Diane Keaton was at the party, a question seconded by Mark and Andrea, as well as Mom. Dad said she'd come with Ann, the associate dean, and that he thought their kids went to school together.

My father and Mark drifted off after a few minutes, and as my mom and Andrea and I continued to chat, a server approached bearing some enticing hors d'oeuvres set out on a mirrored tray. "Mmmm. Those look yummy," Mom said, taking one. "What are they?"

"These are smoked salmon Napoleons on pumpernickel bread with lemon dill sauce and capers."

"Oh, wow. I'd best have one, too," I said, and Andrea followed suit.

I had just popped the canapé into my mouth when Justice Ginsburg came up to my mother to say hello. Mom introduced us, and I mumbled a polite "how-nice-to-see-you-again," trying to hide the fact that my mouth was still full of food.

As I finished chewing and finally managed to swallow, my eyes were drawn to the justice's hands. She was holding a glass of some bright reddish-pink drink, and, set off against her black crocheted gloves, the effect was striking. It seemed the sort of image that Man Ray—had he shot in color—would have photographed. Or perhaps in my addled state that evening, everything simply had a surrealistic slant to it.

I repeated my thought to the justice, who, I figured, was likely wondering why I was staring so intently at her hands.

"Take a picture if you'd like," she replied, extending her arms.

"Uh, that's okay," I said with a nervous laugh, certain she was being sarcastic—that I'd angered or at least annoyed her with my impertinence. "I don't even have a camera with me."

But when I looked up and saw the genuine smile she wore, I realized that the offer was indeed sincere. Even if the justice did think I'd been impudent, she was going to do her best to make me feel at ease.

INTERLUDE

Later in her life, Justice Ginsburg would say that her mother, Celia Amster Bader—whose pay as a bookkeeper was used to send Celia's brother to Cornell—was probably the smartest person the justice ever knew. And she never forgot her mother's sage advice: To always conduct herself civilly and not let emotions like anger or envy get in her way. To hold fast to her convictions and self-respect but be a good teacher and never snap back in anger, because emotions like anger and resentment only waste time and sap energy. These words of wisdom would become a sort of mantra for Celia's daughter, first in her career as advocate, and later as a jurist.

There's a popular conception these days of RBG as a firebrand ninja warrior, a woman who, as director of the ACLU's Women's Rights Project, stormed into courtrooms venting feminist dogma and who, as Supreme Court justice, routinely cut her colleagues to shreds with her scathing dissents.[44] But it's doubtful Ruth Ginsburg would ever have achieved all she did had she engaged in such divisive tactics instead of following her mother's advice.

From that very first case she and Marty took on together, Ruth's weapons of choice consisted of painstakingly researched legal precedent and hard facts. Precision and logic, she knew, were what judges understood and responded to, not fireworks and emotion. And once she was appointed to the DC Circuit bench, Judge Ginsburg's practice was to emphasize collegiality and compromise, as opposed to merely trying to get her way. Unlike the Supreme Court with its nine justices, Circuit Court

44. In her later years of course, RBG *did* become a bit more of the firebrand, reading dissents from the bench and publicly criticizing a certain presidential candidate. Perhaps she was tired of always having to be Ms. Nice Gal, or perhaps she simply felt that collegiality was no longer the most effective plan of action in these factious times.

decisions are rendered by a panel of only three judges, making consensus vitally important. And a unanimous opinion is always stronger than a simple majority of two-to-one.

RBG quickly grasped the benefit of taking into account the personalities of her colleagues when attempting to woo their votes, understanding that individual leanings and quirks can influence a judge's rulings as much the legal theories and facts before the court. In addition, she was always willing to make certain compromises if doing so would sway another to her way of thinking.

As a Supreme Court justice, Ginsburg followed the same course, particularly when she was on the winning side and assigned to write the majority opinion. There are some who find her opinions to be so lacking in emotion as to be bland. But this lack of gloating rhetoric was intentional. She didn't want the result to come across simply as an "I won, you lost" scenario. Rather, it was important to RBG that all the parties felt they were treated fairly and that they retained respect for the workings of the courts, even if they lost.

As said by Learned Hand (another famous Circuit Court judge), and oft-quoted by Ginsburg, if you win at chess, you shouldn't knock your opponent's pieces off the table.

• • •

I was trying to come up with something less inane to say to Justice Ginsburg than my comment about her gloved hands, when we were interrupted by a large man shoving his way between my mother and me. He seemed drunk—and determined to talk with Justice Ginsburg *right that instant*.

Oh, boy. Mom and Andrea and I looked at each other and shrugged, then relinquished our places to the man.

"He's a *big* donor," Mom whispered. I glanced back, hoping the justice could extricate herself soon from the conversation and saw that she'd managed to put on a thin smile for the inebriated donor.

She was in luck. Within moments, Dean Schill started clinking his glass with a spoon to get the room's attention. Everyone hushed and gathered in a circle. The dean thanked Justice Ginsburg once again for coming to the law school to speak and then introduced the UCLA Chancellor, Albert Carnesale.

The Chancellor, a tall man with striking silver hair, came across as a warm and affable guy. He commented on the similar backgrounds that he and Justice Ginsburg shared: he, the Italian son of a cab driver from the Bronx and she, the Jewish daughter of a furrier and haberdasher from Brooklyn. Nevertheless, he went on to become a Harvard professor of international relations and later Chancellor of UCLA; she became the first tenured woman law professor at Columbia and went on to sit on the United States Supreme Court. "It's great to be in a country where stories like these are common," he concluded.

Justice Ginsburg then spoke to us. What I remember best is what she said about being a woman in the law back in the late 1950s, recounting the well-known story of the intimidation she felt as one of only nine women in her Harvard Law School class. But the version she told that night at the dean's home contained amusing details I'd never before heard:

All of the first-year women students had been invited to a dinner at Dean Erwin Griswold's house, the justice recounted, and after the meal she sat smoking a cigarette with an ashtray in her lap. (She long ago gave up smoking, she assured us.) The dean then asked each of the women why she was at Harvard Law School, occupying a place a man could have filled, and when her turn came to mumble a response, the future Supreme Court justice stood up quickly—flustered and nervous—forgetting the ashtray. With dismay, she watched as butts and ashes spilled across the dean's dining room carpet.

Justice Ginsburg also elaborated on the subject of her having been unable to obtain either a job with a law firm or a judicial clerkship after she finished law school, even though she had graduated at the top of her class at Columbia. "Who knows what would have become of me had it not been for Gerry Gunther," she said.

Robin and I—who were across the room from each other—simultaneously let out a plaintive "ohhhh," upon hearing this remark. It had been several years since Gerry had passed away, but the two of us still felt his absence keenly. No one seemed to notice our interjection, however, and Justice Ginsburg continued on with her story about her early years as an attorney.

After the justice finished addressing the crowd, I fetched another glass of wine and resumed my conversation with Andrea. We chatted about England—I had lived there years earlier—and then moved on to cycling and the upcoming Tour of California. We were soon joined by Robin, who had her eyes glued to the hallway in the corner of the room.

"What are you looking at?" I asked.

"Diane Keaton just went into the bathroom. She's been surrounded by people all night, and I haven't wanted to break into their conversation. But I really want to talk to her some more, and I figure the best time to get her alone is when she comes out."

"I found out she came with Ann—the associate dean. Dad told me," I said to Robin.

"Ah," she responded. As Robin watched like a cat at a mouse-hole for Diane to emerge, she gave us her tally of the donor-to-law-professor ratio at the party (two to one, donors to faculty). She then nodded at two men standing near the front door. "Did you notice the marshals?"

"Oh yeah, the marshals! I forgot to look for them." Andrea and I both turned toward where Robin had indicated and saw two men in their late twenties or early thirties, eyes rapidly scanning the room. They had on business suits, and each wore a small round pin in his lapel. One of them saw me looking his way and smiled.

"There are a couple more, over there . . . and over there." Robin pointed to another man and a woman standing at the periphery of the room. "I went over to talk to the two by the front door. The one on the left is the head of the detail, Charles. The other guy, the one on the right, he's from Austin. He was down in the lobby earlier, and he told me he was watching us when we came in."

"I don't remember seeing any marshals down there," I said.

"Well, they were there, and they were watching us, 'cause when I said, 'Oh yeah, sure,' he told me he saw me jab you in the side when Diane Keaton came in." Robin chuckled, then asked me, "Hey, what's the name of that Diane Keaton movie we took with us to Paris?"

"Uh . . . isn't it *As Good As It Gets*?"

"No. That's that Jack Nicholson and Helen Hunt movie." Robin shook her head in frustration. "Damn! I can't remember its name."

"It's odd, but I can't remember either," Andrea said. "It's something like *As Good As It Gets*, I think."

"I want to talk to her about the movie, but it'll be really embarrassing if I can't even remember what it's called." Just then Diane came out of the hallway. Robin pounced.

"I gotta hear this," I said to Andrea, and followed Robin across the room, just in time to hear her tell Diane, ". . . so I wanted to tell you I thought you were really hot in that movie, but I can't remember its damn name. I keep wanting to call it *As Good As It Gets*, but I know that's not it." Robin, who always speaks quickly, was talking even faster than normal, and her words flew out in rapid-fire succession, all in one breath.

Diane laughed. “It’s *Something’s Gotta Give*. And I agree, it’s a *horrible* name. Even *I* call it *As Good As It Gets*.”

“Well, anyway, you *were* hot in that movie.” Robin was gesturing enthusiastically with her hands now, and I watched her glass, willing it not to spill red wine onto the dean’s white carpet. “It’s so great to see a movie where the romantic lead is written for an older woman, instead of someone in her twenties.”

Diane agreed and said she’d been lucky to keep getting good roles, even as she got older.

“I don’t think it’s luck,” I ventured.

“Yeah,” Robin jumped in. She was talking even more rapidly now, and I wondered if Diane would be able to decipher her stream of words. “And your new film—*Family Stone*—I thought the criticism it got was unfair, though Ebert got it right.”

“Uh huh.” Diane nodded.

“I mean, it was poking fun at people like . . . well, the ones at this party.” Robin waved her hand at the room at large. “You know, so-called ‘liberals,’ who may not actually be so accepting of folks who aren’t just like them, and I don’t think the critics got it.”

We chatted a bit more about movies, particularly women’s roles these days and then moved on to the subject of clothes. Robin and I told Diane that we felt that she had personally, by popularizing the *Annie Hall* look—women wearing slacks and men’s shirts and jackets and neckties—made it easier for women in the workplace who don’t feel comfortable wearing dresses and skirts.

“I mean,” I said, “I work at a pretty conservative law firm, and for a long time I was the only woman there who never wore skirts. But no one seems to have a problem with my wearing slacks all the time, and I attribute that largely to you. In some ways, you’ve done as much for women in the workplace as Justice Ginsburg," I added, jabbing my finger in the direction of the justice, who had now once again been surrounded by party guests.

"Well, I don't know about that," answered Diane with a quick smile.

My mom had joined us during this last exchange. "Speaking of clothes," she said to me, "did you notice that you and I are the only ones here wearing any colors?" We all looked around the room and saw that she was right—most everyone was wearing black, and Mom's bright red jacket, and to a lesser extent my olive-green blazer, stood out from the crowd.

"Justice Ginsburg sure looks elegant, though, don't you think?" I said. "And she's not just wearing black—check out that bright gold scarf she's got on."

"And don't you just love those net gloves she's wearing?" Mom added.

"So where are *your* gloves?" Robin asked Diane—who is known for her gloves—in a mock accusatory tone.

"Yeah, I know," Diane sighed in response, gazing down at her bare hands with a shake of the head.

Looking past Diane, I saw the two marshals watching us. "Did you notice all the US marshals here?" I said to her, nodding towards them. Diane glanced over and then leaned towards me and asked in a theatrical whisper, "Do you think they're carrying guns?"

"I imagine so, but I'll go ask."

I walked over to them and said, "Diane Keaton wants to know if you're packing a piece."

The one on the right—the one who had seen Robin jab me down in the lobby—didn't say anything, but he grinned and slowly opened his jacket and let me peek in to see that he did, indeed, have a pistol nestled there under his arm.

"Thanks. I thought so." He closed his jacket back up. "So,

are you guys—the ones here tonight—will you be the same detail with the justice tomorrow night?" I asked him.

"Uh huh. We're with them for their whole stay in LA."

"So you four will be the ones coming to my folks' house tomorrow night, then—I'm cooking dinner for them."

"We'll actually be five, but yep, that's right."

"Five!" I gaped at the two marshals. "That's more than one each to cover my parents and Robin and me. We must be especially dangerous, huh?" I said with a sly smile. "Oh, by the way, I'll have food for you all too, so no need to eat before you come. See you then."

I walked back to Diane and Robin and Mom, who had been watching my conversation from afar, and announced my findings—both about the gun and the number of marshals.

"*Five*?" Mom exclaimed. "Where will we put them all?"

"I'm cooking dinner for Justice Ginsburg and her husband tomorrow night at my parents' house," I explained to Diane.

"You're cooking dinner for Justice *Ginsburg*?" Even through those blue-tinted glasses, I could see Diane's eyes grow big. "Wow. I thought I was lucky just to get to meet her tonight . . ."

She of course wanted to hear about the menu, so I repeated my spiel for her: "Searedseascallopswithgingerlimesauce . . . But *five* marshals," I concluded, shaking my head. "My god. That is rather excessive, I think."

At this point Diane told us she had to leave and needed to make her goodbyes, and she excused herself from our group. I decided I really should eat something more than the couple of hors d'oeuvres I had taken from passing trays and headed over to the buffet table. As I was placing tidbits on my plate, Justice Ginsburg came up to the table and took a plate as well.

"This has red meat in it," I informed her, pointing to the chafing dish of pot stickers that I had tried. "But I think this is salmon, so you can eat it."

"Oh, I love salmon. Thank you," she said, not appearing at all surprised that I would know that she didn't eat meat but would want fish. I later learned that the dark orange spread wasn't salmon at all but was a sun-dried tomato and red pepper torte. I'm sure the justice wondered about my culinary expertise after tasting it and realizing my mistake, perhaps thinking, "and *she's* the one cooking for us tomorrow?" Moreover, it turns out the meat in the pot stickers was chicken, so she could have eaten them after all.

All in all, a bungled attempt at helpfulness.

As Justice Ginsburg was helping herself to the not-salmon torte, I noticed her glance at my sparsely filled plate. "I'm not very hungry," I told her.

"It's important to stay fat," she replied in a motherly tone as she filled up her own plate. This was no doubt a lesson she had learned from her earlier bout with colon cancer. I nodded gravely in agreement.

Notwithstanding Justice Ginsburg's prudent advice, however, I was still feeling way too hyped-up to eat very much. As I nibbled on the warm brie and *crostini* on my plate, Ann Carlson wandered over to the table and said hello. We talked about my dad and the law school for a bit, and then I asked her about Diane's being at the reception.

"Yeah, we became friends because our kids go to school together," she confirmed. "I've been trying to figure out how to get her involved with the law school and, since she's such a news junkie, I figured this would be the perfect thing. And it was; she absolutely loved getting to meet Justice Ginsburg. It was pretty fun getting to see *Diane* be starstruck, for a change," she added with a laugh.

Robin joined us at this point, and Ann told us about what it was like being friends with someone as famous as Diane Keaton. "I've gotten more used to it now," she said, "but when we first started hanging out together it was really weird.

I mean, okay . . ." She leaned towards us conspiratorially. "For example, last year Diane invited me to her fifty-ninth birthday party. When I told her I thought I might be the odd one out, she said, 'Oh no, it'll just be some girls.' Well. It ended up being nine women, including Diane, Meg Ryan, Lisa Kudrow, Diane English, Nancy Meyers, and some other movie industry folk.

"So there we are, all these famous women . . . and me. It was a little intimidating—but fun." Ann paused. "And then in walks Jack Nicholson. He sat at the head of the table and held court, doing a monologue. All those women and Jack." She laughed at the memory. "It was definitely one of the more surreal evenings of my life." Ann shook her head with a smile. "So I've had this wild introduction to Hollywood life through Diane, and it's been both interesting and bizarre."

"I can imagine," I said. "In fact, I think I've been feeling tonight a bit of what you're describing. Of course I was super excited about getting to meet Justice Ginsburg, and—I don't know if Dad's told you, but I'm cooking dinner for her and Marty tomorrow night. So I was already pretty damn amped. But when *Diane Keaton* walked in . . . I mean, that was so unexpected. And talking to her was so, as you say, surreal. Here you are talking to this *movie star*, and she's of course acting like it's totally normal—'cause it *is* for her—and she's so charming and friendly. It was weird."

Robin jumped in: "Oh god, I totally blathered on to her. I told her she was *hot*, and an *icon*. It's pretty embarrassing. I hope she didn't think I'm some kind of freak."

"She *is* great, isn't she?" said Ann. "And no, she did not think you were a freak. In fact, she told me before she left that she was charmed by the two of you."

Robin and I looked at each other. *Diane Keaton was* charmed *by us?* My heart, which had barely stopped pounding since I had stepped into that elevator, started beating even faster, and I felt like I was hyperventilating. I'd already been on a huge adrenaline rush, but now it was as if I'd just been injected with another, stronger dose.

You may be thinking this is hyperbole—Robin does accuse me of exaggerating when I recount stories. But I can assure you I am not doing so here.

Having now experienced this phenomenon, it's become clear to me that your body can undergo powerful chemical changes when you meet a celebrity. And not only had I been hobnobbing that evening with both Ruth Bader Ginsburg and her celebrated tax attorney husband, Marty, but now Diane Keaton had bizarrely been added to the mix.

I think this last bit—which was akin to meeting Paul Newman or Katharine Hepburn . . . or one of the Beatles—was simply too much and pushed me over the edge. For the first time in my life, I'd felt truly starstruck. And as I stood there talking to Ann, I realized that that term, "starstruck," describes an actual physiological state of being: adrenaline floods your body, your perception becomes altered, and you can't think straight. It's a form of temporary insanity.[45]

But the effect on the body caused by this state of mind begs the question, *Why*? Why do we react so to being in the presence of celebrities? Why does merely meeting someone famous cause the body to release a burst of adrenaline? They're just people like the rest of us, after all. I've thought about this quite a bit since that evening at Dean Schill's condo, as I was genuinely surprised by my body's spontaneous and uncontrolled reaction to being in the presence of all those VIPs at one time.

One thing that came to me as I was analyzing the emotions I'd experienced that night is that the feeling of being

---

45. There's a name for a psychosomatic condition similar to this: the Stendhal syndrome, involving rapid heartbeat, fainting, confusion, and even hallucinations, when individuals are exposed to great art.

starstruck—the rapid pulse and heartbeat, the constriction of vascular flow, the distortion of perceptions, and the sensation of euphoria—is exactly the same feeling you experience when you first fall in love with someone. Now, falling in love—unlike meeting celebrities—does seem to have an evolutionary purpose, in that it tends to lead toward procreation, and thus the continuation of the species.

Okay, fine. But why then does the body have this same reaction when it meets a famous person? Well, it's my pet theory that great admiration for someone is similar to—and often mistaken for—love for them. For example, when I was in my teens and early twenties, the people I professed to be "in love" with were often those whom I most admired (teachers and local rock musicians, generally). If this theory is true, and love and admiration are in fact related and similar, it makes sense that the body confuses the feelings and reacts to them the same way. Thus, if you get to know a movie star from seeing all her films—or a Supreme Court justice from learning all she's done for civil rights—and end up with exceedingly high regard for that person, your body will react to meeting her as it would when falling in love: your pulse will race, the blood will rush from your brain to your face, and your senses and perception will get all out of whack.

That was definitely what my body was experiencing as I stood there talking to Ann after spending the evening in the company of Ruth, Marty, and Diane. In addition, Ann herself was pretty darn charming, and—I realized as I spoke with her—she reminded me of a combination of Cynthia Nixon and Charlize Theron. I was thus getting a bit of the starstruck feeling all over again from meeting and talking to *her*.

And now, on top of all that, I was being told that Diane Keaton had been "charmed" by Robin and me. Brain-body overload.

• • •

When my mom came up and said she and Dad would like to leave, I stuffed a few cookies into my mouth, knowing that I needed to put something in my stomach to absorb all the wine I'd drunk that evening, and we all said our goodbyes. My father drove back to where we'd left our car at UCLA, at which time he and Robin got into a bit of a quarrel. Dad was insisting on taking us all the way to our car instead of merely dropping us off outside the parking structure, as he'd heard about some recent attacks on women in campus parking structures at night. Robin, however, who never liked it when others tried to control her behavior, was particularly sensitive to this trait in my father. And she was additionally annoyed that he was being overly protective of us simply because we were women. She protested to Dad that we'd be fine, arguing that he should just let us off outside the building, but at my pleading look she finally let it drop.

Mom and Dad waited until Robin had started the engine and pulled out of the parking spot, and then they drove off. But before we followed, I asked, "Are you okay to drive?" I knew I was in no condition to be operating a motor vehicle and was concerned that Robin might not be either. She turned off the engine.

"I think so. I stopped drinking way before you, but let's see." I watched as she did the 1-2-3-4-4-3-2-1 thumb to finger sobriety test, and she seemed fine.[46] Nevertheless, she drove cautiously to my parents' house.

It was only a little past nine when we got home, so I decided I had to call my sister and tell her about our night. Robin was pouring herself a bourbon-rocks, and I gestured that I wanted one too. I was still feeling a sort of manic-euphoria, and figured I'd never get to sleep unless I medicated myself further.

46. That test, by the way—whereby you touch your thumb to your pinky and then to the other three fingers in turn, and then back again, while counting off the digits—really does work. Try to do it smoothly, quickly, and accurately when you're drunk; I bet you can't.

"Ohmygod, you'll never believe who we hung out with tonight!" I exclaimed when Laura got on the phone. I proceeded to tell her the evening's events in a breathless rush, while Mom and Dad and Robin listened in amusement.

After I hung up, Mom and Dad retired to bed, and Robin and I stood in the kitchen sipping our drinks. I studied the pattern formed by the blue-and-yellow Mexican tiles set into the walls and counter. "Maybe we should invite Diane and Ann to the dinner tomorrow night," I said after a minute. "I have enough food to add two people."

"Yeah, right." Robin chuckled.

"I mean, I'm not really serious, of course. But don't you think Diane would like to come? Ann says she's a news junkie, after all, and she seemed pretty thrilled to meet Justice Ginsburg tonight." I took a sip of bourbon. "She's probably busy, though. It would be pretty short notice."

"There's no way she would be too busy to have dinner with a Supreme Court justice," Robin said, "And I bet she would have a great time. But no way would it work. First of all, it would be the ultimate in level-jumping to even ask her." Robin shuddered at the thought of this *faux pas*. "Plus, I don't think the Ginsburgs are big movie fans—nor are your parents—and it would be, well, *weird* if she were here. It would completely change the dynamic."

"Yeah, I know. But it's a fun fantasy."

We finished our drinks and rinsed the glasses, then climbed the stairs to my old bedroom. Maybe it was my overexcited state or perhaps all the booze I'd consumed, but it seemed warm enough that we wouldn't need to use the sleeping bags we'd brought from home as additional covers.

I got into my old bed and stared at the ceiling. It had certainly been a long and eventful day. But exciting as it had been, there was still tomorrow to come.

CHAPTER 14

D-Day

Saturday—D minus ten hours.

I rolled over the next morning with a groan. Clutching my head, I slowly cracked my eyes to the bright light streaming through the open shutters. My temple throbbed and nausea threatened to overtake me.

Oh, no. This was *not* a good day to start out with a hangover.

Gingerly getting myself up and out of bed, I made my way into the bathroom and stared at the mirror. No actual green was apparent about the gills, but there were certainly bags beneath and circles about the eyes. I downed three Advil and drank a large glass of water, which had the initial result of adding to the nausea, but which I knew from past experience was a necessary remedy. Then I got into the shower, and standing under the stream of hot water helped clear my head.

When I came downstairs, Robin was in the breakfast room with my father, looking cheerful and not the least bit affected by the previous night's excesses. They were both drinking coffee and reading the *LA Times*. I greeted them gamely and then headed for the kitchen, where I surreptitiously mixed myself a Roy Rogers—equal parts milk and Coca-Cola—an elixir that, owing to its blend of protein, sugar, caffeine, and fizz, seems to work well as a hangover cure. Because I was feeling sheepish about having gotten myself into this sorry state—especially given the day and night ahead—I didn't want anyone to know just how lousy I felt, so I gulped down the Roy Rogers in the kitchen, out of sight of Robin and Dad.

That done, I poured myself a cup of coffee with lots of cream (to provide my poor stomach with even more sustenance) and sat down at the breakfast room table. A tall stack of newspapers sat in front of Robin.

"What's all that?" I asked.

It was the previous week's *LA Times*, which she'd fished out of Mom and Dad's recycling, yesterday's *Santa Cruz Sentinel* and *New York Times*, and today's *LA Times*. She'd been working chronologically through them and was now up to Wednesday. Like Diane Keaton, Robin is a news junkie, so this did not surprise me.

As I had a busy day ahead, and was not in the best mental state for reading in any case, I limited myself to scanning yesterday's Santa Cruz paper and today's *LA Times*. While the three of us were reading our papers, Mom came downstairs. She had already been out for her run and taken a shower.

"Okay, what can I do to help?" she asked me brightly.

"Uh, I need to make a list—organize what I have to do and in what order. I'll do that when I finish the paper. But I guess you could set the table, if you want. Let's see . . ." I thought about the courses. "We'll need two small forks and one dinner fork, two knives, a soup spoon, and a dessert fork and coffee spoon. Do you have that many small forks?"

"Oh, heavens yes—I think we have twenty-four of each piece."

"And the two wine glasses and water glasses. Oh, and the napkins. I can fold those in a fancy design I learned in cooking school."

After my cursory reading of the paper, I fetched a pen and paper and jotted down what I needed to do. The entire menu was seared into my consciousness as brightly as a neon sign—I'd been thinking about this meal for nine full months, after all—but it seemed prudent to have a list I could check off as I accomplished the day's tasks. Especially given the current state of my poor hungover head.

There actually wasn't all that much to do, since I'd already made the soup, and the rest of the dinner wasn't terribly complicated. And I couldn't prepare everything this morning, as some of the items—such as the salad and mashed potatoes—shouldn't be made too long before the dinner.

I began by washing and peeling the potatoes and putting them in water in a big pot on the stove. It's not my usual practice to peel potatoes for mashing, but they're more elegant that way, even if less flavorful and nutritious.

Next I chopped walnuts for the soup garnish, grated and juiced the limes for the scallop sauce, and washed and de-stringed the snow peas. I then mixed the dry rub for the fish, combining brown sugar, chili powder, sea salt, wasabi powder, and black sesame seeds in a bowl.

As I worked, I listened to the opera broadcast. The radios in both the kitchen and the living room were tuned to *Così Fan Tutte*, which—as my father had mentioned in his remarks the day before—the Met was performing in honor of Mozart's 250th birthday. While I was mixing the dry rub, my father came into the kitchen and commented on how much he loved the quartet that was being sung at that moment.

"It's a trio," Robin piped up from the breakfast room where she was still going through the newspapers.

"It is?" Dad responded. "It sounds like four voices."

"No. It's definitely a trio—it's my favorite part of the opera."

Robin, as you may have surmised, can be quite competitive, a trait that tended to come out often around my dad, whom she viewed as a worthy opponent.

She's right. My father was indeed an amazing guy, and through the numerous law review articles and books he published over the years, he eventually became known as one of the country's leading authorities on Fourteenth Amendment/equal protection issues. If one were to distill his life's work into one sentence, I suppose it would read something like this: in order to have true equality in America, *all* members of our society must have a sense of inclusion, of citizenship, of *belonging*.[47]

In addition, my dad has been cited in numerous Supreme Court opinions (twelve times, by my count). Alas, these have mostly been dissenting opinions. But as Dad liked to say, "I'd rather be right than precedent."

Like Robin, my father could also be competitive, and he and Robin were both avid game players. As a result, back when Robin was studying for the LSAT and came across a reading comprehension question based on a passage from one of my dad's articles, she couldn't wait to try it out on him. Anyone who's ever taken the SAT or LSAT knows that exams like that test your test-taking skills more than your actual knowledge or ability to comprehend the text. Because Robin had been studying for the test and knew what the examiners were looking for, she got all the answers right on my father's passage. When she had Dad answer the same questions, however, he got two wrong—even though he had *written* the text.

At that time, the *LA Times* had just run a story about the recent publication of the *Encyclopedia of the American Constitution*, of which Dad was the associate editor and for

47. You can read all about this ideology in *Belonging to America: Equal Citizenship and the Constitution*, Kenneth L. Karst (Yale Univ. Press, 1989).

which he had also contributed many of the entries. The author of the newspaper story said regarding my father, "Many of the articles written by [him] make you ask, 'How did he get so smart?'" Well, of course we all had a field day with that quote, and Robin immediately invented a "Ken Karst: How *Did* He Get So Smart?" game, whereby she would read random passages from the *Encyclopedia* and we would have to guess whether they were written by Dad or not.

All this serves to show why Robin was so quick to correct my father with regard to the *Così Fan Tutte* trio. Since Dad was also exceedingly knowledgeable about music, and generally right about opera facts and trivia (and rarely hesitated to correct others when they were mistaken), it gave her great pleasure, she confided to me later, to be the one right that time.[48]

While Robin and Dad discussed the trio, I took the ahi from the refrigerator and patted it dry. It had a bright red glossy sheen to it and still smelled fresh. *Good.* I trimmed off the dark flesh running along one side (the blood line, which has a nasty, gamey flavor), eyeballed the hunk of tuna, then carefully sliced the large end into six thick steaks.

After rewrapping the ahi and returning it to the fridge, I poked my head into the breakfast room to ask Robin when she'd be ready to go get the dessert. Through her internet research, she had discovered a place called Amandine on Wilshire Boulevard that supposedly had fabulous pastries and was particularly famous for their pear tart. She and Mom and I had decided that it would be fun to go together to pick out a selection of pastries. And we needed to get French bread for the marshals' dinner, as well.

---

48. The trio they were discussing is *Soave sia il vento* (may the wind be gentle). Robin actually despises the plot of *Così Fan Tutte*—which is largely about duplicitous and fickle women—but the music is gorgeous, so she prefers that particular opera in a "highlights" format.

"I can't leave till after the opera quiz," Robin informed me. This is the between-act panel quiz they sometimes have on the Metropolitan Opera's Saturday radio broadcast, and—depending on the opera and singers that day—is often Robin's favorite part of the show. "It'll be on at the end of this act, which is soon, and then I can go."

"All right. I'll just keep doing my prep work till you're ready." I leaned against the kitchen counter and took a deep breath. My headache was mostly gone, and I was starting to feel more human, but I still felt slightly queasy.

Shaking it off, I tried to concentrate. *What next?* Oh yeah: garnishes, which I'd neglected to add to my list. I needed to check out what flowers my parents had in their garden before we left, in case I had to get some while we were out. I went to find my mom to ask her what flowers she might have, and she led me out into the patio. This was the first time I'd been outside, and I realized it was another beautiful day: sunny and mild.

"Look at these," Mom said, kneeling down and showing me a leggy dark green plant that was taking over one corner of the patio. I looked more closely and saw that it was an orchid of some sort, with tiny purple blooms at the end of each stalk. "I thought they'd make a good garnish for something."

"Oh, they're so cute!" I exclaimed. "This will be *perfect* for the scallops. It'll add a sort of Hawaiian or Asian feel to the dish. And the purple will look beautiful set off against the black plates and cream-colored sauce, don't you think? *And* orchids are edible—though I doubt anyone will actually eat them."

We stood back up. "I'll wait until later to pick them," I said. "Do you have any nasturtiums in your yard?" I had decided that the orange and red of this flower—which is also edible—would be an attractive compliment to the butternut squash soup, but I couldn't bring any from my garden as they would have been completely wilted by the time of the dinner.

"No, I don't. But let's see if there's anything else out front."

Together we walked back inside and then out to the front yard to see if there were any flowers that would make a good substitute. Mom and I wandered around the yard. This being the dead of winter, however—even though it was Southern California—there wasn't much in bloom, and what there was didn't seem appropriate for use as a garnish.

"Maybe we can find some nasturtiums when we're out and about," I said. "If they're in bloom in Santa Cruz now, they're sure to be blooming down here too."

We headed back inside, and Robin announced that the opera quiz was over and she was ready to go. We all climbed into the car, and as Robin started the engine, I told her we needed to be on the lookout for nasturtiums that I could pick for my soup garnish.

"So you're gonna steal flowers for dinner for a Supreme Court justice, are ya?" Robin raised her eyebrows in mock disapproval. "We'd better not tell her that petty larceny was involved in the food preparation." The three of us giggled like naughty children. "If we find any, maybe we should just knock on their door and tell them we need the flowers for a party for Justice Ginsburg," Robin suggested as she pulled away from the curb. "It worked for the wine and the fish."

I had already forgotten about our flower mission and was spacing out in a hangover daze when Robin turned onto Montana Avenue and shouted, "There!"

"What?" I responded, startled out of my reverie.

"Over there, in front of that apartment building. Look—nasturtiums!" She was right—a whole bed of them, red, orange, and yellow, covered the front yard.

"Good job, Robin!" Mom cried.

"Way to go!" I agreed. "But let's get them on the way back, so I can put them into water right away."

We proceeded on to the *pâtisserie*. There was a long line at the counter ahead of us, which was a good sign. As we waited, we discussed what to buy. Since we didn't know what Ruth and Marty would like, we decided to get a variety, and let them have first pick. Nevertheless, because there was such a wide selection, it took us ages to settle on what we wanted. In fact, by the time it came our turn, we still hadn't decided and had to let several customers go ahead of us.

As we were peering into the display case at all the decadent pastries, tarts, and pies, I realized there was no pear tart, the item for which Amandine was allegedly famous. The man behind the counter confirmed that there were none in the back, that they had already sold out for the day. And it was not even noon; boy, it *must* be good.

This was a disappointment, but we forged on. We finally settled on two slices of the chocolate mousse and praline tart and one each of the lemon chiffon tart, the strawberry and crème fraîche tart, the chocolate ganache tart, and the cheesecake.

"Don't forget the bread for the marshals," Mom reminded me, and we also bought two loaves of crusty French bread.

Our string-tied pink box in hand (don't you just *love* those boxes?), we climbed back in the car and headed home. But first we had our clandestine nasturtium-snatching mission to accomplish.

Robin stopped the car around the corner from the target apartment building, and I strolled as nonchalantly as I could down the sidewalk to the bed of nasturtiums. I think I may even have been whistling. There was a window facing the street—and thus the target flowers—but the shade was down. With a furtive glance up and down the sidewalk, I bent down and started picking blooms.

I tried to do the deed quickly but wanted to get perfect flowers. This one was too small; this one was too big; this one had a blemish. After I had chosen eight flawless blossoms (two extra, just in case), with another glance at the window—the shade was still closed—I picked eight round leaves, being careful to take only ones that weren't too big and that had a bright green color.

Nasturtiums in hand, I dashed down the sidewalk and around the corner into the waiting car. Robin had left the engine running, and we sped off, laughing like crooks who had just pulled off a bank heist.

"Okay, time for lunch," Mom announced as we came through the back door into the kitchen, still chuckling from our clandestine adventure. "We need to fortify ourselves."

While I placed the precious nasturtium blossoms and leaves into a juice glass filled with water, Mom got lunch items out of the fridge. She had bought sliced roast beef and ham from the deli, and with this she set out bread, lettuce, tomatoes, pickles, jack and cheddar cheese, mayo, and mustard. My father came in from the living room where he had been listening to the opera and working on a jigsaw puzzle, and we all made ourselves sandwiches.

"Are you nervous at all?" I asked Dad as he spread Dijon mustard on his slice of rye bread. "You know, about spending a whole evening talking to Ruth?"

"Well, it has been a long time since we've spent much time together," he said.

"And I bet even back then she wasn't what you'd call 'the life of the party.' "

Dad smiled. "Indeed. But at lunch yesterday she was actually quite chatty."

"Yeah, with a bunch of law professors who I'm sure spent the whole time picking her brain about federal jurisdiction and the like. But tonight'll be different—way more of a social evening. Or so I hope, anyway."

"Don't worry," he said, selecting a slice of ham to lay atop the mustard. "It'll be fine. I know you can hold your own in any conversation. And besides, I've known Ruth to be pretty darn amusing when she wants to be."

INTERLUDE

To those who didn't know her well, Ruth Ginsburg could come across as prim and taciturn, a serious woman, not prone to displays of emotion or frivolity. She was rarely seen laughing, and at dinners or cocktail parties, the justice was far more comfortable discussing the law or opera than engaging in idle small talk. Even Bill Clinton, when considering RBG for his Supreme Court nominee, was initially reluctant, having heard she was a "cold fish."

This impression of seriousness has been reinforced over the years by her judicial opinions, which—especially when compared to the wry, acerbic opinions of her one-time sparring partner, Justice Antonin Scalia—can come across as dry and sedate.

Those close to Ruth, however, always knew better. It wasn't that she lacked a sense of humor; far from it. But it tended to be subtle and often held close to her chest. This was a woman, after all, who cared deeply about showing respect, and not scoring unfair points at the expense of others.

In private, however, she allowed her caustic wit to shine. Her handwritten notes on an opposing counsel's brief from back in her Women's Rights Project days[49] demonstrate this sense of humor. Next to the assertion that nature supports the unequal treatment of the sexes, Ginsburg scrawled, "black widow spiders." And in the margin beside the observation that, although women have the right to vote, they have not used the power to repeal the statute in question, she wrote, "Women acquiesce!"

RBG would occasionally poke fun of others in public but only when the fight was fair. Her good friend Nino was thus always fodder for jokes, as he could take it as easily as he dished it out. A photograph used to sit in Ginsburg's chambers of her and the much

49. These notes were made on the appellee's brief in *Reed v. Reed*, 404 US 71 (1971).

more rotund Scalia riding an elephant during a trip to India. When asked by some undisclosed "feminist friends" why the man got to sit in the front, Ruth's wry response was that "it had to do with the distribution of weight."

And with her beloved Marty she was always at ease, ever laughing at his good-natured ribbing about her fondness for prunes or his calling his wife "Her Royal Highness." She even started using his phrase for her position on the nation's highest court, often referring to it as "the good job Marty helped me get."

But in her later years on the Court, we came to see a new public Ruth Ginsburg—one less concerned with placating her colleagues and more interested in voicing her heartfelt beliefs. Within two days in June 2013, for example, she broke a Supreme Court record by reading three dissents from the bench,[50] two of which contain verbal gems worthy of Scalia (though not as acerbic as his could be). One was an affirmative action case in which the Court stated that schools cannot put too much weight on race in their efforts to achieve a racially diverse student body. Pointing to the "deliberate obfuscation" inherent in such a concept, RBG's dissent noted that pretending to believe lies is the shame of the legal profession:

> *Or, as a legendary critic of lawyers put it, "If you think that you can think about a thing inextricably attached to something else without thinking of the thing which it is attached to, then you have a legal mind . . ." Only that kind of legal mind could conclude that an admissions plan specifically designed to produce racial diversity is not race conscious.*[51]

---

50. Reading any dissent from the bench is a rarity and was particularly so for the normally amenable Ginsburg.
51. This is from RBG's dissent in *Fisher v. Univ. of Texas*, 570 US 297 (2013). The "legendary critic of lawyers" is early 20th century law professor Thomas Reed Powell.

In an opinion announced the next day, the Court held unconstitutional the "preclearance" section of the Voting Rights Act of 1965, which required states to check with the Justice Department before changing their election laws, as a way to prevent racial discrimination.[52] Ginsburg's infuriation was palpable as she read her dissent from the bench, citing numerous examples of flagrant voter discrimination still occurring in states such as Alabama, where the case arose. But her most memorable line appears in her written dissent, and it's a zinger:

> *Throwing out preclearance when it has worked and is continuing to work to stop discriminatory changes is like throwing away your umbrella in a rainstorm because you are not getting wet.*

Ouch. No wonder Shana Knizhnik pulled the quote for the very first post on her brand new Tumblr blog, *Notorious R.B.G.*[53]

• • •

Robin went back to her newspapers while she ate her lunch, and Dad retreated to the living room with his ham sandwich to work on the puzzle. According to Robin, he and my mom had just finished another puzzle, so the one he was working on—with tropical fish swimming about a coral reef—had only been set out that morning. Dad had told Robin he wanted to get it put together enough so that it was at the "perfect" stage for the Ginsburgs, in case they wanted to work on it. But my guess is that in reality, notwithstanding his cavalier

---

52. The case is *Shelby County v. Holder*, 570 US 529 (2013).
53. This name was a play on Notorious B.I.G., the nickname of rapper Biggie Smalls, also from Brooklyn.

declarations, he—like the rest of us—was antsy about tonight's dinner, and this provided something to occupy his mind.

My mother and I sat at the breakfast room table to eat our sandwiches and discuss what still needed to be done. I read from my list: "We need to set up the den for the marshals."

"I can do that," Mom said. "We can put a tablecloth on the desk and set it up like a buffet table. What are you serving them again?"

"Soup, salad, and bread. Oh, and Robin is going to get some cookies for their dessert. I forgot I wanted to get some when we were at the pastry shop."

"We can use that soup tureen I bought Dad for his birthday last year," Mom said. I followed her into the dining room, and she pointed out a white porcelain tureen in the china cabinet. "This'll be the first time we've used it." My father had been gung ho at the time about starting to make soups but his initial enthusiasm for cooking had quickly waned.

As Mom set about arranging the den for the marshals, I went back to my prep work. I took the butternut squash soup from the fridge and measured out six bowls' worth for us, decanting this into a small pot. The rest I poured into a bigger pot for the marshals' dinner.

Next I started on the ginger-lime cream sauce for the scallops. Robin came into the kitchen as I was getting all the ingredients ready. "The opera's over, and I finally finished all the newspapers, so I'm gonna go buy the cookies for the marshals. Do you need me to get you anything while I'm out?"

"No, I'm good. But thanks."

And I did feel pretty good—other than my lingering headache, that is. Now that I was actually preparing the meal, it was a lot easier to simply focus on the process without thinking too much about the honored guests to whom it would be served later tonight.

I returned to my sauce, chopping shallots and ginger and

adding them to lime juice, wine, and clam juice, then setting it over a low flame. As I was reducing this concoction, I heard the vacuum cleaner start up. After a minute I saw the business end of the machine poke into the dining room, followed by my father. The carpet in the dining and breakfast rooms is a navy blue, which is really cool looking, but it shows every speck of matter that falls on it and therefore requires frequent cleaning. As I watched, Dad knelt down and examined something on the floor. He picked at whatever it was for a moment, and then stood up and continued vacuuming.

With a smile, I turned away so he wouldn't see me staring. While it wasn't unusual for my father to do the vacuuming, I was touched by the fact that he was concerned about the finer details of tonight's dinner. Or perhaps he truly was nervous and simply looking for more things to do while waiting for the big night to commence.

After the sauce for the scallops had reduced by half, I added the whipping cream and lime zest and let this simmer a bit longer to further reduce. My mom came in as I was stirring the pot, and I asked her to taste it. "I still need to finish it with whisked-in butter, but tell me if you think it needs anything." I had cut in half the amount of lime juice called for by the recipe, as last time I'd made the sauce it had been too tart, but I thought it might still be too acidic.

She took the spoonful of sauce I proffered. "Mmmm. But yes, I think you could add some sugar; it is a bit limey." I added a teaspoon of sugar and let it dissolve, and then we both tasted it again. "Much better," Mom pronounced, and I agreed. I set the sauce aside. I would reheat it and finish it with the butter right before service.

"Come and have a look," my mother said after I'd moved the sauce off the stove. I followed her into the den, where she had covered the desk with a red and white checked tablecloth. On top of this she had placed the empty soup tureen with a ladle, a large wooden bowl for the salad, a breadbasket, a butter plate, a pitcher for ice water, and five each of salad plates, soup bowls, forks, spoons, glasses, and red and white checked cloth napkins. Mom had also set up a TV tray as an additional eating space, as the coffee table wasn't big enough for five.

"Wow! That looks great!" I exclaimed. "I bet they don't get *this* kind of attention every place they go."

Next, I turned my attention to the pea sprout garnish. My plan was to make little bunches and then tie them together with one of the sprouts. I dumped the bag out onto the counter and bunched five of the shoots into a tiny bouquet. As I wound the one sprout around the others, though, it snapped in two. I tried again, this time being as gentle as I could, but it still broke. They just weren't elastic enough to use as a tying agent. *Damn*. What could I use in their stead? I could, of course, simply lay a few sprouts on the ahi without tying them, but it would look far better if they were in little bouquets.

My plan frustrated, I opened the door to the fridge and peered inside. What item could I use as edible string? As I pulled open the vegetable crisper, it hit me. *Of course! Celery—I can use celery string!*

I broke two stalks off the bunch of celery and washed them, then slowly peeled a string from the outside of a stalk. So far so good. Next, I carefully wound the thin string several times around the bunch of pea sprouts and tied it, then cut the ends short. It worked! Now why hadn't they taught me *this* in cooking school?

Just then, Robin returned, a brown paper bag in her hand. "I bought these chocolate chip cookies," she said, taking them out to show me, " 'cause they look like they could be homemade."

Proud of my innovation, I showed her my pea sprout bouquet, telling her excitedly about how the pea sprouts hadn't worked and how I'd figured out I could tie them with celery string.

"All right!" Robin admired my celery-tied garnish, happy that I'd found a solution to my dilemma, but clearly even more pleased with my pleasure about it.

After tying five more tiny bouquets, I placed them in a shot glass filled with water which I put in the fridge so they wouldn't get droopy. I then pulled my list from my pocket and read it over, checking off items I'd completed. The last major prep task was the salads.

I spread six white salad plates out on the tile counter, piled a small mound of spinach on each one, and laid overlapping rounds of sliced blood orange and red onion in an arc shape over the greens. On top of this, I sprinkled crumbled Gorgonzola and dried cranberries. The pine nuts would wait till right before I served the salads, so they wouldn't get soggy. Next I retrieved the wooden salad bowl from the den and made a large salad of the same ingredients for the marshals.

Coming back into the kitchen after stowing all the salads in the fridge out in the Peacock Room, I spied Robin crouched on the floor in the dining room holding an iron, with my father looking on. Curious, I went over to see what she was doing.

"Getting rid of the candle wax in the carpet," she answered in response to my query. This must have been what Dad was picking at earlier, I realized, and he'd asked Robin if she knew how to get it out. Robin is an expert at tasks such as this, as her old job as facilities manager at UCSC had involved much cleaning and repair of damage—including spilled candle wax—caused by students in their apartments.

I watched as Robin placed paper towels on the carpet on top of the wax and ran the hot iron over it, causing the wax to melt and be absorbed by the paper towels. She did this several times with new towels, then showed us the result. "*Voilà*!" she exclaimed, as Dad and I ooh'ed and ah'ed over the now wax-free carpet.

Setting the iron on the table to cool, Robin asked me if I wanted her to set up a drink area in the dining room. "We could do it here," she said, pointing to a tea cart standing against the wall.

"That would be great. Do you have an ice bucket?" I asked Dad.

"I think so. Hon?" he asked my mother as she came into the room, "Do you know where our ice bucket is?"

Mom brought the ice bucket into the dining room, and I set it on the tea cart. "Let's see," I said. "We'll need room for the ice bucket for the white wine and also for the red wine, the fizzy water, and a pitcher of still water. Do you have a nice pitcher we can use?"

"Yep." She led me back into the kitchen and pointed to an elegant glass pitcher on the top shelf of the cupboard. Mom, taller than I, reached up and took down the pitcher and handed it to me. "And here," she said, pulling a tea towel from a drawer. "You can use this to wrap around the white wine, so the condensation doesn't drip when you pour it."

I placed these items on the tea cart next to the ice bucket for Robin to arrange and returned to the kitchen to consult my list one more time. The last thing I needed to do before the *à la minute*, or last-minute steps for the dishes, was to get my *mise en place*—that is, arrange everything I'd need in an orderly fashion, ready for use.

If you've ever been in a restaurant kitchen, you may have noticed all the individual bowls, squirt bottles, and metal insert pans filled with ingredients next to the hot line so that dishes can quickly and efficiently be cooked and plated up once the order to "fire" has been given. Being somewhat obsessive about neatness and order, I take great delight in this part of food preparation.

For my dinner, it would be necessary to have my *mise placée*, if you will, for all four of the savory courses. First would be the scallops in ginger-lime cream sauce. For this, I would need to have the scallops ready for searing in butter, so I grabbed my large cast-iron skillet and pulled the scallops and a stick of butter from the refrigerator to bring to room temperature. The sauce was ready except for the butter finish, but this butter should be cold, so I left it in the fridge. And for the garnish, I would need the lime zest—check—and the orchids.

Oh yeah, I should get those now. I grabbed a pair of scissors and went out to the patio and cut three stalks, each of which had several flowers on it, and placed these in the glass with the nasturtiums. Finally, I got the square black plates from the breakfast room and stacked them on the kitchen counter, ready to be placed in the oven for warming when the time came.

Next course would be the roasted butternut squash soup. The garnishes I would need for this were the chopped walnuts in a bowl, the *crème fraîche*—which I'd put in the squirt bottle I'd brought from home—and the bottle of roasted walnut oil standing by. And, of course, the pilfered nasturtiums. The soup was on the stove, ready to be heated, but I'd make the brown butter at the last minute, and for this I figured I could use the same cast-iron skillet I'd be using for the scallops, since they would be cooked in butter. And I already had a stick of butter out on the counter. I stacked the six white bowls and their base plates on the kitchen counter next to the black plates. Done.

Now for the salads. All I needed for this course was to get a bowl of pine nuts ready and to have the salad dressing on hand. Check.

Finally, the main course. Time to coat the ahi with the dry rub. I fetched the fish from the fridge and rolled each piece in the seasonings, then set them back on the plate, leaving them on the counter to come up to room temperature. Next to the fish, I placed the bottle of sesame oil, which I would use to sear the tuna. As the ahi shouldn't be crowded in the pan when being blackened, I'd need two pans, so I got the second cast-iron skillet I'd brought from home and set it on the stove next to the other.

The sautéed snow peas would also require butter—best take a second stick out of the fridge. The peeled potatoes were already in the water ready to be boiled, but I did need to fill a Pyrex pitcher with cream and butter for last minute heating in the microwave. I placed the can of wasabi powder next to this so I wouldn't forget to add it to the mashed potatoes. Next I got my mom's mixer out of the drawer and set it on the counter by the cream and wasabi. The pea sprout garnishes I would leave in the fridge until later, but I poured some black sesame seeds into a custard cup, which I would sprinkle atop the potatoes.

Scanning my list, I ticked off each course and its required ingredients to make sure I hadn't forgotten anything. And then I let out a slow breath of air. I looked at my watch; it was four-thirty. The Ginsburgs were coming at six, so I had a little time to relax.

If I could.

• • •

Earlier in the day when I'd been feeling queasy, I'd thought that if I got my prep work done early, I would have myself a little lie down. But my hangover had subsided, and I actually felt pretty good, so I decided instead to join my dad and Robin working on the jigsaw puzzle.

On the way through the dining room, however, I was waylaid. Mom had set the table for the dinner, and it looked exquisite. The eight pieces of Gorham Chantilly silverware at each place sat gleaming atop my great-grandmother Nana's lace tablecloth, and all the wine glasses and gold rimmed water glasses were sparkling in the late-afternoon sun. Mom had also set four sterling candle sticks with white candles on the table.

In the center was a low-rimmed, blue-enameled silver bowl with two pink and white camellias floating in water. So they had bloomed in time, after all. At each place sat a white cloth napkin, ready for folding. I took the napkins one by one and folded them into a variation on the bishop's miter—with two extra flaps pulled down facing the diner, like pennants.

Robin and I had already discussed where to seat everyone: Mom and Dad at the ends, with Mom closest to the kitchen; Justice Ginsburg next to Dad; and me in between her and Mom (and thus also near the kitchen); Robin on the other side next to Dad and across from Ruth; and Marty next to Robin, across from me.

I examined Justice Ginsburg's place setting. The wine glasses had some water spots on them, so I fetched a tea towel from the kitchen and cleaned them off. Then, just for good measure, I gave all her silver a final polish. Next, I did the same with Marty's glassware and silver. I didn't bother with the other four place settings.

Satisfied with the table, I headed for the living room to work on the puzzle for a while. By the time I joined them, Dad and Robin had already completed about a dozen separate little wrasses, tang, and triggerfish, some of which were already joined together in a school.

At half past five, I turned on the fire under the potatoes and the marshals' soup pot and put the French bread into the oven at a low heat. Next, I set six champagne flutes on the mantle in the living room and poured the cashews and rice crackers into the two bowls my mom had picked out. The rice crackers went into a Japanese bowl with brown on the outside and a blue and white floral pattern on the inside. For the cashews, Mom had chosen a deep brown ceramic piece made by one of her potter friends. I saw too that she had put out paper cocktail napkins with brightly colored tropical fish on them. We seemed to have a theme going.

As I was placing the nibblies on the coffee table, Robin looked up from the puzzle and commented that we should use the ice bucket for the Champagne, as well. Quite right, I agreed, and she got up to move the bucket from the tea cart in the dining room into the kitchen, ready to be filled with ice.

Next I went into the den to see what still had to be done for the marshals' meal. I needed to put the crème fraîche into the bowl and bring the salad dressing in from the kitchen. Oh, and I couldn't forget the cookies. That all done, I returned to the kitchen to check on the items being heated. I poked the 'taters with a fork—still hard.

The soup pots were bubbling, so I switched off the heat under them. And the bread was now warm, so I turned off the oven as well. I brought the breadbasket in from the den and placed a serrated knife on the cutting board. As I was doing this, Mom and Robin came into the kitchen. "We need a plan," Robin said.

"Right," Mom agreed. "We need to decide who's going to serve which dish, and who will clear. Since you'll be doing the last-minute cooking and arranging the food on the plates, you'll need us to help be your waiters."

"Oh—good idea. Why don't you do two courses each, for both the serving and clearing. I don't care which; you decide."

Robin and Mom conferred for a few minutes and then announced that Mom would help me serve the scallops and salad and would clear the soup and main course, and Robin would assist with serving the soup and main course and would clear the scallops and salad. Mom then went upstairs to change into her party clothes. After she left, Robin came over to the stove, where I was poking the potatoes with a fork. "I want you to monitor my drinking tonight," she told me.

"Uh, huh," I said, stepping around her to grab the pitcher of cream and butter and put it into the microwave to heat.

"I'm serious." She followed me over to the microwave. "I

really don't want to blather on and on to Ruth like I did last night to Diane Keaton. God, that was embarrassing." Robin's upper body twitched in a sudden shudder at the memory.

"C'mon, Diane said she was *charmed* by us. You couldn't have been acting that weird." I stepped around Robin again to go back to the stove.

"Hrumph. In any case, I still want you to watch how much I drink. Don't let me get too talkative, okay?"

"Fine." I turned off the potatoes and carried the steaming pot over to the sink. "I'll give you a signal if I think you're dominating the conversation or acting tipsy." Leaning back to keep from burning my face, I poured the hot water off the potatoes and then covered the pot and set it down on the counter. "And you should do the same for me, all right?"

"Okay. I'm gonna go change. You need anything before I go upstairs?"

"No, I'm fine. I just need to mix the potatoes and slice the bread, and then I'm ready." Taking the hot cream and butter from the microwave, I poured it into the potatoes and turned the mixer on. The trick is to achieve a creamy texture without overmixing, lest they become gummy. Whipping potatoes too long causes their cellular structure to break down and release starch, resulting in a paste-like glop.

Once the potatoes were sufficiently mashed, I added salt and pepper, and a little more butter for good measure. Then I sprinkled in wasabi powder, a little bit at a time, and stirred this in with a wooden spoon.

Mom came into the kitchen at this point. She had changed into an aquamarine cashmere cardigan, offset with a single strand of pearls, and a pair of gray wool slacks.

"You look great," I said. "Nice sweater. Here, would you try the mashed potatoes? I need to know whether I should add more wasabi." I handed a spoonful to her, and she dutifully complied. "Can you even taste it?" I asked.

"Just a little. I think you can add more." I sprinkled in some more powder, and we both tried the potatoes again.

"More," I said. Mom nodded agreement, and I added another dash of the pale green powder. That did the trick. Just enough to know it was there, but not so much that it became overpowering. I put the lid on the potato pot and set it over a larger pot with a little water in it, to act as a double boiler and keep them warm, and set the flame on low.

Next I removed the bread from the oven, sliced it and placed it in the breadbasket wrapped in a tea towel, and took this to the den. I brought the soup tureen back to the kitchen and poured the marshals' soup inside, then returned it to the desk in the den. They'd have to do without the brown butter finish. Finally, I fetched the wooden bowl of salad from the Peacock Room, tossed it with salad dressing, and placed this next to the soup tureen.

I checked my list again and had one last look around the kitchen. That seemed to be everything. It was now a quarter to six; just enough time to dash upstairs and change clothes.

Staring in the mirror as I combed my hair and wetted down a stubborn "wing" that insisted on poking out from behind my ear, I clenched my hands several times before shaking them out with a slow exhale. *You have this*, I mouthed to my solemn reflection. *From here on out, you could prepare tonight's meal in your sleep. Relax and enjoy the moment.*

CHAPTER 15

Justice Is Served

The doorbell rang at 5:55.

Ohmygod, they're early! I came racing downstairs, hurriedly buttoning up my vest, then tried to slow my rapid breathing while my father answered the door. But it was only the head marshal Charles, who, after greeting us, poked his head inside and glanced around the house.

"Are you casing the joint?" Dad joked. Charles smiled politely and said yes, he was making sure they had the right place. The Ginsburgs would be arriving in about five minutes, he informed us and then withdrew back into the night.

Robin went to fetch the Champagne from the fridge and fill the ice bucket, and the rest of us sat down in the living room and fidgeted, counting off the minutes.

Promptly at six the doorbell rang again, and we all jumped up. Dad once more opened the door, and there were Ruth and Marty, smiles on their faces, standing under the warm yellow light of my parents' doorstep.

As it had been meeting Diane Keaton at the dean's reception, I found it supremely surreal seeing the Ginsburgs there on my parents' front porch. This was, after all, the very same porch where I had played Napoleon Solo hiding from T.H.R.U.S.H. agents as a youngster, the porch we'd decorated with jack-o'lanterns and orange and black crepe paper for Halloween.

And now, here were a Supreme Court justice and her distinguished tax attorney/law professor husband standing in that same spot, waiting to come into the house.

Plus, the realization hit me: After all this time—nine months of planning and fretting—it was actually happening. The dinner was *now*. At that moment, a kind of calmness settled over me. Sure, I was still antsy about the evening to come. Concern mostly, notwithstanding that earlier pep talk I'd given myself, that I not mess up the food. But now that the scene had finally been set in motion, now that there was nothing more for me to organize or to plan, I felt the sort of release that comes when one is finally able to relinquish control.

I could now sit back and enjoy the show.

Dad invited Ruth and Marty inside, and I closed the door behind them. As I did so, I peered outside. The marshals were nowhere to be seen. But I knew they were out there somewhere in the dark of the night, keeping a watchful eye on their charges until the door closed behind them and they were safely inside the house.

I took Ruth's purse from her and set it on the bench in the hallway. It was large and surprisingly heavy, and I wondered what she might have in there. Did Supreme Court justices pack pistols? More likely it was merely a book, perhaps a law book; that would explain the weight.

Once again, the justice looked stylish and elegant. She was clad in a simple black dress, black tights, and black shoes, with a long-sleeved, robe-like top over her dress that seemed Asian—or perhaps Persian—in design. It too was predominantly black, but along the edges and around the sleeves ran a thick band of fabric woven into a pattern picked out in delicate shades of brown and orange and pale green. About her neck hung a large elaborate necklace that also looked to be Persian. It was strung with numerous beads of varying sizes, the focal point being a large doughnut-shaped piece of stone sewn onto a rectangle of black fabric.

Marty, though not so strikingly dressed as his wife, looked very dapper, his blue and white pin-striped Oxford cloth shirt complementing a dark blue blazer and olive-green slacks. To top it off he sported a blue tie with alternating diagonals of red stripes and rows of the scales of justice in gold.

He turned to me with a boyish grin. "I've been looking forward to this night. Your father tells me you're quite the cook."

Uh, oh. What have you been saying, Dad? But my father, who was busy greeting Ruth, failed to notice the look I shot his way. "Uh, well," I said, "I did go to a local culinary arts school, but I'm no professional chef, by any means."

"Nor am I," Marty said, "but I do love to cook. And to my mind, that's far more important."

Ruth turned and took me by the hand. "So nice to see you again," she said. "And after hearing what Ken said yesterday, I'm *very* much looking forward to tasting your cooking."

Oh, no . . .

❖ *Hors d'Oeuvres: Salted Cashews and Rice Crackers with Wasabi Peas* ❖

As the four of us were standing in the hall, Robin heard the side door into the kitchen open and close. She went to investigate and discovered Charles in the kitchen. He'd obviously scoped out the house and ascertained that there was another entrance. As the door was not locked, he'd been able to walk right in. (But with five US marshals to protect us, who needed to worry about such things as locking the doors?) Robin took Charles into the den and gave him the lay of the land: the buffet table with their dinner, the bathroom, and the remote for the TV. Charles then headed back outside to fetch his four colleagues.

Mom and Dad led Ruth and Marty into the living room, and while they seated themselves, I opened the Veuve Clicquot and poured it into the six champagne flutes. Ruth sat in the brown velvet chair next to the sofa. Marty wandered over to the chair at the other end of the sofa, stopping briefly to examine the jigsaw puzzle. After all of Dad's work on it, I hoped he noticed Marty's interest. Mom took a place on the sofa at the end nearest Ruth, and I sat down next to her. My father claimed the wingback chair across the coffee table from the sofa.

When Robin returned from getting the marshals settled in their room, she sat at the end of the sofa, between Marty and me, and the six of us toasted each other and sipped our bubbly.

As we sat there on my parents' heirloom furniture, listening to the ticking of the antique clock on the mantelpiece, it struck me that the scene was like the setup for a Golden Age mystery novel—something out an Agatha Christie story. *Maybe that* was *a pistol in Ruth's purse, after all*, I thought, suppressing a giggle. *And maybe she'll be the sleuth who solves the case!* But once again, with five federal marshals down the hall, it seemed doubtful any crime would be committed tonight in my parents' home.

I cleared my throat and turned to Ruth. "So, Dad mentioned that you're going to South Africa right after this trip out west," I said. "That sounds exhausting."

"Well, it's a great honor to have been asked to speak at their Constitutional Court[54]," she replied. "And I can get by without much sleep, so I'll be fine."

---

54. RBG made known over the years how very much she admired the Constitution of South Africa.

"You're lucky. Jet lag turns me into pretty much a zombie. Robin and I were in France last spring, and it took me four days to get back to normal after the flight. Oh," I said, sitting up, "and you should know that one of my goals over there was to discover possible dishes for the dinner tonight."

"Fun research," Mom said, then turned to Ruth. "I seem to remember your children having a connection with France."

The justice smiled. "Yes, Jane has a degree from the Sorbonne in Paris, and James named his classical music record company after the *cédille*.[55] Marty and I love France and have spent quite a bit of time in Paris over the years. It appears to have rubbed off on our children."

"So do you speak French?" I asked, opening the second bottle of Champagne and pouring another round.

"Unfortunately, no. But I was at one time fluent in Swedish."

When Mom and I expressed surprise, she explained how she'd studied the language and then lived in Sweden for two summers in the early 1960s. This then led to a discussion of the use of foreign terms in legal writing. Ruth told us she frowned on the tradition of employing Latin and French words in briefs and legal opinions, preferring to use, for example, the phrases "issue" or "claim preclusion" rather than "*res judicata.*"

"Well, I co-wrote a brief for the US Supreme Court a few years ago," I said, "so I sure hope I wasn't guilty of including too many foreign words."

"Oh, really? What issues were raised in the brief?" Ruth asked.

"Uh . . . we were the respondents in a petition for *cert.*," I answered slowly, trying to remember what the heck the case had been about. "It was denied. Thanks for that." I smiled weakly. For the life of me I couldn't remember what the issues had been. Why on earth had I mentioned that damn brief?

---

55. A *cédille* is that hook that sometimes appears on the letter c in French.

"I think it involved preemption," I finally managed to say,[56] "but to tell you the truth, I can't remember exactly what it was about. I seem to be having a senior moment."

As soon as the words were out of my mouth, I realized how stupid that last comment was. Here I was, not yet fifty, talking to two people in their seventies, and I tell them I'm having a *senior moment*?

My mother and Ruth burst out laughing. "I'm not sure what that makes us," Mom said. "Geriatric?"

Ruth shook her head. "More like decrepit, I'd say."

Oh boy, I thought, hoping the rush of blood that had flooded my cheeks was not as visible as it felt. So much for my first attempt at "law talk." The one good thing about my inane comment, though, was that it sidetracked the earlier discussion, and the Supreme Court justice didn't question me further about my brief.

I took this opportunity to excuse myself and go turn on the fire under the sauce for the scallops and stir the mashed potatoes. Returning to the living room, I topped off our champagne glasses and offered the cashews and rice crackers around. Marty took a couple of rice crackers—probably just to be polite—but everyone else declined, no doubt saving themselves for the big meal ahead.

When I sat back down, I turned to listen to Marty and Dad and Robin's conversation. They were discussing taxes, and I cautioned myself to remain silent to avoid further embarrassment. Although I'd taken a tax law course in law school, what little knowledge I'd once possessed of the subject had quickly dissipated as soon as I'd completed the bar exam.

Robin, however, was and still is fascinated by the world of finance and reads widely on the subject. When she was

---

56. In fact, the brief didn't concern preemption at all. Rather, it involved convoluted issues arising from the California Emergency Medical Services Act and the competitive bid process for ambulance services and whether the ambulance company's petition raised issues of federal law. No wonder I couldn't remember.

considering going to law school, she had thought she might concentrate on tax law. Given Marty's high standing as a tax attorney and professor, she was surely pleased to have the opportunity to discuss the subject with him. "So how would you revamp the tax system?" she asked.

"I don't think that's going to happen any time soon," he replied.

"But hypothetically," Robin pressed. "If you were, say, king of the United States, how would you do it?"

"Ah. If I were king . . ." Marty leaned back in his chair with a smile and thought a moment. "Well. If I were *king*, I suppose I would institute some tax reforms along the lines of those ideas that have been proposed by Mike Graetz—he's a professor of tax law at Yale. Now, I'm not crazy about all of his ideas, but most seem to me good." Marty leaned toward Robin and continued. "For instance, he advocates exempting from the income tax families with incomes under a sizable amount, say $100,000, and initiating a broad-based tax on consumption—a value added tax—the system used widely outside the United States."

Robin was listening keenly and nodding as he spoke. My mind, however, started to drift away from the conversation at this point and to the scallops waiting in the kitchen, so I'm not exactly sure what she said in response, but it was something about employer-based tax-collecting systems resulting in more of a black market for employment.

"That's an astute comment," Marty responded, sounding like the professor he was. I came out of my reverie and glanced at Robin, who was beaming like a proud student. She later told me she'd thought it was a stupid statement as soon as she said it, so she was much relieved by his response.

They continued to talk taxes, and I excused myself once again to check on my sauce. The pan was simmering, so I turned it off. I'd wait a few more minutes and then add the butter and sear the scallops. After popping the black plates into the oven to warm them for the first course, I leaned against the counter and surveyed the room.

All the thought I'd put into tonight's menu—the hours of planning and preparation and attention to detail—was finally paying dividends, and everything seemed to be going smoothly. And, I realized with some surprise as my eyes took in the *mise en place* covering virtually every surface in the kitchen, I was hungry. *Really* hungry—and very much looking forward to eating the fabulous dinner to come.

Allowing myself a self-satisfied smile, I returned to the living room to join the others.

When I sat back down on the sofa, Marty was telling Robin and Dad a story about being a visiting law professor at Stanford the same year Ruth was a fellow there at the Center for Advanced Study in the Behavior Sciences. Being an avid golfer—he'd been on the golf team as an undergraduate at Cornell—he made a habit of playing nine holes in the mornings after dropping Ruth off at work, finishing in time to make it to the class he was teaching which started at ten. One morning after finishing his half-round, he ran into three students from his ten o'clock class who were just teeing off.

"Wanna join us?" they asked.

He replied, "No thanks. I have something else I have to do." Marty smiled at the memory and then told us he especially loved golfing at the Mauna Kea course on the Big Island of Hawai'i. "We used to go to Hawai'i every year," he said with a sigh, "until Ruth got a good job in Washington."

As Robin started to tell Marty about hiking out to see hot lava on the Big Island, I looked at my watch. Time to fire the first course. I interrupted Robin's story momentarily to tell her that everyone could start making their way to the dinner table in a minute or two and then excused myself to go back to the kitchen.

✦ *First Course: Seared Sea Scallop* ✦ *with Ginger-Lime Cream Sauce*

I stirred the cream sauce—it was still hot. Taking the stick of sweet butter from the fridge, I cut off several chunks and whisked them into the sauce one at a time. That done, I heated the skillet and dropped in another generous hunk of butter, smiling at the satisfying sizzle it made as it hit the hot pan. Once it had melted, I placed the six large scallops into the skillet, seasoned side down, and sprinkled pepper and salt on the other side.

Next I took the black plates from the oven, lined them up on the counter, and plucked the six nicest flowers from the orchid stalks I'd taken from the patio and set them next to the plates. The scallops had now browned nicely, so I flipped them over and turned off the heat under the pan. I was *not* going to overcook those tasty morsels.

At a movement in my periphery vision, I glanced up from my work. Robin had herded everyone into the dining room and was getting them seated in their designated places. As I was watching, she turned and came rushing into the kitchen. "The candles!" she said. "Where would I find matches?" I directed her to the drawer by the stove and she hurried back to the dining room.

Returning to the plates, I spooned a ladleful of sauce onto each one and placed a tiny purple orchid bloom on the top corner of each plate. I had just delicately set a plump, toasty-brown sea scallop in the center of each pool of ginger-lime cream sauce when Mom arrived in the kitchen, ready to help serve.

"Perfect timing," I told her. She reached for one of the plates. "Wait. The garnish. Pass me that custard cup, would you?" I sprinkled a dash of lime zest on each scallop, then, examining the plates with a critical eye, determined which two looked the best. "Give this one to Ruth and this one to

Marty," I directed my mom. "Serve the plates points up, like a diamond, and make sure the orchid is at the top corner."

We carried two plates each into the dining room. Robin had opened the Christie chardonnay and was pouring the glasses as we arrived with the scallops, explaining that the wine came from Santa Cruz, as did the red that we'd be having later.

Once everyone had been served, Marty raised his glass in a toast. "To the cook!"

"Thank you." I raised my glass in acknowledgement. "And you should know I'm a cook in more than one way," I said with a wink at my mom, "as that's my mother's maiden name—Cook."

Marty cut off a piece of scallop, dipped it in the sauce, and tasted it. "Mmm, delicious," he pronounced. I smiled proudly. "We just can't get good scallops in DC," he added as he cut off another bite.

Gulp. He obviously thought they were fresh. I didn't have the nerve to tell him they were regular old frozen scallops, same as they could get back East. Luckily, Robin spoke at that moment, so I was saved from having to make a confession.

"I forgot the water," she said, standing up. "Who would like carbonated water, and who would like still?"

"Oh—the fizzy water is Gerolsteiner," I announced enthusiastically. "I bought it in honor of Levi Leipheimer, who rides for their team and who I'm hoping will win the inaugural Tour of California next month." Blank stares from Ruth and Marty. "It's a bicycle race . . ." I started to explain, but I could see this was not a subject of much interest to either of them. "Anyway, here it is, for anyone who wants it." I took the bottle from the tea cart next to me and handed it to Robin.

"No water for me, thank you," Ruth politely responded.

"Nor I," said Marty. Dad declined as well, but Mom and I both asked for the Gerolsteiner. Robin—who did not take any water either—sat back down.

We ate our scallops in silence for a few moments. Before the pause in conversation became obvious, Robin—eager to discuss opera with Ruth—asked her about the time she had been a guest on the Met's opera show. Ruth's eyes lit up. "That was the highlight of my life," she said.

Really? I thought. *That's interesting, given all she's done and accomplished.*

"I remember you told a story about seeing Maria Callas on an elevator," Robin prompted her.

"Yes." Ruth smiled and set her fork down, took a sip of wine, and recounted the story for us. She spoke quietly but deliberately, choosing her words carefully. She had come to Washington, she said, to argue a sex discrimination case before the US Supreme Court and was waiting in the hotel for the elevator.

"And when the door opened, there was Maria Callas, dressed all in white, wearing a white mink coat and holding a white poodle in her arms. I thought to myself, it's a sign; I will surely win this case! And so it turned out." Ruth paused a moment. "Callas has always been a great favorite of mine," she added, eyes gleaming.

During most of the evening up until that point, Ruth had tended to keep her head tilted slightly down, looking at her plate, even as she spoke—a habit that had the effect of making her seem withdrawn. But when she told us the story of seeing Maria Callas, her body language was entirely different; she sat up taller with her head held high and looked us directly in the eyes, a smile on her face. This was the most animated that I saw her the entire night.

She must have felt the same way I did meeting her *for the first time*, I realized. Or Diane Keaton last night. Even Supreme Court justices get starstruck. Fancy that.

"So I gather you're going to see Robert Wilson's *Butterfly* tomorrow," Robin continued. "We just saw his *Parsifal* here last month."

Mom and I giggled at the memory, and Ruth glanced our way. "It was rather heavy handed on the symbolism," I explained. "And the stage direction was bizarrely formal, which seemed at odds with a Wagner opera. Didn't you think so, Robin? She's a great Wagnerian," I added, nodding toward Robin.

"Yes, I've seen his productions." Ruth said with just the hint of a smile.

"Also, Plácido Domingo had a cold, so we didn't get to hear him sing the night we were there," Mom added.

"That's a shame," said Ruth. "He's a *wonder*."

"Too bad the *Butterfly* we're seeing tomorrow is also Robert Wilson." Dad commented and then shrugged. "But that was what the LA Opera was doing this weekend, so we didn't have any choice . . ."

"Oh," Ruth interjected, "but the music is magnificent!"

I stood up from the table at this point to go turn on the fire under the soup, marveling at the justice's take on life—so optimistic and so willing to see all sides of an issue. So very *kind*.

When I returned, Marty was asking the table a riddle. He had written six numbers on a piece of paper—125, 96, 72, 59, 42, and 14—and we were to fill in the next entry in the sequence after 14.

We all pondered for a minute, me wondering if this was a tactic Marty employed at all dinner parties. Did he always have a few party tricks up his sleeve, knowing how taciturn his wife could appear at social engagements? In any case, his riddle was a charming example of a conversation concierge doing his best to put the rest of the table at ease.

"Okay," Dad said after a bit, "they're not all multiples of the same number, and they're not prime numbers . . ." My father, a great fan of games like this, was thinking out loud with his brow furrowed. Marty, as well as Ruth—who no doubt had heard this riddle before—were both smiling, bemused at our cogitation.

"I give up," I said. I don't have much patience for number games; I prefer words.

"Me too," said my mom. Robin and Dad thought about it for another minute and then also said they didn't know.

Marty gave us a hint. "Do not assume it's a math problem." We thought some more and then all shook our heads again. "The next entry is Brooklyn Bridge," Marty prompted us.

As realization started to dawn on me, Marty provided the answer: "They are the express stops on the Lexington Avenue line of the New York subway system," he announced with a triumphant flourish.

"Oh, no fair!" I cried. "We're all Californians and you're from back East and used to live in New York City."

Talking about the New York subway led to a discussion of cars, and Ruth informed us proudly that she still drove a twenty-two-year-old Volvo. "I have a story about that car," she said. While sitting as an appellate judge for the DC Circuit, she told us, she used to drive that Volvo—then rather new—to work. Driving into the parking lot at the courthouse necessitated passing through a bollard that would lower automatically upon proper authorization—either from a key card or a guard, I forget which. The bollard would then rise back up after the car had passed over.

"But one day, being in a hurry, I attempted to follow another car over the bollard before it rose," Ruth said. Alas, she did not succeed. The bollard started to go back up before she passed over, and it raised her car up with Ruth sitting helpless and embarrassed in the driver's seat, suspended in air, until someone was able to get the bollard to lower again. We all laughed, imagining the sight.

Robin stood to clear the first course plates—from the right, as I had shown her. As she started to set my plate on top of Ruth's, I hissed under my breath, "Don't stack the plates when you clear!" This was one of the first rules we had learned waiting tables in the student-run restaurant during cooking school.

"Sorry," Robin whispered back, and took the two plates, one in each hand, to the kitchen. I excused myself and followed her to prepare the next course.

❖ *Second Course: Roasted Butternut Squash Soup with Brown Butter* ❖

The soup had started to boil, forming large thick bubbles that, as they burst, were splattering bright orange soup all over the stove and tile walls. *Oh well, no time to clean that up now.* I stirred the pan and turned it down to low, then set the flame on high under the cast-iron skillet in which I had seared the scallops.

Next I spread the white plates out on the counter and set the bowls on top of them. Choosing the six best of my pilfered nasturtium flowers and leaves, I carefully placed one of each on the plates.

Back to the stove, I shook out my hands to release the pent-up energy that had returned once more to my body. Then, checking the water level under the potatoes—there was still plenty—I gave them another stir. Next I cut off half a stick of butter and slid it into the hot pan. As the butter melted, I used a spatula to scrape up the bits that had settled on the bottom. I let it cook until it turned a hazelnut brown, then poured the brown butter into the pot of soup and stirred it in.

Robin was standing by, ready to serve. I ladled soup into each bowl and then squeezed crème fraîche from my squirt bottle in a spiral pattern on top. Next I drizzled on a bit of roasted walnut oil (Gaby was right; it did provide a lovely, shimmery effect) and finished them off with a sprinkling of chopped nuts.

"*Voilà*. Give these two to Ruth and Marty," I directed Robin, indicated the two I thought had the best spirals and prettiest flowers. "Flowers on the right, with their blooms facing the guests."

"Nice presentation," said Robin. "It looks like something you'd get at The French Laundry—and not just because of where the recipe came from." Grabbing the two soups, she carried them out to the dining room.

Once everyone was served, Robin poured another round of chardonnay. When she asked Ruth if she wanted more wine, the justice gave a slight nod.

Trying not to be obvious, I watched as Ruth tasted the soup. She took a small sip from her spoon and swallowed, then turned to face me. "This is wonderful," she declared. After a slight pause, she added, "And that scallop was scrumptious." I let out a breath of relief. As she hadn't said anything about the scallop during the first course, I'd been afraid she hadn't liked the dish.

I tried a spoonful of soup. It was, indeed, tasty. The nutty flavors of the brown butter, the chopped walnuts, the roasted walnut oil, and the soup itself all complemented each other well. And, I was happy to note, it was not too sweet. Next I tasted the soup followed by a sip of wine. *Heaven*. The notes of acid and pear positively exalted the taste of the soup, and in combination the flavors seemed to sparkle on the tongue.

Delighted, I set down my glass and asked Marty, "So which part of DC do you live in?

He swallowed the spoonful of soup in his mouth before answering. "Foggy Bottom."

"Oh, we stayed in that part of town once. It's the best neighborhood in the city, I think."

"Yes," Robin chimed in. "My sister-in-law's aunt and uncle live there. We met them at my nephew's bar mitzvah a few years ago, and they invited us to come stay with them when we visited DC."

"Oh?" Ruth glanced up from her soup at this remark, and I watched as her eyes were drawn to Dad's beloved mid-century bar behind Robin, upon which sat a large, brass menorah.

Robin told me later that this "Jew-dropping," as she termed it, was deliberate. Her intent had been to signal her affinity with the Jewish culture, as well as cause a mental double take on the part of the Ginsburgs, since—with her ruddy complexion and fair hair—Robin looks about as un-Jewish as anyone can (she's been told by many Jewish friends over the years that she looks like "such a *shiksa*"). She therefore wanted to jog any preconceptions they may have had about her, given her appearance—not to mention her professed love of Wagner—and let them know that she "got" and appreciated their culture.

My family, on the other hand—with our olive skin and dark hair and eyes—apparently looks or acts (whatever that means) quite Jewish. I remember my junior high Spanish teacher, Señorita Esquivel, asking me once, "Now Leslie, as a Jew, what do you think about—?" And just the previous year, our choral director, Cheryl, had asked me how to pronounce the Hebrew text we were singing. Even the piano player in my old country-rock band, whom I'd known for over twenty years—himself a Jew—had always assumed that I was an "M.O.T." (i.e., a "member of the tribe"), I discovered one day.

Watching Ruth gaze at our family's menorah, I realized that she and Marty likely thought we were Jewish, too; had probably assumed so ever since meeting Dad back in the 1960s. And now they had come to my parents' house and there was a menorah in the dining room, substantiating their belief.

But the funny thing is, our family *isn't* Jewish. According to our genealogy (as well as a DNA test I recently took), we're primarily German, Irish, and Welsh. As for that menorah, my mom loved to tell the story of how her mother had purchased it at a rummage sale back in the 1930s, thinking she had gotten a great deal on a marvelous candelabra. Now, my grandmother—Deedee to us grandkids—was most certainly *not* Jewish, and in fact had rather anti-Semitic leanings. My mom and her sister, who knew the truth about the "candle holder," loved this irony and never told Deedee the truth about her precious candelabra.

I smiled to myself and refocused on the group's conversation. Robin was telling the Ginsburgs about her diverse family, which spanned a wide spectrum of spiritual beliefs, including her United Methodist parents; her Jewish brother; her identical twin brothers, one an evangelic Christian and the other a follower of the teachings of Seth and a believer in multiple planes of existence; and herself, an atheist.

As conversations have a way of doing, this one now meandered about, eventually finding its way to the subject of the Virginia Military Institute case, which my father had mentioned the day before in his introductory remarks.

"Nino sent his slings and arrows at *the Chief*, that time," Ruth proclaimed with a sly, cat-who-ate-the-canary smile.

Marty glanced at his wife. "Well, he sent some your way, too," he said.

Ruth chose to ignore this comment and told us gleefully how Justice Scalia, who normally launched his slings and arrows *her* way, had been the lone dissenter in the VMI decision. He therefore instead chose to direct his ire at Chief Justice Rehnquist, who had joined the majority in a concurring opinion.

Having been close friends, Ruth and Nino were surely highly competitive with each other, a competition that was no doubt further fueled by the polar positions they took on so many of the cases that came before the Court. And then, on this issue—the one closest to her heart—she had won a decisive victory, with Nino being the sole holdout.

From the way Ruth described it to us that night, the Virginia Military Institute case seemed to have been a symbolic turning point for her, as it signified her finally having convinced "the Chief" to agree with her on this fundamental issue of equality for women. In a way, her entire legal career had led up to the VMI decision, and with it, her life's work had finally been fulfilled: a woman's place at the table was now assured.

She had earned the right to wear that sly little smile.

INTERLUDE

From the moment she co-founded the ACLU's Women's Rights Project in 1972, Ruth Ginsburg's overarching goal had been to achieve for sex discrimination cases the heightened standard of review applied to cases involving race and national origin—that of strict scrutiny.

In order to survive a court's evaluation under this standard, the law in question must have been enacted to further "a compelling governmental interest" and have been "narrowly tailored" to accomplish that interest. The test is so stringent that it's often said that strict scrutiny is "strict in name, but fatal in practice."

But in all her years as an advocate for the equal citizenship stature of women and men, Ginsburg didn't achieve this goal; the closest she came was an intermediate standard of review, at a level well below that of "strict scrutiny." Then, just three years after joining the Supreme Court, she was presented with the opportunity to finish the job.

The case was *United States v. Virginia*,[57] in which the Justice Department was challenging the Virginia Military Institute's refusal to admit female students. VMI claimed that allowing women into the school would undermine its mission of training its cadets by

57. The opinion, at 518 US 515 (1996), is commonly referred to as the VMI decision.

way of an "adversarial method," which incorporated a culture of ritualized hazing not unlike Marine Corps boot camp. But once the case reached the Supreme Court, it became quickly apparent that the Institute was going to lose.

RBG almost didn't get the chance to pen the opinion that many now consider her crowning achievement. When the votes in conference ended up being six to two in favor of the government (Justice Thomas had recused himself because he had a son at VMI), the opinion was originally assigned to Justice O'Connor. The senior woman justice, however, recognizing the implications of the case and what it meant to her younger colleague, turned it down. "This should be Ruth's," she said.

Ginsburg went to work. Before drafting her opinion, she first had to decide how far she could push the five others in agreement with her (everyone but Rehnquist and Scalia). Should she press for strict scrutiny? This would be risky, for to do so could mean losing the votes of both O'Connor and Kennedy.

Caution prevailed, and she steered the safer course—ultimately swaying even the Chief Justice to her side in the process. But her opinion was a paragon of craftsmanship, and the level of scrutiny RBG invoked, though not technically "strict," was as close to that standard of review as possible without actually bearing the name. In an opinion replete with citations to the cases she herself had won through the years as attorney for the WRP, the justice enunciated a new standard of review, whereby the government must show "exceedingly persuasive justification" for any law or action that differentiates on the basis of gender.

In sum, she held in the Court's majority opinion, "generalizations about 'the way women are,' estimates of what is appropriate for most women, no longer justify denying opportunity to women whose talent and capacity place them outside the average description."

Justice Scalia was the lone dissenter. And in his fuming opinion, he ironically accomplished what Ruth could not, by asserting that the standard of review articulated by Ginsburg in the VMI decision is "indistinguishable from strict scrutiny."

She had finally won the fight.

• • •

The dinner discussion now turned to women in nontraditional employment, and Robin, after telling Ruth and Marty about her various jobs as custodian, journeyman electrician, and facilities manager, excitedly recounted how she'd gotten the candle wax out of the carpet that morning, pointing out the now-clean spot where the wax had been.

She still cringes when she remembers this story, embarrassed how she must have come across as bragging to a Supreme Court justice and celebrated tax attorney about her cleaning prowess. "They both gave me blanks stares when I said it," Robin told me the next morning. But, she insists, the point she was *trying* to make was that through Ruth's work—first as an advocate for equal treatment of women, and later through her judicial decisions such as in the VMI case—the justice had played an important part in making Robin's nontraditional career choices possible.

"I would never have been able to be an electrician without the work that Ruth and others like her had done," she explained to me. "It's amazing, when you think about it." Robin paused and then continued: "And I guess I felt that the wax-free carpet was symbolic of all that." She shook her head with a snort. "But, boy, was that a dorky way of trying to get my point across."

◈ *Third Course: Baby Spinach Salad* ◈ *with Blood Orange, Red Onion, Dried Cranberries, Pine Nuts, and Gorgonzola Cheese*

The next course was easy. While Mom cleared the soup dishes, I fetched the salads from the fridge in the Peacock Room and set them on the kitchen counter. Whisking the vinaigrette one last time, I drizzled it over the six plates. Next, I sprinkled on the pine nuts, and they were set to go.

Robin opened the second bottle of chardonnay (that little nod from Ruth again, when asked if she would like more) as Mom and I served the salads.

"Oooh, blood oranges," Marty exclaimed as I set down his plate.

"Yes, they're from my garden—I've never seen them for sale in this country. I was worried they wouldn't ripen in time for the dinner, but they seem to be okay. They're not too tart, I hope."

Marty tasted one. "Delicious," he proclaimed, and I beamed.

The talk turned to President Bush—W, not Senior. I knew of course that the Ginsburgs were liberals and likely not great fans of his, but I didn't want to put them on the spot by saying anything disparaging about him. After all, in her position as Supreme Court justice, it probably wouldn't be proper for Ruth to bad-mouth the president, or any other government figure for that matter.

So instead, I mentioned that before becoming president, George Bush had stated that he would love to be the commissioner of Major League Baseball. Perhaps that would be a good job for him once his presidential term was up, I suggested.

Marty apparently had no qualms about voicing his opinion of the president. "He couldn't do that either," he snorted, shaking his head dismissively.

Ruth didn't comment on Marty's response and just kept eating her salad. To change the subject, I said something about a television show that had premiered that season. "Well, I think Geena Davis makes a great president. Have you ever seen *Commander in Chief*?" Stupid, *stupid*! I thought to myself immediately. *Like they really have time to watch TV when they get home from work?*

"Martin Sheen is *my* president," Ruth replied with a mischievous grin, then took a sip of wine.

"Really? I mean, yeah, I agree—he's great." I was taken aback by her comment. "Do you watch *The West Wing*?"

"He was in my Lamaze class when I was pregnant with my daughter," the justice responded.

"Was his wife pregnant with Charlie or Emilio?" Robin asked, ever curious about movie trivia.

"It was Charlie, their oldest." Ruth cut a bite of blood orange and smiled. She ate the orange piece and then told us about the time Martin Sheen came to visit the Supreme Court and how everyone was starstruck by him. Robin and I exchanged knowing glances.

As Ruth was telling her Martin Sheen story, a loud noise erupted from the back of the house. She stopped talking and we all looked at each other.

"That sounded like a pack of coyotes," I said, prompting giggles from the table.

"Was that the *marshals*?" Mom wondered aloud.

"I'll go see," I said, pushing back my chair. As I walked down the hall, I heard laughter coming from the den. The five marshals—four men and one woman—were sitting on the couch and easy chairs watching television, empty plates and soup bowls on the coffee table in front of them. They quieted down when I came in.

"I just need to use the restroom," I said, which was partly true. When I came back out, I stopped to chat. "What are you watching?" I asked. It was a rerun of the comedy sketch show *In Living Color*, and they were clearly enjoying the program.

The marshal I had spoken to the night before—the one from Austin with the wry sense of humor—thanked me for the dinner and the others concurred.

"Well, I figure your job is kind of like being in the band that plays at a wedding," I said. "You know, being at parties and social events, but not as one of the guests. I used to be in a band that played at weddings, and I always appreciated it when we got fed."

They might have thought the comparison strange—being a federal marshal who protects a Supreme Court justice is, I grant you, a far more important job than playing music at a wedding. But they laughed politely and let me take a close look at their small round badges, which—I must say—have shrunk considerably since the days of Matt Dillon of *Gunsmoke* fame.

"So, do you always guard Supreme Court justices, or does your detail vary?" I asked. Charles, the head marshal, told me that he was the only one of the five there whose job was limited to guarding Supreme Court justices; the others performed other marshal duties as well.

"I bet that's a plum gig," I told Charles. "You must be a pretty darn good marshal." I turned to the others. "So you all must do the grunt work, like transporting prisoners, huh? Just like Karen Sisco," I added with a grin.

They rolled their collective eyes at this reference to the Elmore Leonard character, a federal marshal who has a habit of falling for her charges. "Sometimes," Mr. Austin replied with an enigmatic smile.

In case you're wondering, federal marshals perform a variety of tasks. As explained on the US Marshals Service website, "among their many duties, they arrest more than half of all federal fugitives, protect the federal judiciary, operate the Witness Security Program, transport federal prisoners and seize property acquired through illegal activities." What amazing stories, I mused, must have been collected over the years by those five individuals who were now sitting around my parents' den, eating my soup, and watching *In Living Color*.

I returned to the dining room and reported that yes, it had been the marshals that we had heard, and that they were entertaining themselves watching television.

"Do you always have *five* marshals when you go out to dinner at someone's house?" Robin asked Marty. "I mean, it seems rather excessive, don't you think?" She stood up to start clearing the salad plates. "I'm thinking maybe I ought to write someone in the federal government to complain about what a waste of the taxpayers' money it is," she teased.

"Don't you dare!" Marty responded quickly in a mock stern voice. But although he knew Robin was kidding, I could tell a part of him was serious: he did *not* want anyone taking away those wonderful marshals.[58] As we all laughed, Robin collected Marty's and Mom's plates, and I followed her out to the kitchen with Dad's and Ruth's. Ruth, I observed, had not eaten her red onions.

Fourth Course: Blackened Ahi, Served with Wasabi Mashed Potatoes and Snow Peas

Glancing at the large dinner plates on the kitchen counter, I realized I'd forgotten to put them in the oven to warm. *Oops*. But if I did it now, they should be warm by the time the course was ready to serve. Next, I lit the flame under the cast-iron skillet I'd used for the scallops, melted a generous chunk of butter in it, then grabbed the bag of snow peas and dumped them into the pan.

As the peas were sautéing, I realized I needed a third skillet,

58. I later learned that both Justice Ginsburg and Justice O'Connor had been targets of death threats less than a year earlier, hence Marty's concern.

since the ahi would require two. I pulled out one of Mom's, moved the peas to the back burner, and set the two pans for the ahi on the front burners and turned them on high. After a quick stir of the mashed potatoes and the snow peas, I poured a little sesame oil into the ahi pans and turned on the fan above the stove.

Once the two skillets were blistering hot, I set three ahi steaks in each one and was rewarded with a gratifying searing sound as they hit the pan. It didn't take long for them to blacken nicely, and I carefully flipped them over with a spatula and immediately turned off the heat under both pans. I wanted to keep that luscious tuna nice and rare inside.

Okay, were the plates ready yet? Opening the oven, I gingerly reached in to touch the stack. *Good.* Spreading the warm plates out on the tile counter, I brought over the pot of mashed potatoes and spooned a dollop onto the top third section of each one.

Now to see if my idea for the snow pea presentation would work. Experimenting with the first plate, I spread seven peas out in a fan shape below and to the left of the potatoes. *Yes!* No one else would likely even notice, but I was ridiculously pleased with myself to see that they resembled a wave erupting from the center of the plate.

Finally, I fetched the ahi skillets and set each steak to the right of the peas, leaning on the mashed potatoes. I retrieved my beloved pea sprout garnishes from the fridge and placed one atop of each piece of fish, finishing the plates with a sprinkling of black sesame seeds on the mashed potatoes.

I then exhaled a deep sigh of relief. All the cooking was done—*fini*! Now I could truly relax.

As I carried two plates into the dining room, Robin jumped up from the table and hurried into the kitchen to get two more. I set Ruth's plate down in front of her.

"How pretty!" she said. "What is it?"

"It's blackened ahi," I announced to the table, "with wasabi mashed potatoes and snow peas."

"Oh, I *love* fish," Ruth responded.

"Yes, I know," I said with a wink at Marty.

By the time I returned with the last two plates, Robin was opening the red wine. She poured glasses for everyone and set the bottle on the table. "It's called le Cigare Volant," Robin explained. "See, there's a drawing on the label of a flying saucer—or cigar—hovering over a vineyard."

"Yeah," I interjected. "And there's a great story on the back of the bottle—*and* it has to do with the law." I picked up the bottle and read aloud to the table:

> *In 1954 the village council of Châteauneuf-du-Pape was quite perturbed and apprehensive that flying saucers or "flying cigars" might do damage to their vineyards were they to land therein. So, right-thinking men all, they passed an ordinance prohibiting the landing of flying saucers or flying cigars . . . in their vineyards. (This ordinance has worked well in discouraging such landings.) Further, any flying saucers or flying cigars that did land were to be taken immediately to the pound.*
>
> *We encourage terrestrial visitation to our winery. Please visit us corporeally [I had a bit of a problem pronouncing this last word, having now imbibed some four glasses of wine during the evening] at 10 Pine Flat Road, Santa Cruz . . .*

I set the bottle back down on the ceramic wine caddy that Mom had made. "Oh, and check this out," I concluded. "It's got a screw cap with an alien's head on the top." They all examined the alien-head screw cap, which I passed around the table for everyone to admire. "More fun than passing around a musty old cork to smell, huh?"

Ruth picked up the bottle and examined it. "In France they don't put the percentage on wine bottles," she observed.

Mistakenly thinking she was referring to the alcohol percentage that was printed on the label (I realized in retrospect that she meant the percentage of the grape varietals), I responded, "Well, in California, they're required by law to put that on." Pause. "But I guess I don't need to tell *you* that . . ." I trailed off lamely. *Dumb, dumb!*

Ruth politely ignored my comment and tried the wine. "That's quite good," she pronounced. Marty and Mom and Dad tasted theirs and they all concurred. We then dug into our main course and the table was momentarily quiet, except for the clicking of silverware against ceramics, punctuated with the odd "*mmm*" and other appreciative utterances.

I tasted my fish. It was crunchy on the outside and rare inside, and the seasoning seemed correctly balanced. Glancing around the table to make sure everyone else's was cooked right, I saw that they all had a bright red center, as they should. The snow peas were good too—still crisp, and nice and buttery. Next I tasted the mashed potatoes.

Uh, oh.

They were way too dry. *Damn!* This was obviously the result of the long period of time they'd spent over the simmering water, during which they had continued to cook. I didn't say anything—one should never apologize for one's own cooking at the table, as it's bad form, and often the guests don't even detect the problem unless it's pointed out to them. But I knew the others couldn't help but notice that the potatoes were not moist and creamy as they should be. (Robin later confirmed that *she* had noticed.) I clearly should have whisked in more hot cream and butter right before service, which would have rehabilitated them from the drying out they suffered sitting over the double boiler for so long. *Oh well, live and learn.*

As I was angsting over my cooking, Marty—who seemed not the least bit troubled by the flawed potatoes—was regaling the table with cooking tales of his own. I shook off my disappointment. So it wouldn't be a perfect dinner; that was okay. I'd heard that Japanese artists always intentionally put a flaw in each work of art, as only God can be perfect. (Of course, this presumes that the artwork *would* be perfect unless one intentionally added the flaw, which seems rather presumptuous, and also contradicts the premise that only God is perfect, but whatever . . .)

I tuned back into the discussion. Marty was explaining how the Ginsburg and Scalia families would always get together each New Year's Eve for a huge dinner party. "Nino goes down to Louisiana every year to kill Bambi," he told us wryly. "After they shoot the poor thing, he and his cohorts do a rough cut and then drag the bloody carcass back to DC for me to prepare for dinner. Last year I carved venison steaks from the loin for *nineteen* people." Marty took another bite of ahi and chewed it with relish. "Ruth, of course, is not keen on venison; she prefers the striped bass."

Her eyes lit up when Marty mentioned the bass. "Oh, yes," she agreed. "One of Marty's assistants fishes Chesapeake Bay on Sundays and often brings back striped bass for us."

Marty turned to me. "I fillet it and drizzle lime juice on top, and then sauté the fillets in butter."

Ruth was nodding as he told me his recipe. "It's delicious," she said when he had finished.

"Yeah, I agree," I jumped in. "I once spent a few days on a houseboat in the Sacramento Delta with some friends, and we caught a few striped bass which I cooked for the group. I fried it in butter too, but with garlic instead of lime. I'd never had it before; it was amazing."

"One of the women on that trip was our friend Valerie, who was the—I guess you'd call it an officiator—at our wedding,"

Robin informed the Ginsburgs. "She started the ceremony by telling the guests that she was neither a minister nor a judge but that she *was* the daughter of a retired California Superior Court Judge, which made the ceremony 'extra legal.'"

Ruth and Marty and my folks smiled at my story, and Ruth remarked that she occasionally performs weddings. "Though in some states I can't," she added.

"Maybe you should become a Universal Life minister," I joked. "Then you could perform weddings in all the states." Although I didn't observe any response from Ruth, this comment prompted a smile from Marty.

"California recently passed a really broad domestic partnership law, though," Robin observed. "I don't know *how* they got that legislation through, but they did. So whereas I used to refer to myself as Ken and Smiley's 'out-law,' I now really am their legal *in*-law." (This was well before the repeal of DOMA and the subsequent Supreme Court ruling invalidating same-sex marriage bans. But thanks in part to RBG, Robin and I are now "officially" married.)

Dad raised his wine glass towards Robin. "And we're glad you are," he said.

"Yay for California," I said, lifting my glass as well.

Marty and Robin and Mom and I continued to chat—about cooking, mostly—and Robin opened the second bottle of Cigare Volant and poured another round. Once again, Ruth gave that little nod of assent when Robin proffered the bottle. I did a quick calculation and figured she'd had some six glasses of wine (counting the Champagne) during the evening, but she was still, dare I say it, sober as a judge.

In fact, she was having a very judge-like and earnest conversation at that moment with my father. I listened in and determined they were discussing some current issue of constitutional law. I was happy for Dad—I knew he must have been pleased finally to have Ruth to himself for some law talk.

But as I watched the two, their faces lit up with joy, a wave of melancholy passed over me. Why couldn't I feel this way about *my* work? Was it worth it, doing a job that provided virtually no pleasure, merely because it paid well? Dad and Ruth hadn't gone into their professions simply for the money. They truly loved the law—it was their life's passion.

Didn't I deserve the same?

With a sigh, I turned back to Marty and Robin and Mom's conversation about the magnificence of Hawaiian papayas. Food. Now *that* gave me pleasure. What if I could write about food and cooking, as opposed to the law?

After a few minutes I stood to clear the main course dishes. Ruth, I couldn't help noticing with a pang, had left some of the too-dry mashed potatoes on her plate. She'd eaten everything else though—even the pea sprout garnish.

❖ *Fifth Course: A Selection of Pastries from Amandine Pâtisserie* ❖

My mother joined me in the kitchen with two more plates while Robin took coffee and tea orders for the dessert course. "I think it's going splendidly!" Mom said, setting down the dishes to give me a tight hug. "Everything has been absolutely *delicious*. I think the Ginsburgs are mighty impressed."

"Maybe. I mean, I hope so. But you know they must have had countless elegant meals over the years."

"Surely none any better than this one," Mom declared. And who was I to argue with my mother? As she went back to get the last of the plates, I fetched the dessert—in that lovely pink box—from the Peacock Room.

"Three coffees, for Ken, Ruth, and Marty—real, not decaf—and no teas," Robin announced, popping her head into the kitchen, then quickly retreating.

"Do you want anything?" I asked Mom when she returned with the dishes.

"None for me," she said.

"Me neither." I can't have caffeine after about 2:00 p.m., or I get terrible insomnia; even having a decaf or a Coke with dinner can have disastrous results. Ending a large meal with a demitasse of espresso is a marvelous thing, however. It fires up the digestion, and it tastes *so good*. I was therefore truly looking forward to retirement, when Robin and I could become "ladies who lunch," and I too could sip coffee as a *digestif*.

"I'll take the cups and saucers out to the dining room," said Mom.

"No, don't," I responded quickly. "Bring them into the kitchen instead. The glass carafe that goes with our coffee maker is chipped and stained and pretty ratty looking."

After grinding the beans and getting the coffee brewing, I set about arranging the pastries on a round glass platter that Mom had discovered going through her dishes in preparation for the dinner. It too had been a wedding present in 1950, and Mom had never used it before now.

My first concept—having the slices face points out, like a star—didn't work, as the platter wasn't large enough, so I had to make do with them arranged like an already-cut pie, points facing the center.

My mom's friend Kirsten had loaned her a silver server—"in case we needed an extra one for the dinner"—and we'd decided to use it for the dessert course so that Kirsten could later brag that it had been used to serve a Supreme Court justice, which was of course the real reason she had loaned it to Mom. I set the server down next to the platter.

Next, I poured half-and-half into the Printemps china creamer and put the sugar cubes in the sugar bowl and took them out to the dining room. "The coffee's almost ready," I announced.

When the coffee had finished brewing, I poured the three cups and Mom helped me carry them out. I returned with the platter of pastries. "These are from a local *pâtisserie*," I explained. "I'm not much of a baker, so I decided to let an expert make our dessert. Robin conducted extensive research and determined that the place these are from—Amandine—had the best pastries in these parts."

I offered the platter for Ruth's inspection. "You get first pick, as the guest of honor." I indicated the slices. "This is a chocolate mousse and praline tart—there are two of those—and this one's chocolate ganache. And these are lemon chiffon, strawberry and crème fraîche, and cheesecake."

Ruth chose a slice of chocolate mousse and praline tart, and I served it to her with Kirsten's silver server. I offered the pastries to Marty next, and he took the slice of lemon chiffon tart. Dad next. As Mom and I had guessed, he opted for the chocolate ganache tart, being ever the chocoholic. Robin chose the cheesecake, and Mom took the other mousse and praline tart, leaving me with the slice of strawberry and crème fraîche tart. This was of course fine with me, since it had *cream*.

After I settled into my chair and we'd all tasted our pastries, Robin caught Mom and me up on the conversation we'd missed. "Marty's been telling us about how he's perfected a method for making the perfect baguette."

"Oh, really?" This was interesting news. It's nearly impossible to get a good baguette in Santa Cruz—you know: with a hard crunchy crust and soft and tender inside. No doubt this is because a true French-style baguette goes stale in only a few hours, and the turn-over simply isn't high enough in our town to justify making them the traditional way. So instead, the bakers tend to add sugar or oil to the dough, which increases their life span but makes for a mediocre baguette. But if I could make them myself . . .

"What's your secret?" I asked eagerly.

"I spent several years tinkering with the recipe until I got it just right," Marty answered. "Several things are key: using the right kind of flour—it should have a high protein content—and the appropriate amount of spring water for the dough. And instant yeast, as well as the correct oven temperature. And you have to use a baking stone." He took a sip of coffee as we waited for him to continue. "And, finally, if you place a very hot pan on the oven floor and throw in a couple of ice cubes, you get the perfect flash of steam, which is necessary to ensure a hard and crunchy crust."

"Would you be willing to share the recipe?" I asked. "I mean, I know I said I'm not much of a baker, but I *would* bake if I could make a real French-style baguette."

"Well, I've never written it down, as it's really all in the method," he said. "But if you want, you can call me sometime and I'll describe to you how I make them."

"I'll do that. Thanks!"[59]

I stood up. "Would anyone like more coffee?" I asked, observing that Ruth had finished her cup. Ruth gave her little nod, and I went to the kitchen to get the pot. Once there, I remembered that I hadn't wanted to bring the carafe into the dining room. *Dang*. Well, I wasn't going to go back for Ruth's cup now; that would be weird. I'd simply have to be quick about it and hope she didn't notice the stains and cracks.

As I refilled her cup, I was relieved to see that Ruth paid no heed; she and Dad had resumed their law talk, which was commanding her full attention. My father declined more coffee, but Marty had seconds.

"Marty says that Ruth drinks fourteen cups of coffee a day," Robin told me as I was pouring his cup.

---

59. I did indeed phone Marty several weeks later, and he explained his baguette method to me. When I tried it out, I found he was right: they were *incroyables*! The transcription I made of his recipe can be found in *Chef Supreme*, the collection of Marty's recipes published by the Supreme Court Historical Society after his death.

“Really?” I looked at him incredulously.

Marty smiled and told me yes, that she did indeed. “Isn’t it true, Ruth?” he said. “That you drink fourteen cups of coffee a day?”

Ruth interrupted her conversation with my father—so she *was* paying attention to what else was going on at the table; impressive—and nodded yes in response to Marty’s question, then turned back to Dad.

She must have the metabolism of a hummingbird, I marveled. To be able to drink that much coffee (not to mention wine), and to eat meals like we’d had and stay so petite. *Except instead of having wings that flap thousands of times a minute, it’s her brain that’s constantly in overdrive.*

I took the coffee pot back to the kitchen and returned to the table. Dad and Ruth were still deep in conversation, and Mom and Marty were discussing the plans for tomorrow, with Robin listening in. The marshals would pick my parents up at UCLA and drive them downtown along with Ruth and Marty. (*What fun to get to ride in the marshals’ car!*) First would be a private tour of the Disney Hall, then lunch across the street at Kendall’s Brasserie, and then the opera at the Dorothy Chandler Pavilion.

We were chatting gaily about the following day’s activities when Marty glanced over at Ruth and announced, “I think it’s time to go.”

Robin and I looked at each other. Had Marty seen something that we’d missed? Although Ruth seemed completely engrossed in her conversation with Dad, maybe he could tell she was tired. Or maybe he was the one who was tired. It was almost eleven o’clock, after all. And they were no doubt still on DC time. Given the jam-packed weekend they were having, I could certainly understand their wanting to get back to the hotel.

We all stood. I retrieved Ruth’s purse from the hall, again intrigued by its weight, and we commenced the obligatory, drawn-out leave-taking process. Marty and I exchanged

French-style *bises*, and he thanked me for the dinner. I told him I'd call about the baguette recipe.

Everyone else said their goodbyes, and Ruth told Dad she really did want to co-teach a class with him some time in the near future. This was obviously something they had spoken about during their law talk.

I turned to Ruth. "That was a wonderful dinner, Leslie," she said to me.

This was the first time she'd called me by name, and it gave me a bit of a thrill, hearing her say it aloud. I stepped forward to shake her hand . . . or something—I wasn't quite sure what was appropriate—but she saved me from having to decide what to do by initiating a warm hug.

As we separated, I wished her good luck in the rest of the term, which was to recommence a few weeks hence. This would be her first time sitting on the Supreme Court as the sole woman on the bench. Moreover, many feared that the Court had taken a swing to the right with the loss of Justice O'Connor, and Ruth's ability to garner a majority would now more than ever be put to the test.

Ruth took my hand in hers and looked me in the eyes. What she said was brief—only a sentence or two—but it was poignant and deeply moving. And I'll never forget the look of sadness in her face as she said it.

The problem is, I don't remember her exact words. I blame it on the wine and maybe the excitement of the evening. But I do know that it was about her fear of isolation on the bench, as a woman and as a jurist.

Dad shut the door behind them. The four of us turned to face each other and broke into broad smiles. Mom and I exchanged high fives, and Robin slapped me on the back. "Well done," said Dad.

I went to check on the marshals. They had all gone as well, slipping out the side door as stealthily as they had arrived.

Coda

Not again.

Rolling onto my side, I curled up in the fetal position in an attempt to suppress the queasiness in my stomach and cursed myself for having indulged in that celebratory, post-dinner nightcap with Robin. Across the room I could see that the other twin bed was empty, the covers thrown back.

I took a slow breath. Okay, lying on my side wasn't helping. Rolling onto my back, I stared up at the cracks in the plaster ceiling. They were numerous, due to the age of the house and the not infrequent earthquakes it had experienced during its life. As a teenager I had identified various animals in the shapes caused by the cracks, but they had changed over the years and new ones had appeared.

I squinted, trying to make out the shapes above me, but my throbbing temple and the fact that I hadn't yet put in my contact lenses made it difficult to focus. Yes, that one looked like a rabbit, and that one . . . a stag, with huge antlers.

This reminded me of Marty's "killing Bambi" story from the night before, and I smiled. So what if my head ached and my stomach was in turmoil; it didn't matter how I felt today. It was over. I could relax.

Closing my eyes, I dozed a little longer.

• • •

Robin was at the sink, finishing up the last of the dishes, when I finally made it downstairs. She rarely suffers from hangovers, and no matter how late a party has gone, she'll generally rise early the next morning and often have the entire kitchen clean by the time I get up. I fetched myself a cup of coffee and, glancing at the stove area, cracked up.

"What?" Robin stopped scrubbing the mashed potato pot and looked my way.

"Can you *believe* all the butternut soup that's splashed all over the place?" I indicated the bright orange splotches on the stove, on the blue-and-yellow tiled counter and wall, and all over the floor.

"Yeah, I decided I'd let you clean that up," she said with a grin and returned to her scrubbing.

"I'll do it in a bit." I poured milk into my coffee, then sat down in the breakfast room and stared out the window. It was another sunny day.

After a while my dad joined me. "You look nice," I commented. He was already dressed for the day's activities in a suit and tie. This was unusual for him, as he generally wore a sports coat rather than a suit to the opera.

Mom came downstairs soon thereafter. She too looked grand, in a pale blue pant suit, black sweater, and brightly colored silk scarf.

"My!" I exclaimed.

"Well, I have to keep up with Ruth," she responded, twirling around for me to admire her outfit. "You know she'll be dressed to the nines today for the Disney Hall tour and opera."

I finished my coffee, after which Mom helped me pack up all the kitchenware and glasses I'd brought down for the dinner. The leftover soup and (too dry) mashed potatoes, as well as the spinach, Gorgonzola cheese, and other perishable items, I left with her. Minus all the food and the box of wines we'd brought down, there'd be a lot more room in the car going home.

Next I went back upstairs to pack my suitcase. As I was folding my black slacks, which I'd tossed over the chair the night before, I spied spots of butternut squash soup on the bottom of the left pant leg. I picked up my black dress shoes. Yup, it was splashed on my left shoe as well. *I wonder if Ruth or Marty noticed*, I thought, then with a shrug, rinsed out the slacks, wiped off the shoe, and packed them away.

Once Robin had loaded up the car and I'd cleaned the stove and environs of all signs of orange soup, Mom and Dad came into the kitchen to bid us goodbye.

"Well, you did it," said Mom.

"No, *we* did it," I responded. "This weekend could never have happened without all of us working together. We make a great team."

And as we stood there in the kitchen laughing about Ruth's weighty purse, Marty's subway riddle, and the five federal marshals who'd camped out in our den the night before, it struck me that this wasn't simply an offhand cliché—we truly *had* come together as quite the team.

Many families, of course, get along just fine.[60] And I'd always taken for granted the warmth and closeness within my own. We had lots of fun whenever we gathered for holidays or other reunions and were good about keeping in touch with each other during the rest of the year. But this dinner party—and all that went into its planning and preparation—had created a new sort of connection between my parents and Robin and me.

Dad, who'd been leaning against the counter as Robin chuckled about Ruth's Maria Callas story, turned my way. "And didn't you *love* that bit about Scalia's 'slings and

60. Though, sadly, I've worked on enough probate litigation cases to know firsthand how nasty and hurtful members of a family can be to each other, as well.

arrows'?" he said with a smile I took to mean, "You're a fellow lawyer, so I know *you* get it."

I returned his grin.

Yes, I'd been an attorney by this time for nearly twenty years, but my father and I hadn't often discussed the law. Partly it was because we lived in vastly different legal realms—he in the theoretical world of thorny constitutional questions; I in the practical world of depositions, jury instructions, and motions to change venue. But it was also partly me—that I felt working at a civil law firm, spending my days hustling those endless billable hours, wasn't as important or worthwhile as Dad's lofty life of an academic.

Hosting this dinner, however, had somehow changed that. It was as if, having shared all the exhilaration and hubbub leading up to the event—and my having been initiated into "the world of Ruth"—Dad and I had forged a new and special connection. We were now in the same club, with the same in-jokes and knowing glances.

As for my mom, I've always felt we were in the same club, one that revolved around food, art, mystery novels, and a shared sense of silliness. But I can't remember an instance where she and I were as jointly involved in a project as we were with this meal. And something about those excited emails we'd exchanged, all the discussions concerning china and flowers and ginger-lime cream sauce had served to bring us even closer yet. In the years following the dinner, all I'd have to do was mention the story of my buying those square black plates, and Mom would burst out laughing.

Robin slapped her hands on her knees. "Well, I guess we should get out of your hair," she said. "You've got yet another big day ahead." But I knew she was also anxious to get on the road for our long drive back up to Santa Cruz.

We hugged and kissed goodbye, and Mom and Dad followed us out to the curb. I climbed into the car and rolled down the window. "What an amazing weekend it's been," I said, leaning out to take them both by the hand. "Thanks so much for including us."

My folks waved as we drove off, and Robin and I waved back until they were tiny specks in the distance.

• • •

This being a Sunday morning, traffic was light heading north on Highway 405.[61] I settled back in the passenger seat and studied the Getty Center as it came into view, its bright white travertine walls seeming to grow out of the surrounding hillside.

"So what was your favorite part of the weekend," Robin asked, interrupting my musings about whether the museum more resembled a space-age habitat or a medieval fortress.

"Wow. That's a hard one." I thought a moment, frowning in concentration. "I guess it would have to be when Ruth called me by my name, 'Leslie.' It kind of sent a shiver down my spine."

"Really?" Robin glanced my way, then returned her focus to the cars zipping by us in the fast lane.

"Yeah. I know it seems odd, but I think it wasn't till that moment that she stopped being 'Ruth Bader Ginsburg, Supreme Court justice' for me and became simply 'Ruth.' You know, a friend of the family—a regular person."

"A regular person?" Robin asked, eyebrow arched in skepticism.

"Okay, maybe she'll never be just 'regular.' But it was then, at the end of the night, when I realized I'd stopping thinking of her as some sort of a celebrity. She'd become more, I dunno . . . real, I guess."

---

61. I'd grown up calling this highway "the San Diego Freeway," but Angelenos now refer to it as "the 405." An easy way to tell Northern from Southern Californians is by whether they say "highway" or "the" before freeway numbers.

Robin nodded, staring at the ginormous silver Hummer ahead of us. "Yeah, I know what you mean. It's like, when you're starstruck by someone—"

"Like Diane Keaton?"

"Right, perfect example. So, you know how weird that was, seeing her there at the dean's condo and then later talking to her. And you're trying to act all cool and normal, but it's pretty much impossible because you're feeling so amped up and giddy."

"I know," I said with a laugh. "And of course what's really funny is that at the same time, Diane was completely starstruck about getting to meet Ruth Ginsburg."

Robin slapped the steering wheel with her palm. "Exactly! And then Ruth tells us how in awe *she* was when she met Maria Callas—and Martin Sheen. So it just goes to show that even for celebrities, there's always someone they'll go all fangirl over, too."

Fed up with following the silver behemoth, Robin flicked on her turn signal, checked her blind spot, and jumped into the left lane to pass the Hummer. "Anyway," she went on, "the point is, I'm pretty sure if I ever met Diane Keaton again, even if she was super warm and friendly, I'd still be pretty starstruck—though probably not as much as the other night. But I agree that if I ever see Ruth again, I think I'll be pretty normal."

"As normal as anyone can be around someone like her. But, of course, that has nothing to do with her being famous." And then I groaned. "But if we ever *do* meet again, I sure as hell hope she doesn't bring up what I said about having a *senior moment*. Ohmygod, that was *so* embarrassing."

"Not nearly as embarrassing as my bragging to her and Marty about how I got that candle wax out of the carpet." Robin's upper body flinched at the memory, and she had to catch the steering wheel to keep from propelling us into the center concrete divide.

We continued on in silence for a while, each contemplating our cringeworthy moments from the night before. As we merged with I-5 and headed north through Santa Clarita and the Los Padres National Forest, my thoughts turned to the next day, at which time my life would be going back to "normal" once again. A vision of myself at the law library desk sifting through pages of Civil Code annotations flashed through my brain. And then I shuddered.

No. I just can't. Not after all I've experienced over the past nine months.

I'd now had a clear look at what life was like for those who had sought to follow their passion—for Ruth, and Marty, and my mother and father. And Robin, too. They were all spending their days doing what brought them satisfaction and pleasure.

Maybe, after all was said and done, *that* was what this whole event had been about. Not the planning and cooking of the meal, but how much it had meant for me to do it. It was as if I'd finally gained an insight into the purpose of my own existence: Life shouldn't be about making money or having a "good" job—and certainly not about pleasing your father. *No*. Your life should be about being honest with yourself and about following your own dreams.

I mused on all this as we negotiated the treacherous Grapevine, and then once we were making our way up the Central Valley, I turned to face Robin. "How would you feel if I quit my job?" I asked. "Not immediately, of course, but in like a year or two? We'd be able to afford it, right?"

Robin nodded. "Sure," she said. "I think we'd be fine. Though we'd probably have to start cutting some corners—you know, watching our budget more carefully. But why this sudden decision to leave the firm? I mean, I get that you've never been in love with the law, but why *now*?"

"It's partly 'cause of Ruth. And Dad."

She laughed. "Well, there's an irony."

"Yeah, I know. But as you said, you know how hard it's been for me at work lately—for a long time, actually. And I guess it was just my realizing over these past months how much Dad and Ruth truly love their work—how *vital* it is to their very being. And the more I thought about it, the more it made me, I dunno . . . jealous. I want that in *my* life."

"And I want that for you, too," said Robin. "You've put in close to twenty years at the firm; I think you've earned the right to move on." She glanced over at me. "But what else will you do? 'Cause I certainly don't see you lying around the house all day watching TV."

I hesitated before answering. Although I did in fact have an idea, it was a little scary to speak the words out loud.

"I want to write a mystery novel," I finally responded. "About food and cooking. A culinary mystery."

Robin beamed and reached over to pat me on the knee. "That's *perfect*, hon! I love it."

"Really? You don't think it's a crazy idea?" At that moment, I realized how nervous I'd been, not only about my father's reaction to this wild notion of mine but also about what Robin would think—probably even more so than Dad's opinion. And to hear these words of encouragement from her meant the world to me. Maybe it wasn't such a crazy idea after all. Maybe it was in fact my destiny—my true *vocation*.

We drove on for a few miles, Robin humming to herself, me plotting insidious ways to poison someone at a fictional restaurant. Then, passing a sign for a fast-food joint, I realized I was hungry. "So, speaking of culinary mysteries," I said, "you wanna stop soon for an early lunch?"

"Sounds good. We could go to that Indian place." Robin had told me about an Indian restaurant she'd once tried while driving home from LA, one incongruously in the middle of nowhere, right smack in the center of the Central Valley. "It's not too far from here—in Buttonwillow, I think."

We drove a bit longer, and there it was. We could see the sign from the freeway: Taste of India Restaurant. "I hope it's open," I said, glancing at my watch. It was a little after eleven. Robin took the exit and we pulled into the parking lot.

The restaurant was indeed open, though no one was inside except a young woman at the register. She was watching the television in the corner of the dining room, which was tuned to a channel showing a rodeo. We weren't too far from Bakersfield, home of Merle Haggard and Buck Owens, so this wasn't terribly surprising—even though the woman seemed authentically Indian, rather than a transplanted Okie like many of the folks in these parts.

We perused the menu and decided to get two lunch specials, which came with a variety of items such as Tandoori chicken and dal.

"For here or to go?" the woman asked.

Robin looked at me. "Well, it would be hard to eat in the car," I said, "but it's so nice today. Maybe we should get it to go and eat outside somewhere."

While I waited for the food and watched the bull riding on TV, Robin fetched the blanket we kept in the trunk and spread it on a grassy area next to the parking lot. This wasn't the most picturesque of picnic sites—bordered on one side by the parking lot, on another by a Super 8 Motel, and on the third side by the freeway overpass above—but the sun was shining, and it was warm for a January day.

I brought the food out, and we had our picnic, listening to the big rigs roar by overhead. I ripped off a piece of naan and scooped up some dal. It was good—spicy and hearty and just what my hungover body needed. But after a few bites of dal and Tandoori chicken, I couldn't eat any more. I set the chicken leg back down in its Styrofoam box.

"Aren't you hungry?" Robin asked.

"I am, but I just can't eat. I'm still way too hyper."

"Yeah, I'm not all that hungry either." Robin and I looked at all the uneaten food we'd ordered. "Well, we can take it home and have it for dinner tonight."

I nodded and put the lid back on the dal container. "Good idea," I said. " 'Cause I sure as hell don't feel like *cooking*."

Epilogue

Many years have now passed since my dinner with Ruth, but the experience still burns brightly within me as one of the most important and meaningful of my life.

I can still call to mind with startling clarity the morning Mom and I played "grown-ups" as we decided on the china for the meal, the tartness and creamy mouthfeel of those seared scallops, and the soul-stirring sight of Ruth's satisfied smile as she recounted to us her glorious victory in the VMI case.

And yes, a little over two years after the events of this book I did indeed quit my job as an attorney and set to work penning a murder mystery. Being free from the daily grind of motions to compel and billable hours was (and remains) exhilarating, and—notwithstanding my fears of disappointing him—my father was one of the first to congratulate me with warmth and pride when the book was finally published. I now find myself the author of an entire culinary mystery series, so my dream of combining my passions for both food and writing has been fully realized.

Oh yeah, and I'm also now well-equipped to hold my own with any celebrities I might meet in the days ahead.

You never know where one dinner is going to take you.

Recipes

❖ *Seared Sea Scallop with* ❖ *Ginger-Lime Cream Sauce*

(serves 6)

I adore scallops, and this dish shows them off in grand style, with its mouth-watering combination of briny shellfish, savory shallots, rich cream, and sweet-and-sour ginger and lime.

Notwithstanding their reputation as a "fancy" food, scallops are actually one of the simplest dishes to prepare; you simply sear them quickly on each side and serve them with either a sauce made from deglazing the pan or—as here—one made separately in advance. The trick is to not overcook the delectable mollusks. Start with a very hot pan and fry them just long enough to brown, then flip and let them cook only another 30 to 60 seconds. They should be warm throughout, but the center should be close to raw—otherwise they become tough.

I served only one large scallop apiece at the Ruth dinner, as we had so much food to follow, but you could certainly prepare three or four per person and use this recipe as a main dish.

Ingredients for Sauce

¾ cup clam juice
½ cup dry white wine
1 tablespoon fresh lime juice (zest lime first, then cut in half and squeeze for juice)
2 teaspoons sugar
2 tablespoons shallots, minced
1 teaspoon ginger, minced
½ teaspoon lime zest
1 cup heavy whipping cream
4 tablespoons butter, chilled
salt, to taste

Ingredients for Scallops

6 large sea scallops, at room temperature
salt and fresh-cracked black pepper
1 tablespoon butter
½ teaspoon lime zest (for garnish)

DIRECTIONS

Place clam juice, wine, lime juice, sugar, shallots, and ginger in a medium-size sauce pan and cook over medium heat until reduced by half, stirring occasionally. Add the ½ teaspoon lime zest and the cream, and continue cooking until reduced to 1 cup, stirring often. *Watch the pan, as the cream has a tendency to boil over and make a big mess.* (The sauce can be prepared up to this point and stored, covered, in the refrigerator until needed.)

Reheat sauce, if necessary. Over low heat, add the butter one tablespoon at a time to the sauce, while stirring constantly, until incorporated. Taste, then add salt as needed. Turn off heat and let sauce sit, covered, while cooking scallops.

Sprinkle scallops lightly with salt and pepper on both sides. Heat a skillet over medium-high heat, and once hot, add the butter. As soon as the butter has melted, place the scallops in the pan and fry until a golden brown, then flip. Cook scallops 30 to 60 seconds more, then remove from pan to a plate with a paper towel.

Spoon sauce onto six plates, then place one scallop atop the sauce on each plate. Garnish with lime zest and more black pepper, if desired.

✦ *Roasted Butternut Squash Soup with* ✦ *Brown Butter, Garnished with Crème Fraîche, Walnut Oil, and Chopped Walnuts*

(serves 6)

This soup is adapted from a recipe created by the famed French Laundry chef, Thomas Keller, but my version is less sweet and incorporates walnuts and walnut oil for a more savory flavor than that of the original recipe. Not only can most of it be prepared a day in advance, the dish is actually improved by doing so, as this allows the flavors to better meld.

Served with a tangy green salad and crunchy baguette, this hearty soup makes for a delicious main course all on its own.

Ingredients

1 3-3½ pound butternut squash
2 tablespoons neutral oil (such as canola)
salt and fresh-ground black pepper
2 sprigs fresh sage
¼ cup thinly sliced carrots
1 cup thinly sliced leeks
½ cup thinly sliced shallots
½ cup thinly sliced onions
6 garlic cloves, smashed
6 cups chicken or vegetable stock
1 bouquet garni of 8 sprigs thyme, 2 sprigs parsley, 2 bay leaves, and ½ teaspoon black peppercorns, wrapped in cheese cloth and secured with string
4 tablespoons unsalted butter
¼ cup crème fraîche (for garnish)
½ cup roasted walnuts, chopped (for garnish)
roasted walnut oil (for garnish)

DIRECTIONS

Preheat oven to 350° F.

Cut off the neck of the squash and set aside. Slice body of squash in half and remove seeds. Brush each half with oil (about 1½ teaspoons each side) and sprinkle with salt and pepper. Place a sprig of sage in each cavity and set squash halves face-down on a baking sheet lined with aluminum foil. Roast until tender, about an hour. Remove squash from oven and let cool, then scoop out the flesh (discarding the sage and skin).

While squash body is roasting, peel skin off the neck using a paring knife, and cut the orange flesh into ½-inch pieces.

Heat the remaining oil in a large stockpot over medium-high heat. When the oil is shimmering, add the carrots, leeks, shallots, and onions and cook, stirring often, until soft—about five minutes. Lower the heat to medium and add the diced squash, the garlic, 1 teaspoon salt, and ½ teaspoon black pepper. Cook, stirring often, for 3 minutes, making sure the garlic and squash don't brown. Add the stock and bouquet garni and bring to a simmer. Cook 10-15 minutes, until squash is tender. Add the roasted squash pulp and simmer for another 30 minutes.

Remove pot from heat and discard the bouquet garni. Once cooled down enough to do so, purée the soup in batches in a blender (or use a handheld immersion blender). Let cool completely, then refrigerate, covered, until ready to serve. (This much of the recipe can be prepared a day or two ahead.)

Reheat the soup over a low heat, stirring occasionally so it doesn't burn. While the soup is warming up, heat a medium skillet over high heat. When very hot, add the butter and let melt. Stir and scrape the bottom of the pan, cooking until the butter turns a hazelnut brown. *Don't let it burn.* When browned, pour the butter carefully into the soup (it may spatter), then stir to mix in.

Whisk the crème fraîche until smooth.

Ladle the soup into bowls. Top with crème fraîche (you can make spirals by putting it into a squirt bottle), then drizzle with roasted walnut oil and top with chopped walnuts.

✦ *Baby Spinach Salad with* ✦ *Blood Orange, Red Onion, Dried Cranberries, Gorgonzola Cheese, Pine Nuts, and Dijon Vinaigrette Dressing*

(serves 6)

This recipe uses what Robin calls my "house dressing." It can be made in advance and keeps well in the fridge; just remember to take it out about a half hour before you need it, and give it a stir before using. You can add more or less of the seasonings and sugar, to taste. Don't overdo it on the dressing; a little goes a long way, and this recipe makes more than you'll likely need for six servings of salad.

Ingredients for Dressing

- 2 tablespoons Dijon mustard
- ¼ teaspoon garlic powder
- ¼ teaspoon black pepper
- 1 teaspoon brown sugar
- 2 tablespoons balsamic vinegar
- ½ cup extra virgin olive oil
- 1 teaspoon water

Ingredients for Salad

- 8 oz. baby spinach
- 3 blood oranges, peeled and sliced into thin rounds
- ¼ red onion, sliced into thin rounds
- ½ cup crumbled Gorgonzola cheese
- ½ cup dried cranberries
- ½ cup pine nuts

DIRECTIONS

Mix the mustard, garlic powder, pepper, sugar, and vinegar together in a bowl and stir until smooth. Slowly drizzle in the olive oil, using a wire whisk to mix it in. Don't beat it too hard, or the olive oil can become bitter. Finish it by whisking in the water. (I find that this last step helps to thicken and bind the dressing.)

Place a mound of spinach on each of six plates. Lay an arc of overlapping rounds of orange and onion atop each salad. Sprinkle with gorgonzola cheese and cranberries. (The salads can be prepared up to this point several hours before service and kept chilled in the refrigerator.) To finish, drizzle each salad with the dressing, then top with pine nuts.

❖ *Blackened Ahi Coated in a Dry Rub of Spices and Black Sesame Seeds* ❖

(serves 6)

This recipe is my riff on the blackened redfish invented back in the 1980s by Chef Paul Prudhomme, but with an Asian twist. Don't be put off by the fact that it calls for the ahi to be basically raw in the center—it's perfectly safe, as long as you buy sushi-grade tuna, and will not be nearly as tender and flavorful if you overcook the fish.

Ingredients

4 teaspoons brown sugar
1 teaspoon chili powder
½ teaspoon wasabi powder
½ teaspoon sea salt
1 tablespoon black sesame seeds
3 lbs. sushi-grade ahi tuna (or enough for 6 large or 12 small steaks, once blood line is removed)
4 teaspoons sesame oil

DIRECTIONS

Remove the blood line—the dark red part of the fish running down the center, which may also have bones—from the ahi, and discard. Slice the fish into 6 large or 12 small steaks, at least 1" thick.

Mix all the dry ingredients together in a bowl. Pat the ahi steaks dry, and sprinkle both sides with half of the dry rub. Set steaks aside until time to fry the fish.

Right before frying them, sprinkle the rest of the dry rub on both sides of the ahi steaks.

Heat two skillets (preferably cast-iron) over high heat till very hot, then add 2 teaspoons of sesame oil to each pan. Once the oil is sizzling, lay the ahi gently in the pans, making sure not to crowd them. As soon as they are dark brown (i.e., "blackened), flip them over and turn off the heat. Once the bottom sides start to brown, remove the fish from the pan to a plate atop a paper towel. The idea is to sear and brown the fish as quickly as possible, so that it's still pretty much raw—though warm—in the middle. Serve immediately.

❖ *Wasabi Mashed Potatoes* ❖

(serves 6)

Mashed potatoes are a truly marvelous thing—light and creamy mouthfuls of savory wonder. Unless they're not. We've all had the experience of eating mashed potatoes that were dry and mealy, or even worse, gummy and paste-like. The trick is to use hot butter and milk, to not overbeat them, and to stir in more liquid right before service if you prepare them in advance.

Ingredients

3 lbs. russet potatoes
5 tablespoons butter
½ cup whipping cream (plus ¼ cup more,
  if preparing dish in advance)
1 to 2 teaspoons wasabi powder, to taste
½ to 1 teaspoon salt, to taste
1 teaspoon black sesame seeds (for garnish)

DIRECTIONS

Peel the potatoes (or not, if you like them with the skins on), cut them into 2" chunks, and place in a large pot with enough water to cover the potatoes completely. Cook the potatoes at a low boil until a fork goes into them easily.

While the potatoes are cooking, pour the butter and milk into a large pitcher and heat in a microwave till the butter is melted and the mixture is hot. Or heat them in a saucepan, if you prefer. (In either event, watch that the milk doesn't boil over.)

Drain the potatoes and return them to the pot, then set the pot back over the heat for a few seconds until the residual water in the pot evaporates.

Remove the pot from the heat and mash the potatoes with a handheld masher, ricer, or fork. Using an electric beater, slowly add the heated butter and milk as you mix the liquid into the potatoes. As soon as the potatoes are creamy, stop beating. *Don't overmix, as the starch in the potatoes can cause them to quickly become gummy.*

Add salt and wasabi powder to the potatoes, mixing them in with a wooden spoon. Taste, and add more salt and wasabi powder as needed.

If you're going to make the potatoes in advance, they can be kept warm over a double boiler, covered, on a low simmer. Right before service, stir in ¼ cup more hot cream, till they are once again smooth and creamy in texture. Serve garnished with a scattering of the sesame seeds.

❖ *Sautéed Snow Peas* ❖

(serves 6)

This simple sauté shows off the fresh, bright flavor of the crunchy snow peas. It has no added seasoning other than the butter and salt and pepper, as it was meant to be served with two other dishes (the blackened ahi and wasabi mashed potatoes) which already had strong, pronounced flavors.

But it you want to spice the peas up a little, feel free to add flavorings such as sesame oil, minced garlic, citrus juice or zest, or red pepper flakes to the sauté.

Ingredients

1 pound snow peas
1 tablespoon butter
salt and pepper to taste

DIRECTIONS

Heat a large skillet over a medium-high heat, then add the butter. Once the butter is melted and bubbling, add the snow peas and sauté, tossing or stirring often, until they are warmed through (3 or 4 minutes), then turn off the heat. You want them to retain their crisp snap, and overcooking will make them limp. Season lightly with salt and pepper and serve immediately.

Author's Note and Acknowledgments

I hadn't planned to write a memoir about the events contained in this book. But on the trip back north to Santa Cruz from Los Angeles the morning after the dinner, as Robin and I were reliving all the marvelous, amusing, and occasionally bizarre occurrences leading up to and including the big night, we both came to the same conclusion: I had to write it all down. Right then, before I forgot the details.

I grabbed a pen and the sheaf of office paper we kept in our car, and as Robin navigated Highway 5, the two of us brainstormed regarding everything we could remember of the previous nine months—including all the conversations from the night before. Scribbling furiously, I took everything down, eventually covering some twenty pages with my notes.

As soon as I was home, I commenced writing the memoir. The draft was finished within a few months, but then there it sat for years on my computer while I was sidetracked first by my legal work, then by writing my culinary mystery series. Finally, after much egging-on by Robin, her mother, and various others who knew of the manuscript's existence, I decided that they were right. The extraordinary story needed to be out there for others to read.

So, notwithstanding that this book is being released over fifteen years after my dinner with the Ginsburgs, the events described herein are as accurate as possible—with some literary license, of course. (As for Ruth's talk and the Q&A session at the UCLA law school, the recounting is close to verbatim, as I was later provided with a DVD of the event.)

With regard to the "interlude" sections of this memoir, these are based on extensive reading that I did regarding the life and work of Ruth Bader Ginsburg, including books, law review articles, magazine pieces, letters between RBG and my father, and other materials. Any factual mistakes therein are entirely mine.

On a sad note, not only are Ruth and Marty now gone, but both my mother and father have also passed away in the last few years (though my parents were, thankfully, able to read an early draft of the manuscript).

This book would not have been possible without the kindness and generosity of a host of others. I'm grateful most of all to my wife, Robin McDuff, for all she did (and what she put up with) during the crazy period I was so completely obsessed with the dinner and also for her dogged encouragement with regard to this memoir, as well as her continued support in my quest to pursue my true calling as a writer. And I'm eternally grateful, as well, to my parents, Kenneth L. Karst and Smiley Karst, who played such an important role in all the events recounted herein.

Thanks also go out to all of my terrific beta readers: Robin, Mom and Dad, my sister Laura Karst, Marty Ginsburg (who provided useful and—not surprisingly—witty comments on excerpts of the manuscript relevant to himself and his esteemed wife), Scott Lankford, Winnie Baer, John Dizikes, Ellen Byron, Roberta Isleib, and Edith Maxwell.

I'm grateful also to the UCLA School of Law for allowing me to have a DVD of Justice Ginsburg's talk; to Leigh Iwanaga,

Special Events Manager at the law school, for providing me details regarding the reception at the dean's residence; to Derrick Wang, for granting permission to quote from the libretto of his marvelous comic opera, *Scalia/Ginsburg*; to editors supreme, Kristen Havens, Barbara Boyd, and Jodi Fodor for their invaluable insights and assistance in revising and polishing the MS to prepare it for publication; to Shirley Tessler, for her assistance in editing the recipes; to my fabulous agent, Erin Niumata of Folio Literary Management; to Crystal Patriarche, Grace Fell, and Leilani Fitzpatrick at BookSparks publicity; and to publishers Brooke Warner and Lauren Wise, cover designer Lindsey Cleworth, editor Krissa Lagos, and all the other amazing gals at She Writes Press who made this book a reality.

Finally, thanks to Ruth, for agreeing to come to dinner.

About the Author

The daughter of a law professor and a potter, Leslie Karst waited tables and sang in a new wave rock band before deciding she was ready for "real" job and ending up at Stanford Law School. It was during her career as a research and appellate attorney in Santa Cruz, California, that she rediscovered her youthful passion for food and cooking, at which point she once again returned to school—this time to earn a degree in culinary arts. Now retired from the law, Leslie spends her days penning the Sally Solari culinary mystery series, as well as cooking, gardening, cycling, and singing alto in her local community chorus. She and her wife and their Jack Russell mix split their time between Santa Cruz and Hilo, Hawai'i.

Author photo © Robin McDuff

SELECTED TITLES FROM SHE WRITES PRESS

She Writes Press is an independent publishing company founded to serve women writers everywhere. Visit us at www.shewritespress.com.

Brave(ish): A Memoir of a Recovering Perfectionist by Margaret Davis Ghielmetti. $16.95, 978-1-63152-747-0. An intrepid traveler sets off at forty to live the expatriate dream overseas—only to discover that she has no idea how to live even her own life. Part travelogue and part transformation tale, Ghielmetti's memoir, narrated with humor and warmth, proves that it's never too late to reconnect with our authentic selves—if we dare to put our own lives first at last.

In the Game: The Highs and Lows of a Trailblazing Trial Lawyer by Peggy Garrity. $16.95, 978-1-63152-105-8. Admitted to the California State Bar in 1975—when less than 3 percent of lawyers were women—Peggy Garrity refuses to choose between family and profession, and succeeds at both beyond anything she could have imagined.

Life's Hourglass: A Memoir of Chasing Success at a Cost by Janice Mock. $16.95, 978-1-63152-005-5. When Janice Mock's stage four cancer diagnosis causes her to examine her career as a successful trial lawyer and the relentless drive for wealth and excess that corporate America promotes, she comes to the realization that she must change in order to make the most of the rest of her life.

Sacred & Delicious: A Modern Ayurvedic Cookbook by Lisa Joy Mitchell. $28.95, 978-1-63152-347-2. Both a cookbook and food memoir, this book gives down-to-earth information and instructions for cooking tasty and healing Ayurvedic dishes, celebrating the healing power of food and spices andembodying ancient Ayurvedic wisdom while appealing to a modern American palate and dietary needs.

Hedgebrook Cookbook: Celebrating Radical Hospitality by Denise Barr & Julie Rosten. $24.95, 978-1-93831-422-3. Delectable recipes and inspiring writing, straight from Hedgebrook's farmhouse table to yours.

Searching for Family and Traditions at the French Table, Book One by Carole Bumpus. $16.95, 978-1-63152-896-5. Part culinary memoir and part travelogue, this compilation of intimate interviews, conversations, stories, and traditional family recipes (*cuisine pauvre*) in the kitchens of French families, gathered by Carole Bumpus as she traveled throughout France's countryside, is about people savoring the life they have been given.